MW01530894

Civil Society Networks in China and Vietnam

Non-Governmental Public Action

Series Editor: **Jude Howell**, Professor and Director of the Centre for Civil Society, London School of Economics and Political Science, UK

Non-governmental public action (NGPA) by and for disadvantaged and marginalized people has become increasingly significant over the past two decades. This new book series is designed to make a fresh and original contribution to the understanding of NGPA. It presents the findings of innovative and policy-relevant research carried out by established and new scholars working in collaboration with researchers across the world. The series is international in scope and includes both theoretical and empirical work.

The series marks a departure from previous studies in this area in at least two important respects. First, it goes beyond a singular focus on developmental NGOs or the voluntary sector to include a range of non-governmental public actors such as advocacy networks, campaigns and coalitions, trades unions, peace groups, rights-based groups, cooperatives and social movements. Second, the series is innovative in stimulating a new approach to international comparative research that promotes comparison of the so-called developing world with the so-called developed world, thereby querying the conceptual utility and relevance of categories such as North and South.

Titles include:

Barbara Bompani and Maria Frahm-Arp *(editors)*
DEVELOPMENT AND POLITICS FROM BELOW
Exploring Religious Spaces in the African State

Jude Howell and Jeremy Lind
COUNTER-TERRORISM, AID AND CIVIL SOCIETY
Before and After the War on Terror

Jenny Pearce *(editor)*
PARTICIPATION AND DEMOCRACY IN THE TWENTY-FIRST CENTURY

Tim Pringle and Simon Clarke
THE CHALLENGE OF TRANSITION
Trade Unions in Russia, China and Vietnam

Andrew Wells-Dang
CIVIL SOCIETY NETWORKS IN CHINA AND VIETNAM
Informal Pathbreakers in Health and the Environment

Thomas Yarrow
DEVELOPMENT BEYOND POLITICS
Aid, Activism and NGOs in Ghana

Non-Governmental Public Action Series
Series Standing Order ISBN 978-0–230–22939–6 (hardback) and 978-0–230–22940–2 (paperback)

You can receive future titles in this series as they are published by placing a standing order. Please contact your bookseller or, in case of difficulty, write to us at the address below with your name and address, the title of the series and the ISBN quoted above.

Customer Services Department, Macmillan Distribution Ltd, Houndmills, Basingstoke, Hampshire RG21 6XS, England

Civil Society Networks in China and Vietnam

Informal Pathbreakers in Health and the Environment

Andrew Wells-Dang

palgrave
macmillan

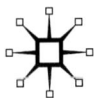

First published 2012 by
PALGRAVE MACMILLAN

Palgrave Macmillan in the UK is an imprint of Macmillan Publishers Limited, registered in England, company number 785998, of Houndmills, Basingstoke, Hampshire RG21 6XS.

Palgrave Macmillan in the US is a division of St Martin's Press LLC, 175 Fifth Avenue, New York, NY 10010.

Palgrave Macmillan is the global academic imprint of the above companies and has companies and representatives throughout the world.

Palgrave® and Macmillan® are registered trademarks in the United States, the United Kingdom, Europe and other countries

ISBN 978-0-230-38020-2

This book is printed on paper suitable for recycling and made from fully managed and sustained forest sources. Logging, pulping and manufacturing processes are expected to conform to the environmental regulations of the country of origin.

A catalogue record for this book is available from the British Library.

A catalog record for this book is available from the Library of Congress.

10   9   8   7   6   5   4   3   2   1
21 20 19 18 17 16 15 14 13 12

Printed and bound in the United States of America

For Giang, who holds up half the sky

Contents

List of Tables, Figures, and Maps   ix

Preface   x

Chapter 1   **The Dynamic Societies of China and Vietnam**   1
             New agents of political action   2
             Changing visions of civil society   4
             A genealogy of networks   10
             Comparing networks in China and Vietnam   16
             Plan of the book   21

Chapter 2   **Redefining Civil Society: Networks and**   24
             Advocacy
             Network analysis   29
             A typology of civil society networks   33
             Varieties of network advocacy   41
             Embedded advocacy   44
             Media advocacy   50
             Community advocacy   53
             Hypotheses on network effectiveness   56
             Tightrope acts   59

Chapter 3   **The Bright Future Group of People with**   61
             Disabilities
             Network formation and history   63
             Network membership and structure   65
             Advocacy strategies   68
             International linkages   73
             Network effectiveness: Policy change   75
             Network effectiveness: Sustainability   78
             Network effectiveness: Political space   82
             Conclusion   83

Chapter 4   **The China Women's Network against AIDS**   85
             Network formation and history   87
             Network membership and structure   90
             Advocacy strategies   94
             International linkages   96

	Network effectiveness: Policy change	100
	Network effectiveness: Sustainability and political space	102
	Conclusion	104
Chapter 5	**Preserving Hanoi's Reunification Park**	**106**
	Network formation and history	108
	Network membership and structure	121
	Advocacy strategies	122
	International linkages	128
	Network effectiveness: Policy change	128
	Network effectiveness: Sustainability	130
	Network effectiveness: Political space	131
	Conclusion	134
Chapter 6	**The China Rivers Network**	**136**
	Network formation and history	139
	Network membership and structure	144
	Advocacy strategies	148
	International linkages	157
	Network effectiveness: Policy change	159
	Network effectiveness: Sustainability	161
	Network effectiveness: Political space	164
	Conclusion	167
Chapter 7	**Conclusion: Civil Society Networks and Political Change**	**169**
	Network formation and leadership	173
	Formal and informal structures	175
	Resources and donor roles	178
	Effectiveness	181
	Civil society networks, social movements and political change	184
Notes		188
Bibliography		201
Index		229

List of Tables, Figures, and Maps

Tables

2.1	A typology of networks	35
2.2	Illustrative examples of network types	37
2.3	Features of selected civil society networks in China and Vietnam	38
3.1	Advocacy tactics – Bright Future network	72
4.1	Members of the China Women's Network against AIDS	92
4.2	Advocacy tactics – Women's Network against AIDS	94
5.1	Advocacy tactics – Reunification Park network	126
6.1	Advocacy tactics – China Rivers Network	154
7.1	Comparison of network case studies	171

Figures

2.1	Networks, social movements and civil society: A nesting paradigm	28
2.2	Network structures	31
2.3	Overview of civil society networks' advocacy strategies and tactics	45
3.1	Bright Future network structures over time	67
4.1	Structure of the Women's Network against AIDS	93
4.2	WNAC advocacy strategy	97
5.1	Reunification Park network structure	121
6.1	Formal and informal CRN structures	145

Maps

5.1	Major parks and lakes in Hanoi	109
6.1	Proposed and completed dams on the Nu, Lancang and Jinsha rivers	138

Preface

Non-democratic states are often assumed to lack functioning civil societies or to constrain their development through rigid systems of control. In spite of apparent restrictions, however, citizens in such contexts actively create informal pathways for social action through cross-sectoral networks. Members of environmental and health networks, among others, engage with policy-makers and corporate elites through creative advocacy strategies. Using personal relationships, media allies, and new technologies, activist networks are transforming public discourse and expanding political spaces.

In contrast to portrayals of civil society in terms of autonomous organisations, a state-civil society dichotomy, and links to democratisation, a focus on networks is more revealing of the dynamics of civil society development and its complex relations with the state. Through a mixture of primary interview data, participatory observation and secondary sources, the case studies presented in this book illustrate examples of network formation, structure and relationships and show how informal and virtual networks, rather than corporatist associations or non-governmental organisations (NGOs), may be seen as the building blocks of civil society.

This book is the product of lived experience in China and Vietnam spanning nearly two decades. I first worked in China in 1993–95 as a volunteer teacher and have made multiple return trips in the intervening years. Since 1997, I have been based largely in Vietnam, with the privilege of working alongside Vietnamese and international colleagues in many organisations and educational projects. Thus, I began research on civil society with an existing set of ties that widened over time and led to deeper connections and friendships, both professional and personal. In this way, I first came in contact with members of various networks, including the four profiled in this volume: the Bright Future Group of people with disabilities (Chapter 3), China Women's Network against AIDS (Chapter 4), Hanoi public space network (Chapter 5), and China Rivers Network (Chapter 6).

The empirical core of the book comes from over 150 semi-structured interviews carried out from 2008–10 in multiple locations, primarily Beijing and Hanoi, in a mixture of languages (Mandarin Chinese, Vietnamese and English). Most interviews were one-on-one conversations lasting an average of two hours and sometimes extending over several sessions, offering a chance to speak at length and develop rapport with informants. Befitting the subject matter of social networks, all interviews were arranged via introduction from another network member or the recommendation of an intermediary. Many interviews were fascinating, even exhilarating experiences. As one Vietnamese respondent said, 'It's I who should thank you for this interview, because you've given me an opportunity to talk about experiences that are so important for me!'

Although China and Vietnam are conventionally held to be challenging research settings, I did not encounter significant obstacles or delays: everyone interviewed was willing, even eager to talk about their work, although many preferred not to be quoted by name. In order to preserve the anonymity of respondents who requested it, the names of people interviewed are not mentioned in the text. However, networks and organisations are referred to by their actual names, as are the authors of public printed sources (including web materials), even if these authors are also network members and/or interview subjects, as this is information in the public domain.

The smoothness of research arrangements was a salutary result of the chosen design and methods. Since interviews were almost exclusively with network members, there was no need to set up formal appointments, submit paperwork to a sponsor or intermediary, or obtain anyone's advance approval. Research in Vietnam took place while living and working there. In China, the authorities appeared to apply the same 'hidden rules' of 'no recognition, no banning, no intervention' to informal research as to many unregistered foreign and domestic NGOs (Deng 2010).

During the period of research for this book, I was employed with Catholic Relief Services in Vietnam, who graciously allowed me time and flexibility to pursue interests outside of my normal responsibilities. On one of my research visits to Beijing, I was hosted on a voluntary basis at China Development Brief (中国发展简报), which produces an indispensable magazine and website in Chinese and now once again in English. Finally, part of the writing process was undertaken in space provided by a Vietnamese NGO, Action for the City (*Trung tâm Hành động vì Đô thị*), which was founded by my wife, Giang in 2006 with a mission of improving the urban environment and quality of life in Hanoi.

I hope that these organisational relationships were as productive for Chinese and Vietnamese colleagues as they were for me. However, the research and interviews were all conducted by me as an individual without any affiliation or sponsorship. I began all interviews by clarifying that my research is personal and not connected with any organisation. To the extent that respondents already knew and respected me, this made appointments easier to arrange, helped me know what questions to ask, and probably led to sharing of more information than to a stranger. On first meetings, my hyphenated married name provided an entry into the 'politics of self-representation' (Mullings 1999: 340) and in China, often led to an ironic explanation that Dang is the Vietnamese equivalent of Deng, as in Xiaoping. In this and other ways, it often happened that 'research participants interviewed me before I interviewed them' (Miraftab 2004: 599). My status could also be a potential source of bias, if respondents wished to overemphasise their effectiveness or the role of international support, although this could occur with any external interviewer. Possible bias was controlled by triangulating interview data with printed materials, observations, and impressions of secondary informants.

I am grateful to the many network members, NGO leaders, and academics in China and Vietnam who provided invaluable research suggestions, contacts and introductions, although they are not mentioned by name in the text. In addition, the research and writing of this book profited from written and verbal comments, criticisms and moral support from, among others, Greg Auberry, Michael Büsgen, Luis Cabrera, Wararak Chalermpuntusak, Catharin Dalpino, Jim Delaney, Dinh Thi Nguyet, Chris Eberhardt, Fu Tao, Martin Gainsborough, Gao Ming, Julie Gilson, Jude Howell, Caroline Hughes, Hy Luong, Mian Liping, Jason Morris-Jung, Tam Ngo, Henry Rosemont, Shawn Shieh, Pana Stitsart, Vu Thi Tuyet Mai, Wen Bo, and several anonymous reviewers. Of course, responsibility for the analysis and all remaining errors is mine alone.

Hoi An, Vietnam

1
The Dynamic Societies of China and Vietnam

'Now who do I know who might be able to help you?'

The Chinese director of a non-profit development organisation leaned back in a comfortable chair. We had not met before, but had been introduced by former colleagues from the 1990s. I explained my interest in networks of individuals and organisations who engage in advocacy. The director listened politely, then pulled out a cell phone and began searching for contacts. 'When you go to Beijing, you should talk to [this person]. And [this professor]. You can say that I recommended you. You can speak Chinese, right?'

My Chinese was a little rusty, but passable enough for interviews. It was near the beginning of a research visit to the mainland. I had not been to this city for nearly a decade, and it had changed to be almost unrecognisable. So had the social landscape.

'You should be fine then', the director said. 'They can both speak some English. Here are their cell phone numbers... No, even better, I will call them for you and set up appointments!'

A few smiles, laughs, and high-speed Chinese conversations later (with the English phrase 'civil society' interposed in the middle), the director had arranged two meetings for me the following week with specialists I would have had little chance of reaching on my own. The Beijing professor later told me, 'I don't usually meet with foreign researchers. But it's interesting that you live in Vietnam. And when [the director] told me you were coming, of course I made time!' The two meetings resulted in a series of introductions to organisation and network leaders.

The director could be of such help to me because, in Chinese terms, a person at the centre of social networks can 'pull *guanxi*' (关系,

Vietnamese *quan hệ).* In the language of sociology, the director had both a broad stock of social capital and high status in the social system (Lin 2001), with a wide-ranging network of ties to other non-governmental organisations, academics, and government officials.

The terms 'network' and 'social network' have become ubiquitous, especially in reference to the Internet: sociologist Manuel Castells calls networks 'the emblematic organisational form of the computer age and global informational economy...the new social morphology of our societies' (1996: 469). The idea of personal *guanxi* networks, moreover, has been common in Asian societies for decades (Yang 1994). But the application of the term (网络 *wǎnglùo*, Vietnamese *mạng lưới*) to civil society is more recent; words such as 'group', 'platform', 'forum', 'alliance', and 'coalition' are more frequent. In some locations, a 'network' might sound threatening to insecure authorities, while 'a group of organisations' is less so. Yet even if certain networks call themselves by other names, 'network' is still the best general term, precisely because of its connotations of personal ties and the Internet.

Chinese and Vietnamese networks take form and develop their identities in a complex context of social change, negotiation for space from authorities, and international influences. These networks are built on personal connections and develop into flexible, often informal structures that engage in path-breaking advocacy with authorities and elites. Civil society may thus be re-conceptualised as a process of building cross-sectoral networks, rather than a set of autonomous organisations. Looking at civil society through the lens of informal networks reveals a wider range of advocacy techniques and strategies in both countries than previously documented in non-democratic political systems. In the restricting political contexts of China and Vietnam, civil society networks have brought about significant social change.

New agents of political action

In most scholarly and journalistic portrayals, China and Vietnam are undergoing economic reforms without any corresponding political change (Abuza 2001, Hom and Mosher 2007, Ho 2008a, Hayton 2010). China is depicted as 'a country that bans independent non-governmental organizations and has no organized philanthropy' (Rucker 2008), with a 'repressed civil society' (Alagappa 2004: vi). Chinese civil society actors are 'loosely arranged and fragmented, with no self-conscious participation in a larger project or sphere' (Howell and Pearce 2001: 140); the 'absence of networks' is held to be a 'serious problem' (Ma 2006: 199).

In Vietnam, likewise, 'anything resembling the various definitions of civil society seems to be lacking' and pseudo-NGOs 'try to pass themselves off as "genuine"' (Salemink 2006: 121, Thayer 2009: 10–11). 'The presence of the state is so overwhelming that civil society has yet to truly develop', says another researcher; it only exists in the 'wishes and imaginations' of foreign observers (London 2009: 393).

In cross-country comparative studies, China and Vietnam are presented as negative examples, when they are mentioned at all: divided domestic movements with weak leverage (Keck and Sikkink 1998: 118), counterexamples where little change occurs (Potter 1996: 14), or among the last remaining Communist countries with little participation in 'global civil society' (Ougaard and Higgott 2002: 152). Implicit in many of these accounts is an identification of civil society with a linear model of democratisation and 'transition from authoritarianism' (Linz and Stepan 1997, O'Donnell and Schmitter 1986), which is not presently occurring in China or Vietnam.

Reality is more complex: China and Vietnam are not and may never be fully open and democratic societies, yet political change is demonstrably possible. Although each of the above negative statements may have been accurate at one time or in certain settings, they do not capture contemporary dynamics and result in a skewed picture (Luong 2005: 124). Contrary to the picture of a political system that 'remains frozen', there have been sweeping changes in 'a period of extraordinary contention' (Perry and Selden 2003: 6,20). In spite of 'political wraps' (Heinrich Böll Foundation 2006), citizens are not passive, apathetic, or ignorant; instead, they 'develop new ways to articulate their interests in the political system' (Shi 1997: 264). Legal and extra-legal structures set limits on network activities, yet network members can and do engage parts of the state and mould political opportunities through advocacy.

In particular, many activists, NGO leaders, journalists and academics are highly strategic and independent in their thinking, whatever their connections, negotiations and conflicts with state authorities. They are pathbreakers in constructing new forms of organising and ways to engage in advocacy. With few exceptions, network members are not anti-government dissidents, but neither are they afraid to express critical views. Although the systemic constraints they face are real, their agency as civil society actors is absent or undervalued in much existing literature (Büsgen 2006: 14).

One reason that existing portrayals of China and Vietnam are insufficient is that they depend on conceptions of civil society that, for all their varied philosophical roots, insist on identifying independent organisations that are voluntary and autonomous from the state. If these criteria are applied strictly, one could conclude that no civil society exists in either country. Alternately, one could qualify the cases as 'diminished subtypes' (Collier and Levitsky 1997).[1] Yet size and strategic considerations alone suggest that China and Vietnam are too important to be dismissed as exceptions. Moreover, the social conditions of globalisation and industrialisation in a single-party authoritarian regime are far from unique in today's world. Rather than fit China and Vietnam into 'precooked historical or theoretical scenarios' (Mulder 2003: 233), a more productive research agenda begins with empirical realities in both countries and suggests ways that concepts of civil society might be revised and updated to account for these findings. This network-based theory of civil society is outlined further in Chapter 2.

Changing visions of civil society

Recent analysis by Chinese, Vietnamese and international scholars on civil society may be grouped in three general approaches, corresponding roughly to the early 1990s, late 1990s–early 2000s, and 2005 to the present. In the first period, scholars imported existing theories of 'civil society against the state' (Cohen and Arato 1992: 29) and applied them to 'the great unknown' of Asian Communist regimes (Potter 1993: 375).[2] A thorough, if at times sterile debate took place about the historical (non-) applicability of civil society and the public sphere in China (Wakeman 1993, Gu 1993, He Baogang 1997). In the post-Tiananmen years, researchers who arrived with binary opposition models encountered 'common frustration' (Perry 1995: 297) and found little or no evidence of civil society according to their definitions. 'An organization that is "non-governmental" is practically unheard of in Vietnam or China', wrote Kerkvliet and Porter (1995: 26; see also Gray 1999). Some observers found Vietnamese NGOs 'virtually non-existent' (Potter and Taylor 1996: 14). Chinese NGOs did exist but were found to be 'very tame' and 'deeply compromised', since they 'either work closely with the state or are repressed' (Weller 1999: 127–8). The problem in Vietnam, wrote one academic, is the lack of 'agents of change', defined as 'organized and autonomous groups with their own authority system' (Abuza 2001: 9). If civil society depended on autonomy, there was little of it to be seen in the 'mono-organisational socialism' (Thayer 1995) under the central authority of the Communist Party.

In the second, more nuanced phase of scholarship, researchers sought to compare Asian realities with a theory of civil society based on European experience; the most in-depth example of this genre is White, Howell and Shang (1996), *In Search of Civil Society*. The authors conclude that something is occurring in China that fits under the rubric of 'civil society', but that it differs in several important respects from the imported definition, particularly in the lack of clear separation between civil society and the state. This finding led several China specialists to argue that state-society relations can be better understood in terms of corporatism, rather than civil society (Unger and Chan 1995), an approach that has also been influential in Vietnam studies (Jeong 1997). In state corporatism, the state creates a system of formal interest representation and recognises or licences only one association per constituency (Schmitter 1974: 93, Unger 2008: 7). In this system, also labelled as 'mobilisational' or 'soft authoritarian-corporatist', a fragmented state may delegate some roles to society while retaining overall control over national development (Kerkvliet 2001a: 180, Dixon 2004: 25–6).

From the level of analysis of the state, advocates of corporatism have a strong case in China and Vietnam. The legal systems in both countries conform to the key assumptions that all social organisations 'belong' to state agencies at either the central or provincial/local levels, with 'government-organised NGOs' (GONGOs) receiving preferential treatment. Specific examples of corporatist legal structures include China's dual registration system, in which social organisations must have both an administrative 'mother-in-law' and a legal government sponsor, and Vietnam's use of quasi-governmental umbrella organisations to register and limit the activities of domestic NGOs. Both countries' regulations also state that no more than one association may represent a given constituency in the same geographic area, though this rule is more strictly observed in China.

Official sponsors, in the corporatist view, 'completely dominate' associations, while grassroots organisations remain at the periphery with 'delicate, precarious' status (Unger and Chan 2008: 55–64). Research on business associations has found that entrepreneurs seek embeddedness, not autonomy, confirming a corporatist hypothesis (Dickson 2002, Gallagher 2004). Gallagher notes that the Chinese state is capable of enforcing its corporatist regulations, but instead allows 'unofficial civil society' to grow outside of the corporatist framework since capturing it would serve to legitimise these groups. Instead, marginal social groups such as migrants and religious sects build 'informal, flexible networks' outside the state, building internal social capital but not contributing to civil society (2004: 436–9).

In the view of certain Chinese and Vietnamese respondents, the state does not actually have the capacity to carry out all of the regulations it issues, but uses them selectively or arbitrarily 'like a stick' to make an example of organisations that 'cross the line'. The two countries' regimes no longer seek to control all aspects of society (a goal that was never fully achieved, at least in Vietnam), and instead pursue policies of 'small government, big society' (小政府大社会) or the Vietnamese euphemism for privatisation, 'socialisation' (*xã hội hoá*). The Party-sponsored mass organisations in Vietnam are relatively stronger than their Chinese equivalents; together with their coordinating 'umbrella' body, the National or 'Fatherland' Front (*Mặt trận Tổ quốc*) they have the ambiguous dual function to 'pre-empt the emergence of auto-nomous civil society bodies', while simultaneously representing inter-ests of constituents and serving as channels through which people can organise (Shanks et al 2004: xiv).

At the same time, scholars who looked less at legal structures and more at the grassroots level noticed a significant change: the emer-gence of semi-independent NGOs. As one observer noted, Vietnamese were forming 'what they believed were independent organisations', and they felt free 'to decide their own agenda and to raise money to act' (Beaulieu 1994, quoted in Kerkvliet 2003: 1). These groups num-bered 'at least in the hundreds' and were 'among the most exciting, dynamic sectors' in the country (Sidel 1996: 293). Vietnam specialists began to see signs of 'creeping pluralism', in which newly-formed organisations engaged in a process of negotiation or contestation with state authorities (Kerkvliet and Porter 1995: 86).

By the early 2000s, observers noted greater numbers and variety of organisations, improved though not complete legal structures, more discussion of civil society in the media, and less state repression (Luong 2003, Kerkvliet 2003: 15–16, Gray 2003). The initiative, however, lay with the state's decision to employ more or less repression or incen-tives for civil society (Kerkvliet 2003: 18). Organisations were still 'deeply entangled with each other and the state' (Nørlund 2008: 2); they engaged in some forms of advocacy, but within bounds set by state authorities (Hannah 2005: 109). In China, similarly, shifting boundaries between state and society resulted in 'many groups hav[ing] a fair degree of operational autonomy' (Gallagher 2004: 419, 446).

Partly as a result of this scholarship, the term 'civil society' began to be used widely by scholars, donors and organisations in both China and Vietnam (Nørlund 2008: 2, Alagappa 2004: 14). Some authors pre-ferred to qualify civil society with adjectives – a 'partial and patchy' or 'semi-civil society' (White 1996: 207, He Baogang 1997), a 'state-led civil society' (Frolic 1997, Lux and Straussman 2004), or infantilising metaphors such as 'nascent', 'embryonic', 'immature', or 'fledgling' (Thayer 1992, He 2003, Nørlund 2006, Xie 2007). Other writers described contradictory puzzles of 'dependent autonomy' (Lu 2008), 'embedded activism' (Ho and Edmonds 2008), or 'civil society and corporatism simultaneously' (Ma 2006: 137), in which large associations are corporatist while grassroots NGOs fit a civil society model. Autonomy remains an important determining factor in these analyses, as a range instead of a binary variable. Many analyses place organisations in categories on a spectrum from most to least autonomous (White et al 1996, Gallagher 2004, Watson 2008). Ma Qiusha, likewise, argues that autonomy is 'not the only important question' for Chinese NGOs (2006: 13), but still emphasises a typology of organisations grouped according to relative autonomy.

The comprehensive works by Ma, Lu Yiyi (2008) and Ho and Edmonds (2008) make a number of convincing arguments about state-society relations in China: the political and social structure offers opportunities as well as restrictions for NGOs; state corporatism no longer applies very well as an explanatory model; civil society can develop without leading inexorably to democracy; and NGOs are enmeshed in a web of *guanxi* with the state. All, however, focus on NGOs as their unit of analysis, not considering networks or informal groups. Regarding Vietnam, Benedict J. Tria Kerkvliet has outlined three contrasting interpretations of state-society relations: the 'dominating state' model, authoritarian/corporatist, and dialogical, premised on the actions of 'organized activists beyond official channels to voice citizens' concerns and demands' (2001a, 2001b: 248). Although Kerkvliet is clearly partial to the dialogical model, he is careful to point out that each has evidence to support it and may be relevant in differing situations. The apparent incompatibility of corporatist, statist and civil society theories may also lie in a lag in observers' ability to account for these changes. Asian Communist parties did indeed pursue mono-organisational strategies at one time, and corporatism may have applied quite well to the Chinese and Vietnamese contexts in the 1990s, but is no longer sufficient (Howell 2004a: 162–4).

Both China and Vietnam now have societies that are far more diverse than a corporatist or 'partial civil society' model would predict. Many non-profit organisations, religious groups, and informal local associations have found alternate means to operate beyond the corporatist structures set by the state, either registering as for-profit businesses, as a subsidiary of other legal organisations such as universities and the media, or by simply not registering at all (Howell 2004a: 151–9, Ma 2006: 76–94). One informant, a Chinese government official, explained this by drawing a pyramid on a scrap of paper. The base of the pyramid, she said, is formed of unregistered groups, followed by a thin layer of NGOs registered as businesses, and registered social organisations at the top. Since it is difficult to register with the Ministry of Civil Affairs (民政部), most groups remain unregistered, but this does not stop them from many activities.

Individual leaders and members of these groups demonstrate independent thinking and strategising (Büsgen 2006, Wells-Dang 2010) beyond the loyalty and subservience expected of them by the state. Even official associations such as mass organisations and GONGOs may have significant autonomy to pursue their own objectives (Ma 2006: 96). One study of NGOs in China concludes that the legal registration status of an organisation actually has no value as a predictor of an organisation's behaviour towards the state (Lu 2008: 30).

The third and newest phase of scholarship has moved beyond organisational characteristics to look at how informal groups and activists legitimate activities and engage with authorities (Büsgen 2006, Kerkvliet et al 2008: 49). Realising that the term NGO has set many researchers on the wrong track, this analysis emphasises agency as well as structural limitations, brings in insights from social movement studies, and considers informal as well as formal organisations and networks. Gao Bingzhong (2007) considers forms of legitimacy other than legal registration; an organisation or network can also be recognised as legitimate by society, then say, 'Yes, we do not have your permission, nor have we registered, but what we have done is right in nature' (62). As long as groups are not perceived as anti-state, they have significant freedom to act.

Once scholars look beyond formal organisations, the picture of civil society appears different – in part because Chinese and Vietnamese societies have changed, but also due to a new and liberating concept of what makes up civil society. Jude Howell describes 'a new multi-tiered configuration of organising, reaching from registered social organisations at the top to substrata of affiliated centres, networks, groups and projects'. Groups and individual activists are promoting a public sphere in the sense of 'making an issue a public issue', even though the Chinese government still can determine what is or is not public (2004a: 151, 153). A public sphere forms, in this interpretation, as actors act to bring about changes in social and government policy through 'invited consultation'. But the result is far from the encompassing public sphere envisioned by Habermas; instead Howell finds 'a multiplicity of protopublic spheres that are occupied by technical and intellectual elites, that are evolving separately and unevenly, and because of their uncertain and episodic relation with the Party/state, are both transient and fragile' (2004a: 160–1). Some of these multiple spheres are now developing in a more substantial and stable way than Howell observed nearly a decade previously.

As international scholarship takes steps away from a three-sector model of state-market-civil society, ironically, the concept is increasingly being accepted by Chinese and Vietnamese authorities. In Vietnam, official publications have printed theoretical articles on civil society (Vu D 2008, Bui 2007, Van 2006). Another article urged, 'Don't be afraid of civil society!' (Khiet 2006). The main argument of these writers is that civil society is not in opposition to the state but is a separate axis that can be complementary, and even help the state to do things. As one respondent notes, 'the line is in different places at different times. Before, no one was allowed to talk about "civil society"; now the term is being used in the National Assembly'. Since the authorities have already acknowledged the importance of a separate market sector, the argument proceeds, the 'third sector' is just one more step along the path to government decentralisation or a defence to minimise negative impacts of market and government failures (Dang 2007: 308). Most Chinese and Vietnamese writing is based on foreign sources from the liberal individualist side of civil society theory, influenced by economic management and public policy discourses, as well as some discussion of social capital (Gao and Yuan 2008, Nguyen M 2009). Analysts have taken a generally positive view of the greater acceptance of civil society terminology as 'evidence of a developing and widening civic space' and a move beyond corporatism (Kerkvliet et al 2008: 28, 49, Wischermann 2010).

A sharply different view comes from dissidents such as 2010 Nobel Peace laureate Liu Xiaobo, who identifies civil society with 'resistance movements' on the part of a united 'people' opposing the 'officials' (2006: 121). Liu believes 'there are no Chinese NGOs in the internationally-accepted sense', since registered organisations 'all are covertly manipulated by the Communist Party and their very existence depends on the Party's estimation of how much of a threat they pose to power' (2007: 116–19). With due respect to Liu's activism and sacrifices, he undervalues the ways that registered and unregistered organisations and networks find ways to work through and around the existing system. In Vietnam studies, the strongest advocate for a confrontational model is Carlyle Thayer, who defines civil society as 'the creation of public space where Vietnam's one-party state can be challenged by the non-violent political mobilization of ordinary citizens' in a 'struggle for democracy against the authoritarian Vietnamese state' (2009: 10). The possibility that NGOs, religious groups and others could form networks that cut across classes and regions and form a 'base against the party-state' is exactly what authorities most fear (Gold 1998: 176, Yang 2008: 137), but aside from small networks of individual dissidents who are willing to take on immense personal risks, few domestic activists share this vision. The dissidents and critics correctly point out that civil society is fundamentally political, is not comprised solely of formal organisations, and depends on what people actually do. However, a definition based on total opposition to the state is far too narrow and misses contestation that takes place within, around and among the state and society.

A genealogy of networks

Compared to the extensive literature on NGOs, there is as yet no systematic study of networks in China or Vietnam. Howell's 2004 *Governance in China* mentions several emerging networks in HIV, gender and labour sectors as 'a direction that civil society may be moving towards', though this was 'risky' at the time (163). Joseph Hannah (2007: 224–5) noted several networks forming in Vietnam in 2002–03, in most cases limited to 'personal networks and informal ties'. Since then, several case studies have been published on Chinese environmental networks (Büsgen 2006, Xie 2007), community and homeowners' networks (Shi and Cai 2006, Read 2009), Vietnamese NGO networks (Desmond et al 2007, Hoang and Bui 2008), and relief networks that formed after the 2008 Sichuan earthquake (Shieh and Deng 2011). Most of this research has focused on horizontal networks among participants, rather than vertical networking between citizens and officials (Shi and Cai 2006: 316).

Personal and local networks have existed in Vietnam and China for centuries. Vietnamese academics associate historical civil society with networks and connections among villages, which had partial autonomy from the state, as reflected in the oft-quoted proverb that 'the king's edict stops at the village gates'. China had a stronger national state, but its civil society was also made up of local traditional social associations (Pye 1996, Tsai 2007). Many observers saw the emergence of informal associations in Beijing and other cities in 1989 as the beginning of a new civil society, but their hopes were dashed afterwards (Saich 1990, Pye 1996). Since 1989, there have been many popular protests in China but no major social movements, with the exception of Falun Gong (Lin 2001, Shue 2004, Johnson 2004, Hu Ping 2007). Informal social network ties have been critically important in maintaining Chinese associations and tradition through periods when formal organisations have been repressed or co-opted (Weller 1999).

The potential of informal 'rhizomatic networks', operating with no permanent members or titles, is illustrated in Mayfair Yang's study of *guanxi:*

> The flexibility, relative anonymity, and weak integration that characterize guanxi networks are what enable them to withstand incursions made by the state. The quasi-group can continue to function even though occasionally a few members get caught. Given the current political conditions in China, quasi-groups are better off not becoming crystallized and institutionalized into full-fledged and visible formal associations and corporate groups.... Most likely, this form is only a transitional phase, so that once the state can guarantee the legitimacy of formal associations...quasi-groups can be transformed into open associations that contribute to the welfare of a community or the larger public. (Yang 1994: 304–5)

Twenty years after Yang's research, political conditions have shifted greatly, and Chinese and Vietnamese authorities allow many types of formal social organisations to register. Yet such informal 'quasi-groups' continue to function, for some of the same reasons. Legal requirements do not encourage horizontal networks, but loose connections do form, based on personal relations, not institutional ones. There is no legal category for networks in either Vietnam or China (Kerkvliet et al 2008: 27, Schwartz and Shieh 2009: 9). Some networks have managed to register as organisations or as branches of a larger association, but most are unregistered. As with organisations, being unregistered 'doesn't mean you're illegal or legal; if you do good things', says one informant, 'the government doesn't pay too much attention'. Authorities use registration requirements to restrain the formation of networks; in China, there is an added regulation that organisations (even GONGOs) may not set up branches in other cities and provinces. But due to the lack of a legal framework, government control of networks is weak.

One NGO director points to the 1995 United Nations World Conference on Women as a key turning point in grassroots organising, as Chinese had opportunities to meet and network with international counterparts. At that time, Chinese activists were 'isolated islands' and didn't even know each other. The first formal network among Chinese non-profit organisations began in 1999 with the sponsorship of the NGO Research Institute at Tsinghua University in Beijing and the China Youth Development Foundation's Project Hope. This led to a large capacity building conference in 2001 among 18 NGOs, which became the China NPO Network.

Samantha Keech-Marx (2008) considers women's networks as well as organisations in Beijing, treating networks as a type of organisation or association, not a distinct category. She analyses civil society as made up of personal networks across institutions, citing Perry's description (1995: 297) of Chinese associational activity as a 'peculiar blend of public, private and state'. Lu's survey of Chinese NGOs found that a desire to expand personal networks, including internationally, can be a key reason to form a new organisation (2008: 121). NGOs use informal ties to compensate for inadequate institutional capacity (106). Overall, however, personal networks contribute to civil society development, and 'millions of Chinese are participating in some sort of formal or informal network' outside of registered organisations (Ma 2006: 108–15, 135).

Given China's immense size, many networks operate regionally rather than nationally; for instance, several informal community development networks cover Yunnan, Sichuan, and Guizhou provinces in southwest China, with links to southern networks in Guangdong and Guangxi, as well as to Hong Kong. In one donor's view, provincial or regional networks may have a better chance of sustaining themselves than national ones. 'Different networks should exist at different levels and sectors', says a Chinese HIV/AIDS activist. 'National-level networks should be spontaneous and develop naturally, not be man-made by outside forces... Real networks grow up from the bottom; they are not artificially created. There is conflict and opposition, but it's real.'

Many networks are nameless, as it could be risky to draw attention to a large group: 'Having a name is too much trouble!' says the coordinator of one network in China's Yunnan province. Such groups have little contact with government and primarily provide training and support for their members and local NGOs, rather than engage in public advocacy, but they have latent potential for civil society involvement, as demonstrated in the case of the 2008 Sichuan earthquake. The earthquake was 'a shock of consciousness' (Gadsden 2008), a turning point in government attitudes towards NGOs and networks (Ford 2009). After the earthquake, two NGO networks came together rapidly to channel materials and information to affected communities (Teets 2009). These networks were able to form quickly because members were already connected to each other through existing social ties, including regional NGO training pro-grammes and rivers advocacy experience. Unregistered NGOs who joined the earthquake relief effort were found to rely more on networks than did registered, business, or individual-based organisations (Shieh and Deng 2011: 187).

In addition to regional networks, national sectoral federations would be desirable but are more difficult to form. One organisation in Shanghai reports 'close ties' with other local NGOs through project cooperation in the same geographic areas; they intend to form a more formal alliance, but this requires cooperation with local government. There are different levels of networks including GONGOs at the outer level, but a core of grassroots groups in the centre. In contrast to membership organisations, which are closed and only for members, such informal networks operate flexibly among organisations whose staff meet each other at conferences, workshops and salons. Closer to Yang's 'rhizomatic networks' are unregis-tered Buddhist women's groups that meet in informal groups and con-nect through the Internet in both China and Vietnam. These groups have names that are known internally but not mentioned to outsiders; if members speak to the media to promote their activities, they do so as individuals and not as members of any group. Unlike large Buddhist organisations in Taiwan and some other Asian settings, these networks exist with a semi-underground status, but their goal is the same: to attract Buddhists to social service, including not a few government officials and Party members who would not be able to take part in a public group.

Perhaps the best-developed networks in China and Vietnam are in the area of environmental protection, as environmental groups have 'crossed the bridge' from a service orientation to advocacy (Wells-Dang 2011a). In Vietnam, there are formal networks on river protection and climate change, as well as many informal task forces. An informal network among anti-wildlife trade campaigners, with a 'strident cam-paigning agenda and access to top politicians' (Hayton 2010: 166–7), operates in small cells known simply as the 'bear group', the 'tiger group', and so on, with assigned members from different organisations. Task forces share information, avoid overlap, and strategise jointly on policy advocacy. 'There are only 100 bears and 30 tigers left in the wild, so there's no space for us to be competitive!' says one activist.

In China, besides the anti-dam network profiled in Chapter 6, a water pollution network holds an annual conference along with several net-works of mostly unregistered grassroots groups funded by the same donor. An environmental education network is based in Sichuan, while almost every province has networks of student environmental groups. These groups are very well connected online; the amount of information is staggering. Since environmental issues affect everyone, it is possible to stimulate broad participation and international donor interest (Futrell 2008). Chinese activists equate environmental development with the public involvement of 'a participatory group of citizens who share the same views' (Liang and Yang 2007: xv).

Environmental networks provide the clearest evidence of a growing generational transition in membership. Civil society networks formed in the 1990s or earlier, such as women's networks dating from the 1995 Beijing conference, were initially led by a generation of activists who matured during the Cultural Revolution and its aftermath in China, or the American War and 'subsidised period' in Vietnam. By the 2000s, these pioneers were increasingly joined by students and younger professionals who grew up during the decades of reform and economic development. Compared to the older generation, the younger activists have relatively lower anxiety about politics, more international connections and exposure, and higher use of information technologies. The younger network members also tend to be pragmatic rather than ideological, with repertoires of collective action based more on international and regional NGO campaigning and less on socialist-era mass struggles. The tension among generations is a consistent element of Chinese and Vietnamese networks, offering diversity and also at times sharp differences of opinion on strategy and tactics.

Some networks (or their organisational members) have been able to access international funding, most often through foundations, bilateral or multilateral donors with programmes in China and Vietnam. Funding decisions and mechanisms have had undeniable influence on network capacities and structures, whether through deliberate conditionality of funding or underlying attitudes towards civil society. Donor support, though welcomed by most networks, is not always an unmitigated blessing; as with government regulations, networks have also developed strategies to engage and manage funding relationships.

For example, donors in Vietnam have focused attention on 'collaborative groups' (*tổ hợp tác*), informal networks in rural areas focused largely on agricultural production, as a form of 'surrogate civil society' on the assumption that 'a vibrant, genuinely independent civil society does not yet exist' (Fritzen 2003: 3, 25). While this strategy may have resulted in temporary gains for participants in local groups, it created issues of sustainability and dependence. A workshop in 2007 found that collaborative groups established independently by local residents are more sustainable than those set up through external projects (PPWG

2007). As there has been no sign yet of aggregation of these local networks into larger federations with advocacy capacity, collaborative groups might be said to have more potential than actual civil society features. In this and other cases, donors thought networks were important, but Vietnamese participants had other priorities.

Donors and international NGOs have also funded large projects to create new nationwide networks, with international study tours, capacity building training, and all-expenses-paid meetings, among people who had not previously worked together. The results have been disappointing. In one case of a donor-initiated network, an evaluation found that individuals participated in training provided for their own benefit, but there was no sustainable network after the conclusion of the project or observed net effect on civil society development (Desmond et al 2007). Similar counterproductive results have been documented by other NGOs including CARE and ActionAid. Larger donors, such as bilateral and UN agencies, may at times be too far removed from the implementation of their projects to notice how their funding is used.

At a workshop in October 2008, one Vietnamese NGO delegate worried whether donor-funded workshops on advocacy and networking were becoming a 'fashion'. In addition to four workshops on advocacy-related topics the author attended in 2007–08 in Hanoi, at least three others took place, with as many as 90 participants each (Vu T 2008). Vietnamese observers sense that much network advocacy has not been as effective as expected (Hoang and Bui 2008, Vu T 2008). 'A lot of organisations want to do advocacy, but only some are able to', according to one conference speaker, due to both lack of resources and knowledge. In one case,

> advocacy went no further than issue identification and training, [with] no impacts on the local policy-making process…. An underlying assumption of networking is that the whole can be greater than the sum of the parts. If the network only serves as an umbrella…it is not realising its value-added potential. (Hoang and Bui 2008: 17–18)

Lack of skills and confidence on the part of network members was one explanation, together with resistance and lack of recognition of the network's legitimacy by policy-makers. Some government officials still perceive advocacy as a threat to their power (Vu T 2008: 26); this may also be because they do not understand activists' use of terms like 'civil society' and confuse this with Party warnings about 'colour revolutions.' It is also worth acknowledging that many organisations and networks are not themselves representative or transparent (Vu T 2008: 28).

Lu (2008) cites several examples of unsuccessful networks and campaigns in which Chinese NGOs had difficulty working together, presenting a perhaps overly negative picture of the possibilities of network success.

In a more promising example, one community development organisation in China forms networks through participatory organising involving local leaders, social workers, and resident committees. In some areas, multiple community networks then assemble into a 'platform' with a newsletter and cooperation in community services with local governments. The degree of advocacy is limited, but the model has possibilities to expand, as one interview respondent states:

> There are obstacles on the government side: they are sometimes not transparent, wanting to capture the project and not share information. But NGOs can work together and form alliances among organisations in the community, for instance bringing groups of elderly people and cultural groups together, or holding festivals for migrant workers.

Labour activists are less networked, by design. Workers practice 'cellular activism' with few cross-factory protests, due both to state opposition and the perceptions and repertoire of workers (Lee 2007b, Chen 2008). For Bernstein and Lu (2003: 17, 117), peasant protests do not aggregate into a social movement since they have no urban allies. The level of rural-to-rural networking is also limited, as cross-jurisdictional protests are more likely to provoke repressive responses. International NGOs and donors often find it difficult to fund such networks since they have no legal status to receive donations, and especially in China, the funder may not have legal status either. Instead, many donors channel funds to one or more organisations that are network members or act on behalf of a network; while this often works smoothly, it is less than ideal.

Comparing networks in China and Vietnam

This book compares networks, not nation-states: the sample of civil society networks examined is taken from a field encompassing both countries. A focus on networks increases the size of the sample and compares among multiple smaller units (King et al 1994), in place of the 'methodological nationalism' (Anheier et al 2003: 4) and other limitations of a binary comparative analysis between two nations (Dogan and Pelassy 1984). Comparison among networks is nevertheless based on an assumption that

China and Vietnam share enough social, historical, cultural and political characteristics to be considered an 'area of homogeneity' (Ragin et al 1996: 752).

No published literature compares civil society or networks in China and Vietnam.[3] The comparisons of China and Vietnam undertaken to date mostly focus on history (Womack 2006, Woodside 1988) and economic reforms (Chan et al 1999, Abrami et al 2008). Two of the few scholars engaging in full-scale bi-national comparisons are Woodside (1988, 1998, 2006) and Womack (1987, 2006).[4] Although China has always been much larger and more powerful, these comparisons show that influence has not been unidirectional, but rather the two countries have related in a process of co-evolution and adaptation. Vietnam is not a mere subset of China or a secondary variant of 'Confucian society' (Alagappa 2004: 13).

A common feature of much Chinese (and some foreign) writing is a claim that civil society in China is irreconcilably different from 'the West', due to a unique 'traditional Chinese collective identity' (He Xirong 1997: 116, Xie 2007, Gu 2008). Such thinking seems less prevalent in Vietnam, perhaps since it is a smaller country with greater historical exposure to foreign influences, both benign and invasive (from both China and 'the West'). In this book, Chinese and Vietnamese cases are considered together in order to focus attention on the common trajectories of networks, rather than on the particularities of a single country (Womack 1987: 480). To the extent that China and Vietnam are similar, neither country is unique; to the extent that China and Vietnam are different, it is hard to maintain the illusion of a unified Asia.

Surprisingly, given the countries' proximity and apparent similarity, there has been little dialogue among the respective literatures. Vietnam is mentioned as a footnote in some studies of civil society in China (Bell 2006: 251, Howell and Pearce 2001: 146), while Vietnam-focused studies do not refer to Chinese civil society at all. Comparisons between Vietnam and other ASEAN countries are more common: one paper on public administration reform (Vasavakul et al 2009) compares Vietnamese experience to Southeast Asian neighbours and to Taiwan and South Korea, but makes no mention of the elephant to the north. In what Woodside (2006: 15) terms one of the 'idols of the postwar Western academic (and strategic) mind', the border between China and Vietnam also forms an imagined boundary between the regions of East and Southeast Asia. More than actual border controls, this arbitrary division inhibits the emergence of a coherent approach to commonalities and intersections between China and Southeast Asia (Liu 2001: 261).

The discontinuity extends to civil society actors in both countries, who have little if any contact with each other. As a Vietnamese respondent notes, 'we only meet Chinese colleagues at international meetings in a third country'. Third-country meetings can offer important opportunities for information exchange and network-building, but are expensive and time-consuming to organise. Language barriers form a significant obstacle to direct interaction, as do mental barriers. Many Vietnamese are fearful and suspicious of China (Hayton 2010: 188–92), and Vietnamese civil society actors feel they have nothing to learn from people in another single-party, communist state: they would rather emulate what they see as more successful instances of civil society in developed countries. On the Chinese side, most people are unaware of Vietnamese sentiments, and unless they happen to live near the Vietnamese border, they pay little attention to their neighbour. As a result, there is little cross-border networking between groups in China and Vietnam (Hinton 2000). The civil society networks examined in this book are primarily domestic, not transnational, in their nature and structure. External links may be important, as may expatriate or diaspora membership in some cases, but for most networks, the local context remains of primary importance (Edwards and Gaventa 2001, Kalland and Persoon 1998, Florini 2000).

Many studies assume that 'socialist states have weak civil society because of the predominance of the party and state in social and political affairs and the absence or weakness of domestic capital' (Howell and Pearce 2001: 123). Yet comparative political analysts conclude that Vietnam is relatively more open than China. Kerkvliet, Chan and Unger (1998: 6) describe Vietnamese policies as 'less ideologically strident' and 'divisive' than China's. Labour experts find Vietnam's legal protections more effective than China's, resulting in a 'less abusive' system (Chan and Wang 2003: 5). A series of liberal Chinese writers, led by a former deputy editor of the *People's Daily* (人民日报), have argued that Vietnam has greater 'intra-party democracy' and has made progress on political reform that China should emulate (Xu 2006, Fu 2006, Liu Zhenting 2006, Qian 2010, Lam 2007b). While these issues were widely discussed in the Chinese media, analysts conclude that Vietnam's state-owned media is freer than China's (London 2009). More inclusive governance structures have also been found to explain Vietnam's apparently slower increase in income inequality (Abrami et al 2008).

Given this record, one might assume that the political space for civil society networks to engage in advocacy is relatively greater in Vietnam

than in China. Indeed, some features of civil society in Vietnam confirm this impression. It is, on the whole, easier to register a new NGO
in Vietnam (Kerkvliet et al 2008: 12, Wexler et al 2006: 127), although
many groups still experience lengthy delays (Hannah 2007: 148). A
Chinese network leader says, 'I have the impression that Vietnamese
people are better networked and organised. China is too big for this!'
Yet other Chinese activists who have been to Vietnam find it 'difficult
and chaotic'. Laws and regulations are often less rigidly enforced in
Vietnam. Donors are under more scrutiny in China, and fundraising is
harder: some Chinese NGOs have been closed or threatened with closure
because they accepted funding from unwelcome donors. International
NGOs are more numerous and active in Vietnam and can usually register
without obstacles (Kerkvliet 2003, Wells-Dang 2007), while most international NGOs in China operate without legal registration (Ma 2006:
174). Both domestic and international NGOs routinely work directly
with Vietnamese government ministries and provincial authorities,
who usually welcome aid and take credit for positive results. This is
sometimes the case in China, but stories of the reverse are also common:
following a successful project, a local government feels threatened by
the NGO and forces it to leave the area.

Other factors point towards greater potential for civil society in
China. Many Chinese networks and organisations are larger, more professional and have existed for longer than their Vietnamese counterparts. This sophistication applies not only to certain NGOs and GONGOs,
but also to religious organisations, media, and research institutes. The
university system in China is better established than in Vietnam, with
higher relative levels of scholarship and academic freedom, including
several well-known civil society-related research centres in key national
institutions. China's growing prosperity has also fostered the development of a new sector of domestic private foundations, which hold the
potential to transform fundraising and philanthropy; nothing of the
sort has yet occurred in Vietnam. And although international NGOs
and foreign aid in general are thinner on the ground in China, certain
groups that are barred from Vietnam are able to operate openly in China,
including the Salvation Army, Peace Corps, and International Republican
Institute.

When making any such comparisons, it is crucial to consider the distorting effects of size and time. The most obvious difference between
China and Vietnam (or indeed, between China and any country besides
India) is that China is much larger: about 15 times larger in population
than Vietnam. Vietnam is not a small country – at 87 million people, it

is the thirteenth largest in the world – but it is barely the size of a single large Chinese province (Womack 2006: 12). There are significant regional differences within China (Lee 2007a), and also to some extent in Vietnam, though the latter may be overstated by outsiders who recall the relatively short historical period (1954-75) of forced division into North and South. A more appropriate geographical comparison might be between regions or cities: say, Vietnam's northern mountains with Yunnan province of China, the capital cities of Hanoi and Beijing, or the economic centres of Ho Chi Minh City and Guangzhou (Turley and Womack 1998).

A national-level comparison shows that there are, in absolute terms, many more social organisations operating in China than Vietnam. No statistics are available for networks; for NGOs, the most recent surveys count 386,916 registered social organisations in China (Gao and Yuan 2008: 34), about half of which are NGOs, but only perhaps 20 per cent grassroots-based (Chan 2005: 26). In Vietnam, 1,700 local NGOs are registered (VUSTA 2010). The number of informal and unregistered organisations is estimated to be several times higher (Gao and Yuan 2008: 19, Watson 2008: 37). In the 2000 World Values Survey, China was found to have low membership in NGOs but high levels of volunteering, while Vietnam was high in both areas, presumably because membership in mass organisations was included (Anheier et al 2002: 363–4). Considering the scale difference between the countries, the per-capita density of civil society involvement appears to be higher in Vietnam.

Time sequencing is also an important distinction. Although Vietnam began some economic reforms before China (Fforde 2009), China began 'reform and opening' (改革开放) from a much stronger economic position than Vietnam's 'Renewal', or *đổi mới* (Chan et al 1999: 9). Chinese society also liberalised significantly in the 1980s, and the first independent Chinese NGOs, such as the Protestant Church-led Amity Foundation (爱德基金会), formed at this time (Fiedler and Zhang 2005). These 'drops in the ocean' (Howell 1996) expanded when political space opened again in the early 1990s: China's best-known environmental NGO was established in 1994, and others formed in subsequent years (Ma 2006: 116–25, Sun and Zhao 2007). By contrast, comparable Vietnamese organisations mostly date to the early 2000s. Analysts routinely state that Vietnam's reforms are a decade or more behind China's (Chang 1997: 147–8, Vu 2009, Oxford Analytica 2010); one need not follow stage-theory reasoning to agree that the most appropriate direct comparison might be between a present-day Vietnamese network and a Chinese network when it was at the same age or state of formation.

Overseas diasporas and networks play a role in advocacy in both China and Vietnam, especially in the internet age (see Chapter 2). There is no

Vietnamese corollary, however, to the offshore islands of Hong Kong, Macau and Taiwan with their different histories and political systems. Hong Kong has followed 'a unique middle path' (Thomas 1999: viii), playing an influential role in development of civil society in China (Ma 2006: 179). With a mixture of inside and outside identities, Hong Kong Chinese act as cultural and linguistic network brokers (Smart and Smart 1998). Hong Kong connections with the mainland are not a question of citizenship but rather context, geography and social networks, perhaps also cultural sensitivity. Weller's comparisons of China, Taiwan and Hong Kong (1999, 2005, 2008) form 'close to a natural experiment' (1999: 11) to show that cultural factors do not determine socio-political outcomes, since all share a Chinese identity but have diverging trajectories. On the other hand, despite clear political differences, sometimes China and Taiwan share common social outcomes (Read 2009). Weller and Read hardly mention Vietnam, but the parallels are clear. These connections and common features form the basis for understanding the development of civil society networks in China and Vietnam.

Plan of the book

This book seeks to demonstrate that civil society networks exist in the political contexts of China and Vietnam and understand how they engage in advocacy, through answering the following questions:

- How are civil society networks formed? How do they operate?
- How do networks interact with state actors? What strategies do they select to influence other stakeholders?
- How effective are networks' advocacy efforts, in terms of policy impact, sustainability, and opening of political space?

This chapter presents an overview of civil society and networks in China and Vietnam, a brief comparison between the two contexts, and the methodologies employed in research. Chapter 2 develops a framework for understanding networks and advocacy, then introduces a typology of networks with illustrative examples from China and Vietnam. Primary source interviews and secondary data from both countries are juxtaposed in dialogue with each other. The chapter concludes by detailing three overall advocacy strategies observed among Chinese and Vietnamese networks, followed by a series of hypotheses on how networks employ these strategies.

The successive four chapters, comprising the heart of the book, present in-depth case studies of selected networks in different sectors, two in Vietnam and two in China. The Bright Future Group of people with disabilities (Chapter 3) is a longstanding informal network of individual activists that has supported the development of disability organisations and policy in Vietnam. The China Women's Network against AIDS (Chapter 4) is a newer network that began as a virtual support group for HIV-positive women and now faces conflicting pressures from its membership and donors. The Reunification Park public space network (Chapter 5) has successfully struggled to preserve Hanoi's largest park from private development, while keeping a very low profile. The China Rivers Network (Chapter 6) has experienced both formal and informal periods in its multi-faceted advocacy campaigns against dams in south-western China. Finally, the Conclusion identifies commonalities and variation among the case studies and assesses the results of research questions and hypotheses. The findings on the formation, roles and effectiveness of civil society networks are not only of value for observers of China and Vietnam, but also contribute to 'middle-range theory' (Klandermans and Staggenborg 2002: 317) that can inform theory-driven empirical research on other networks and in other research contexts.

This book employs a comparative case study method to illustrate the history, structure and advocacy strategies of selected civil society networks in China and Vietnam. The case study, as used here, is 'an empirical inquiry that investigates a contemporary phenomenon within its real-life context, especially when the boundaries between phenomenon and context are not clearly evident' (Yin 1994: 13). The comparative use of cases allows for in-depth analysis of complex and changing issues and 'engenders an extensive dialogue between the investigator's ideas and the data' (Ragin 1987: 49).

Research began with a scoping survey, which identified dozens of civil society networks in both countries that fit initial definitional criteria. The next step was identification of case studies, selected from the networks identified in the scoping survey using a purposive sampling method aiming to 'select information-rich cases' (Patton 1990: 169) that illustrate a diversity of sectors, network forms, size and prominence. Selection did not deliberately focus on extreme cases, either of success (Shi and Cai 2006) or resistance (O'Brien and Li 2006: 114). As the focus of the argument is on networks and advocacy as forms of political organisation, networks were selected with four different areas of focus (environment, health, disability and land rights) rather than from a single social sector. The majority of networks identified in both countries work in one of these four focus areas. The sample includes long-established and new networks; more formal and less formal structures; and networks with individual membership, organisational membership, and a combination of the two.

Each case study chapter follows a consistent protocol (Yin 1994: 64–5), consisting of information about the issue, history of network formation, membership and structure of the network, advocacy strategies, and political implications. The empirical chapters offer detailed and context-specific 'thick descriptions' (Geertz 1973) of each network, focusing less on content than on the framing of meaning and political space (Gamson and Meyer 1996). Since the level of analysis is the network, not the individual or organisation, case studies tell a collective narrative instead of individual stories of network members and activists, as compelling as these frequently are. The presentation of case studies is based to the greatest degree possible on interview data and primary source documents written by network members themselves.

Research was conducted through a combination of individual interviews, direct observation, and published materials, the latter including reports, websites, media articles, and academic publications. The amount of available documentation varied from very little in the case of the Vietnam disability network to immense for the China rivers network. Overall, much more secondary data is available on civil society and networks in China than in Vietnam, both in English and the local language. This balanced the author's greater access and linguistic fluency in Vietnam.

Interviews allowed for in-depth understanding of networks from members' perspectives, bringing human agency to the centre (Blee and Taylor 2002: 90, 96). Multiple interviews with informants within and outside the network, using a variant of a snowball sampling method, were the primary check to ensure balance and accuracy. In no case did anyone appear afraid to speak for political or security reasons.[5] The fact that the interviewer was a non-Asian foreigner did not seem to present any impediment.[6] There were also no observed gender differences in responsiveness; an equal number of men and women were interviewed in both countries. Where available, secondary literature formed the third leg of triangulation, allowing for multiple observations that increase the reliability of findings (Yin 1994: 87, Patton 1990: 187–8). Each draft case study chapter was circulated among one or more network members and secondary informants for review and comment, a form of 'peer debriefing' (Erlandson et al 1993: 31). Each of the cases may stand on its own, as an example of what Charles Tilly calls 'individualized comparison' (1984: 81–2). Taken together, the four case studies provide a composite picture of some of the range and extent of civil society networks and advocacy in present-day China and Vietnam.

2
Redefining Civil Society: Networks and Advocacy

Civil society is a process of collective action that occurs and develops when organisations and individuals join together to influence power and promote positive, non-violent social change. The basic units that comprise civil society in this analysis are networks of organisations, informal groups and individual activists, rather than non-governmental organisations alone. A *network* is defined as any set of individuals, informal groups and/or organisations linked together for a common purpose. One subset of networks consists of *civil society networks*, which engage in advocacy in pursuit of a shared agenda for social change. Such networks frequently span traditional social and political boundaries between state and non-state actors.

Network theory offers the basis for a re-theorisation of civil society, not as a sector or an arena but as a political process of collective action and alliance-building. This definition resonates with approaches that have become more influential in the literature on civil society and social movements in recent years.[1] It requires three key adjustments to existing civil society theory. First, the component parts of civil society are networks, not only autonomous organisations; these networks include individual and/or organisational members. Second, civil society occurs as networks act, therefore the question is no longer who is 'in' or 'out' of civil society, but what civil society actually does (Uphoff and Krishna 2004). Third, the actions of civil society networks cross boundaries between society, family, the market and the state, which are not monolithic but must be disaggregated according to their roles and positions.

Civil society in a network analysis is relational, made up of the links among individuals and organisations. Surprisingly, the connection between networks and civil society has rarely if ever been made, as most social

24

movement and network theorists keep a distance from civil society. The few existing references to 'civil society networks', such as on CIVICUS' website, describe links among NGOs.[2] Other related, but not identical concepts include 'solidary groups' (Tsai 2007) and 'action groups' (Haynes 1997). Perhaps the closest definition is in a discussion of civil society in Singapore, made up of 'networks of voluntary organisations...formed by citizens to pursue mutual interests or beliefs' (Kadir 2004: 330). This definition is still organisation-based, but Kadir notes that activists have 'ad hoc gatherings as a way of strengthening informal networks' (332).

Civil society networks are networks of individuals and/or organisations that engage in advocacy towards state authorities and elites. Such networks may have individual members, organisational participants, or both (Diani 2002: 174, Wilson-Grau and Nuñez 2006), ranging in size from a small group of individuals to a formal organisational coalition. Their structures may be formal or informal, with a variety of leadership and coordination models. In mixed networks, participants have some degree of individual participation as well as associational identity. NGOs and other associations form part of civil society networks to the extent they join in collaborative actions with others and are embedded in network structures (Potter and Taylor 1996: 2, Khagram et al 2002: 17–20). Simply having non-profit status is insufficient, as organisations may act in their own private interests as grant-seekers or service providers, even if they are not distributing profits to members or shareholders. This differs somewhat from Putnam's conception of membership in associations having value in itself for building social capital and democratic values (1993: 167); in a process view of civil society, formal or informal association membership has the *potential* to bring about these effects, but only when and if associations join in networks with others to pursue shared goals and engage authority. Networks and organisations may also have legitimate differences concerning goals and strategies, leading to intra- or inter-network conflicts.

Networks may include other individual and collective actors, such as for-profit businesses and media outlets, to the extent that they work together with others for perceived public benefit in addition to their own private interests. It is even conceivable that some component parts of states, such as local governments, ministry departments, or research institutes, may participate in civil society networks. This does not mean that GONGOs should be lumped into civil society. Rather, civil society can arise from within parts of the state to the extent that civil servants or agencies adopt 'amphibious' identities alongside their official roles (Ding 1994). Specifically, individual government officials may act in their own capacities as part of collective efforts to address climate change, improve women's rights, or numerous other possibilities. As one Chinese environmental official has said, 'During the day, I work as a government official. But that is just eight hours a day! For the rest of the time, I am an environmental activist'.

Not all networks are civil society networks. Many networks among individuals remain at the level of personal ties and have no public or advocacy component: for instance, most private clubs and business networks exist only to serve the interests of their members. Religious groups, by contrast, often have a vision of the common good but are identity-based and do not engage in advocacy. Social capital theorists sometimes claim that whether groups operate in the public interest or in private interests, they build social capital and civility, which foster civil society (Ma 2006: 206). This is too naïve; certain networks may be harmful. States may set up networks or corporatist arrangements of their own and co-opt other social actors to join (Lee and Rhyu 2008). The same possibility exists for corporate-initiated networks, let alone networks operating in illegal or semi-legal domains such as mafia or terrorist groups. In greyer areas, some networks may have multiple functions, incorporating certain civil society features while also pursuing private interests. Such actors require informed, context-specific yet ultimately subjective evaluations; analysts should 'stick with the empirical facts and scrutinize each and every civic organisation carefully, as to whether or not they might be contributing to "civil society-building"' (Krishna, cited in Wischermann 2006: 209).

Information technology is key to the communications and operations of civil society networks. Many newer networks have emerged parallel to the growth of IT access, and network members use information and communication technology – e-mail, chatting and cell phones/texting – as their main modes of communication. In fact, many network activities would be impossible without these technologies. This does not imply that the Internet has inherently liberating tendencies (Diamond 2010) or is responsible for creating networks, but rather that technology is a tool that has changed the operating realities of networks as well as state and private actors (Lehmann 2011).

Civil society networks' actions offer the potential, though no inevitable guarantee, of positive social change. The content of this change and its valuation as positive is an object of contestation within and across circumstances and cultures. For instance, liberals may assume that individual freedom is of ultimate value, and that civil society should be rights-based (Kaldor 2003: 14, 46). Theorists operating from other interpretative approaches disagree, positing alternative values such as liberation and fulfilment in place of individual autonomy (Mohanty 1998). It is precisely this divergence across societies that makes qualitative comparisons interesting and valuable, and provides direction for cross-societal research.

A process-based definition of civil society brings time and human agency back into what can be a static and structural form of analysis (Fay 1996: 242). The dynamics of civil society cannot be quantified on a linear scale or graphed in a box; they must be understood within national and local contexts. Furthermore, static pictures of the nature of civil society cannot do justice to the historical processes at work in social and political change; a time dimension is essential (Sztompka 1993: 277–8). Networks may originate in one form and change into another, from civil society-initiated to state-dominated or vice versa. Social change, in this concept, is an interactive process of ideas, values, networks and interests, rather than forms or structures. It is 'ecological' in the sense that what happens now depends on what has already happened and what is happening elsewhere at the same time. As political opportunities shift and waves of contention rise and fall, change is both contingent and path-dependent: once a tipping point is reached, there is no return (Koopmans 2004: 40–1).

Social movements are a subset of civil society networks that are large, sustained and highly coordinated – 'a network of networks' (della Porta et al 2006: 31). The same is true for an intermediate form, advocacy campaigns, which have certain features of social movements but on a smaller scale. The differences among networks, campaigns and movements are not fixed but are rather a question of perspective, size, and degree. As collective action becomes more complex, the difficulties of cohesion and sustainability increase. Hence there are fewer past or present examples of full-fledged social movements than focused campaigns, fewer campaigns than civil society networks, and fewer networks than social organisations (Khagram et al 2002: 6–9); 'the transformation from network to movement is not always intended or attained' (Bandy and Smith 2005: 3).

This paradigm differs from traditional depictions of civil society in that it describes the relationships among the components, showing that social movements and campaigns are subsets of the broader phenomenon of civil society networks, and that all forms of networks are based on underlying social relations. This schema also has the advantage of not posing civil society as a separate component that is contrasted with other types of social and political organisation. By looking at a sample of networks, each of which includes a number of organisations and numerous

Figure 2.1   Networks, social movements and civil society: A nesting paradigm[3]

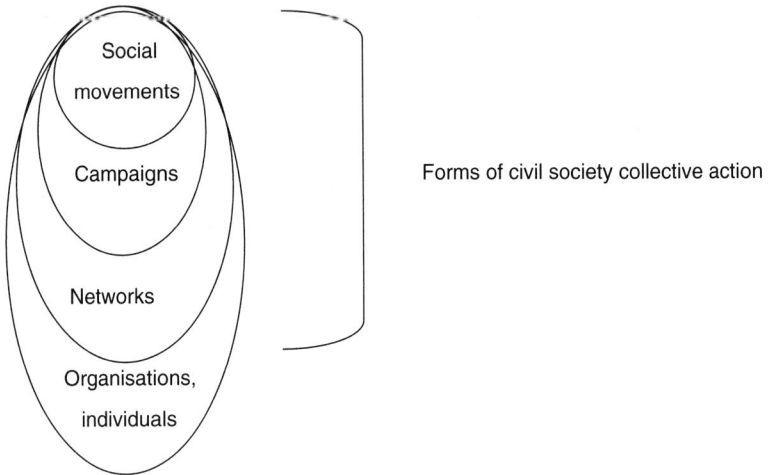

individuals, it becomes possible to describe the 'organisational ecology' of a civil society in which 'movements are comprised of more than the sum of their affiliated organisations' (Minkoff 2002: 261). Such an approach is flexible enough to apply in all societies, while offering a context and direction for comparative research.

Civil society networks engage in **advocacy**, defined as 'any attempt to influence the decisions of any institutional elite on behalf of a collective interest' (Jenkins 1987: 267). This definition is broader than policy change alone: advocacy also can focus on policy implementation or public opinion (O'Brien and Li 2006: 85, 96). In the development and public policy literature, advocacy models have also been used to explain policy processes *within* the state. The concept of advocacy coalitions, 'composed of people from various governmental and private organisations who share a set of normative and causal beliefs and who often act in concert' (Sabatier and Jenkins-Smith 1993: 17), is closely related to civil society networks as used here. Other writers describe 'policy networks' made up of individual actors (Marsh and Rhodes 1992) and 'governance networks', multi-stakeholder groups involving members inside and outside the state (Schiffer and Waale 2008). Nooteboom looks at 'adaptive networks' in the Netherlands, defined as people from multiple sectors who cooperate to find solutions to social problems and 'try to connect thinking and acting in different parts of society' (2006: 21). Such networks are based on interpersonal relationships within and outside government; they self-organise or 'coagulate' from loose personal networks and rely on high levels of trust among members. Contrasted with 'power networks' which are wholly within the state, adaptive networks have no formal power or resources; their effectiveness depends on influence on the public agenda (Nooteboom 2006: 155–76). Many advocacy networks depend on individual 'policy entrepreneurs' in or out of government who invest resources and take personal risks for the sake of an idea, sometimes joining with other specialists to form a 'policy community' (Kingdon 2003: 117–22).

Advocacy coalitions, issue networks and adaptive networks share many common features with civil society networks as profiled here. Given the longer history of democracy and collaborative experiences in Euro-American societies, these networks are larger, stronger and better established than many in China and Vietnam, but not necessarily more formalised structurally. Though based on models of interest group politics, the advocacy literature transposes rather well to the fragmented authoritarian political structures of Asian single-party regimes. Nothing in the concept of civil society networks requires democratic forms of government; the only requirement is that there are interests within the ruling authorities that tolerate advocacy. This implies a complex set of relationships and interactions between social actors and the state, from information sharing to engaging the state along a range of advocacy strategies from dialogue to contention.

Network analysis

Networks consist of relations among actors, 'a set of links or ties connecting nodes' or 'a set of interconnected nodes' (Katz and Anheier 2006: 242, Castells 1996: 470). The size of nodes can range from individuals in personal networks up to nation-states (Knoke and Kuklinski 1982: 14–15); together, network 'relationships and roles...construct politics' (Knoke 1990: 7).

As a field of social research, network analysis offers a clear example of relational thinking (Emirbayer 1997: 298–9). Networks are, by definition, 'interstitial'– they cut across discrete clusters, groups and communities – though in certain cases they may also congeal into identifiable units, termed 'category networks' or 'catnets' (Tilly 1984: 29). At the meso-level of social analysis, networks form key links between individual agency and macro-level social processes and structures (Diani and McAdam 2003: 4, 284, Marsh and Rhodes 1992: 1). Thus, networks are an appropriate modal unit of analysis for social research, more than separate organisations (Castells 1996: 198; della Porta and Tarrow 2005: 240). In the words of social theorists Wellman and Berkowitz, 'the world is composed of networks, not groups', since networks may not be divisible into discrete organisations (1988: 20, 37). The renowned sociologist Fei Xiaotong (1992) saw Chinese society in similar network- and kinship-based terms, which lie at the core of Confucianism (Rosemont 2002: 361). Both anthropologists and business analysts have seen network approaches as appropriate in Asian contexts; at the least, the concept is not out of place there.

Common network structures include the pyramid, hub-and-spokes wheel, and web. Other structures shown in Figure 2.2 are a 'clique', an egalitarian but closed structure in which all nodes are adjacent to each other; a polycephalous structure in which a few main groups are linked by bridges, or a 'segmented decentralized' structure with weak network identity and high organisational loyalty (Diani and McAdam 2003: 306–12). Networks that are highly centralised (hub structures) are seen as more susceptible to external shocks, since if the hub stops functioning the network will collapse (Schiffer and Waale 2008: 14). The choice of network structures also has power implications: a centralised network (in which a few nodes have many ties, while other nodes have only a few ties) is implicitly more hierarchical. Boundary spanning between networks increases the informal power of individual leaders and of the group as a whole, but offers diminishing returns the more bridges are built (Krebs 2004). Such brokerage or bridging is often carried out by loose-knit connections such as acquaintances, since strong ties such as kinship are already assumed to be networked (Granovetter 1973: 1376).

A core problem in network analysis is boundary specification, differentiating members or participants from mere supporters (Emirbayer 1997: 303). Using the so-called 'realist' criterion, 'the network analyst adopts the presumed subjective perceptions of system actors themselves, defining the boundaries of a social entity as the limits that are consciously experienced by all or most of the actors that are members of the identity' (Knoke and Kuklinski 1982: 22, Diani 2002: 176). Actor-centred mapping of network boundaries enables people to speak for themselves as to who is part of the network, rather than impose external criteria.

Individuals join networks through relational channels such as existing friendships, not as single individuals (Melucci 1996: 330). Movements grow out of informal networks, communities and organisations (Crossley 2002: 93), and people are mobilised to join networks by people they already know (Katz and Anheier 2006: 246). Thus, networks demon-

Figure 2.2 Network structures[4]

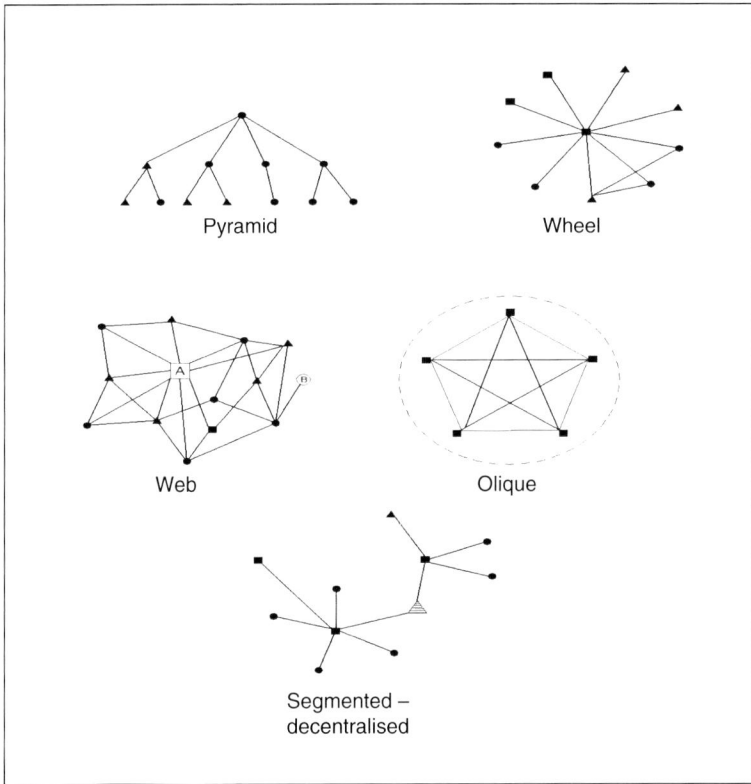

strate social capital and 'bounded solidarity' (Coleman 1990), referring to the level of trust and cooperation among members; a network's social capital consists of the sum of ties it includes. 'Prior ties' and 'network capital' are thought to matter even more in authoritarian and communist regimes, where people rely on networks for transactions (such as access to power holders or acquisition of restricted goods) that would otherwise be structured through markets or state institutions (Osa 2003: 78–9, Vala and O'Brien 2008: 109). Dense yet informal, network ties extend beyond instrumental linkages to include shared meanings, stories and identities (Keck and Sikkink 1998: 3, Diani and McAdam 2003: 5, 23).

In a prescient article, David Korten (1990b: 2) found that 'the power of voluntary action arises not from the size and resources of individual voluntary organizations' but rather from 'vast and constantly evolving networks' that reach across sectors:

> As our understanding grows, we see that strategic networks are the building blocks of social movements. A strategic network is a temporary alliance of individuals and organizations though which their resources are combined in pursuit of shared, defined and consequential goals that strengthen the movement's position in relation to major opposing forces. These alliances commonly reach beyond the formal voluntary sector to engage students, media, universities, agencies of government, and responsible business organizations (1990b: 2–3).

Korten expects networks to be large and 'energize spontaneous voluntary action on a considerable scale' (1990b: 3), but not exist permanently: 'Participants in successful movements collaborate in continuously shifting networks and coalitions' (106).[5] These loose networks do not always function smoothly. Hirsch and Warren (1998: 11) note that networks and coalitions in the environmental sector 'typically build and dissolve around particular issues, prevailing sentiments and even personalities'. Mayfair Yang quotes a Chinese artist: 'Guanxi networks are like casting a fishnet into the sea; when the fish have been caught, the people (holding the net) disperse. When the net is recast, not all the same people are in the new network' (1994: 304).

The best-known work linking network analysis with civil society and social movements is Keck and Sikkink's *Activists Beyond Borders* (1998), which depicts transnational solidarity networks engaged in 'production, exchange, and strategic use of information' (3), in contrast to the information-suppressing habits of states and other actors. 'Network campaigns' (McCarthy et al 2004), such as Jubilee 2000 or the International Campaign to Ban Landmines, can reframe debates, contribute new ideas, norms and identities, and enhance political resources available to domestic actors.[6] Keck and Sikkink insist that networks be formed of 'non-state forces', but they do not have to use only confrontational means. Transnational advocacy networks include both NGOs and other actors, with NGOs 'play[ing] prominent roles'. Such networks are primarily horizontal and reciprocal in their patterns of communication and exchange (1998: 1–3). Although a desirable ideal, this may not always apply to networks' internal structures: as with other forms of social organisation, networks may reproduce existing social norms of vertical or even authoritarian structures led by a charismatic individual or a core clique (Encarnación 2006: 370).

NGOs or individuals may act as 'bridgers' or 'gappers' brokering among networks, often transnationally as 'rooted cosmopolitans' (Cunningham et al 2007: 19, 70, Tarrow 2005: 29, 190) or 'strategic network catalysts' (Korten 1990a: 124). According to one analyst, NGOs' 'most promising long term future…is to become nodes, hubs, enablers and supporters of civic networks' (Fowler 1997: 233). Compared to formal organisations, according to network promoters, these structures are cheaper, quicker, better at sharing information, more fun, and ultimately more effective (McCarthy et al 2004: 212–13).

Network theory is not without detractors. Accountability can be missing, and large networks are difficult and expensive to maintain (McCarthy et al 2004: 214). The claims of network theorists have been criticised for overreach, while the more technical side of network analysis is viewed as static and disembodied (McDonald 2006: 37). A simple map of nodes and ties does not indicate who in a network is more influential or why; 'meaning does not stem automatically from ties' (Diani 2002: 194–5). Network theory has also been critiqued as structurally biased (Emirbayer and Goodwin 1994); since everyone is potentially part of networks, they have little effect as mobilising structures (Goodwin and Jasper 1999: 46). Network analysis should not stand on its own, but link to the broader process of civil society in specific contexts.

A typology of civil society networks

Civil society networks carry out multiple activities, showing a combination of internal and external orientations. They train and support their members, raise funds, share information, link with international partners, and conduct advocacy campaigns. One way to categorise networks is by their varying priorities among these activities, summarised as 'capacity building' and 'advocacy'. Respondents emphasise that networks should keep a balance among these activities.

A second key distinction is the formal or informal structure of a network. This is not the same as legal status, as nearly all networks are unregistered, although legal recognition is a strong indicator of formality. Some networks have organisational members who themselves have legal status, but others do not. Formal networks ('The X Network') have organisational structures, fixed membership, regular meetings, by-laws, mission statements and strategic plans, and set means of internal communication. They may or may not have other organisational features such as paid staff and a permanent office, which depend on stable funding. By contrast, informal networks ('my friends and allies') have none of the trappings of an organisation and may not even have a proper name. They cover a wide range from virtual networks and volunteer groups to information sharing fora and self-help groups. The self-attributed use of the term 'network' is not required. Externally, they may be nearly invisible, or appear indistinguishable from personal networks. But they are personal networks with a public purpose.

Both informal and formal networks maintain websites, organise events, and conduct advocacy campaigns. A Chinese activist distinguishes between two categories of formal and Internet-based networks: the first type have websites, some form of registration, and funding, but exist mainly for information sharing, while the second type of 'informal networks are more action-oriented'.

Closely associated with formality is the size of a network. Most informal networks are by nature relatively small; as they grow, issues of formal organisation inevitably arise. At the opposite extreme, federation-type formal networks can have highly complex structures with thousands of members, as witnessed in some NGO networks in the Philippines (Silliman and Noble 1998: 11–20). Networks may follow any of the basic structures outlined in Figure 2.2, or variations on them, including a mixture of horizontal and vertical ties. It is sometimes useful to differentiate the formal structure of a network with its actual operation; for instance, some networks are rhetorically committed to equality among members, but in reality a small core makes key decisions.

Individual, organisational, or mixed membership types can be found among both formal and informal networks. An 'NGO network' is typically a formal network of organisations (Heyzer et al 1995), but there are also informal alliances of organisations cooperating on particular issues. Many NGO networks contribute to civil society, but not all necessarily meet the definition of civil society networks as engaging in advocacy in pursuit of a social change agenda. Conversely, individual membership networks may be highly formalised. Individual members may be committed, full-time activists, or retired or current government officials wearing multiple 'hats' (Bentley 2004).[7] Thus, a binary division of NGO networks and informal networks, or 'strong coupling' and 'weak link' models (Tong 2009) is not sufficient, nor should all networks be categorised together with unregistered and underground organisations (Schwartz and Shieh 2009: 9, 33).[8]

Table 2.1 categorises networks vertically into four types.[9] *Coalitions* have a high degree of formality, an organisation chart (hierarchical)

Table 2.1 A typology of networks

	NGO networks	Issue-based networks		
	Cross-sector	Intra-sector	Advocacy	Individual
Coalition	1. NGO membership coalitions	2. Sectoral coalitions		
Forum		3. NGO information sharing fora	5. Issue-based fora	
Informal network		4. NGO task forces	6. Informal advocacy networks	7. Semi-formal membership groups
Personal network				8. Social groups

Organisation-based ←——————————————→ Individual-based

Larger ←——————→ Smaller

More formal ←——————→ Less formal

structure, and usually a large membership. Their main purpose is representation with government and society. *Forums* are also formal structures, but their main purpose is information sharing among members. *Informal networks* are less structured civil society groups, differentiated from *personal networks* or *social groups* among individuals. The two columns of NGO networks both have organisational members only; issue-based networks may have a combination of organisational and/or individual members; individual-based networks have individual members only. Of course, some NGOs themselves have members, though this is rarer in China and Vietnam than other settings. In NGO networks, however, the organisation participates at a head-office level, not via its own membership base.

Personal networks are pictured directly beneath informal membership groups. Virtual networks are not considered as a separate type, but rather as a subset of informal advocacy or personal networks that have selected a particular communication structure. Virtual organising is employed by a variety of networks but is a particular feature of dissident networks such as Vietnam's Bloc 8406 (Thayer 2008, Hayton 2010: 113–34) and anti-bauxite mining campaign (Thayer 2010). Whether networks can be considered as civil society networks depends on their relative position in this typology as well as the extent to which they share other characteristics described in Chapter 1.

Type 1 (NGO membership coalitions) can be divided into three subtypes depending on their membership. The first, and primary form is made up of NGO members only; the second by both NGO and government representatives; and the third is the 'umbrella organisation' (Vasavakul 2003), a government-organised entity for the purpose of representing, registering, managing and/or controlling NGOs. These distinctions are particularly salient in Vietnam, where legal associations (*hội*) take various forms of Party-sponsored mass organisations (*tổ chức đoàn thể*) such as the Vietnam Women's Union, government-organised professional 'umbrella organisations' such as VUSTA, and quasi-governmental social associations (*tổ chức xã hội*) (Nørlund 2006: 32).

Tables 2.2 and 2.3 present a selection of the more than 20 civil society networks identified in each country. Few have been previously described in print. The Asia Foundation (2008: 85–6) includes mention of eight networks in Vietnam in a publication on organisational advocacy, all of which are categorised here as issue-based fora or NGO task forces.[10]

Table 2.2   Illustrative examples of network types

Network types	Examples in China	Examples in Vietnam	Other Asian countries
1a. NGO membership coalitions	None	None	NGO Forum on Cambodia; CODE-NGO (Philippines); Asia NGO Coalition
1b. NGO-Govt membership coalitions	CANGO	VUFO-NGO Resource Centre	
1c. Umbrella organisations	Yunnan International NGO Society (YINGOS)	VUSTA	
2. Sectoral federations	China AIDS CBO Network	Vietnam Civil Society Partnership on AIDS	Myanmar NGO Network
3. NGO information networks	Climate Change Action Network	NGO Resource Centre working groups	
4. NGO task forces	5-12 Sichuan Earthquake network	Working for Advocacy and People's Initiatives (WAPI)	
5. Issue-based fora	**Women's Network against AIDS (see chapter 4)**	Disability Forum (ch. 4), Vietnam Rivers Network, CIFPEN, GenComNet	
6. Informal advocacy networks	**China rivers network (ch. 6)**	**Reunification Park network (ch. 5)**, bauxite network, Bloc 8406	
7. Semi-formal membership groups	HIV self-help groups, such as Henan Golden Sunshine (ch. 5)	**Bright Future Group of People with Disabilities (ch. 3)**	Micmac (Micro-Macro) network, Laos
8. Personal networks	Birdwatchers groups	Bright Future Group before 1995	
Mass organisations	All-China Women's Federation	Ho Chi Minh Communist Youth Union	Lao Front for National Reconstruction
Organisations calling themselves networks	China HIV/AIDS Information Network (CHAIN)	None	Southeast Asia Rivers Network

Table 2.3 Features of selected civil society networks in China and Vietnam

Network	Location	Sector	Year estab.	# of members	Network funding?	Network website?	Structure/ leadership	Advocacy involv't
China AIDS CBO Network (CNNAC)	China (national)	Health	2004	133 orgs	Open Society Inst.	None	Rotating chair, but one leading org	Legal aid and advocacy for gays/lesbians, HIV+
Vietnam Civil Society Partnership on AIDS	Vietnam (national)	Health	2007	160 orgs and groups	Global Fund, Ford	www.vcspa.org.vn	Coordinator, steering committee	Govt and donor policy on HIV; UN reports
China Civil Climate Action Network	China (Beijing)	Environt	2007	8 core, 31 participnts	Member-supported	None	Core group led by one org	Policy research, energy saving campaigns
Climate Change Working Group (NGO Resource Cen.)	Vietnam (Hanoi)	Environt	2007	~40 orgs + indiv	None	ngocentre.org.vn/ccwg	Core group of 7 intl + local NGOs	Statements to govt/donor consult group
5-12 Sichuan Earthquake network	China (Sichuan)	Emerg relief	2008	40 orgs (a few intl)	Member-supported	www.512ngo.org.cn	'Centre' hosted at one local NGO	Coordinate NGO support to quake victims
Working for Advocacy and People's Initiatives (WAPI)	Vietnam (Lang Son)	Rural devel	2007	3 orgs. (orig. 4)	Member-supported	None	Rotating chair	Input to National Front on ethnic minor policy

Table 2.3 Features of selected civil society networks in China and Vietnam – *continued*

Network	Location	Sector	Year estab.	# of members	Network funding?	Network website?	Structure/ leadership	Advocacy involv't
Women's Network against AIDS	China (national)	Health	2007	21 orgs.	UNAIDS	wnac.csr-pioneers.org	Secretariat, 3 paid staff	Improve policies for women affected by HIV
Vietnam Rivers Network	Vietnam (national)	Environt	2005	150 indiv + 20 orgs	ICCO (NL), McKnight Found. (US)	www.ware-cod.org.vn	1 coordinating org, sub-groups in north/centre/ south	Research on impacts of dams and flooding
Building Civil Society Inclusion in Food Security and Poverty Elimination Network (CIFPEN)	Vietnam (mostly Hanoi)	Rural devel	2005	43 orgs + 2 observers	EU, Action-Aid	www.cifpen.org	1 coordinator, exec committee	Influence local govt socio-economic planning
Gender and Community Development (GenComNet)	Vietnam (Hanoi)	Gender	2006	12 orgs + 11 indiv	ActionAid	www.gen-comnet.org	4-person exec committee, elected	Wrote shadow reports on gender for CEDAW
China Rivers Network	China (national)	Environt	2003	~20 indiv; orig. 7 orgs	Member-supported	Not at present	Core group of individual activists	Protect rivers, prevent dam construction

Table 2.3 Features of selected civil society networks in China and Vietnam – *continued*

Network	Location	Sector	Year estab.	# of members	Network funding?	Network website?	Structure/ leadership	Advocacy involv't
Reunification Park network	Vietnam (Hanoi)	Land rights	2007	~15 indiv + 2 orgs	None	None	Web structure, 1 core org + indivs	Prevent privatisation of parks
Bright Future Group	Vietnam (Hanoi)	Disability	1988	30 indiv	DTU (Denmark)	www.ttsong-doclaphn. vn	Chair and elected exec committee	Disability laws; created national association
Bauxite mining network	Vietnam (virtual)	Environt	2009	~30 key indiv + supporters	None	www.bauxite-vietnam. info	Segmented-decentralised, multiple nodes	Stop Chinese-invested bauxite mine; political website and blogs
Bloc 8406	Vietnam (national)	Democy, h. rts	2006	2,000 indiv signers	None	None	Underground core group	Circulated manifesto. Members arrested.

Varieties of network advocacy

Advocacy consists of a range of strategies for engaging the state and public opinion.[11] Within a particular advocacy strategy, networks choose among multiple tactics, meaning approaches or methods to reach an objective: personal lobbying and blogging are two of many possible tactics. A network may have more than one strategy and use multiple tactics within these strategies, constituting an advocacy repertoire. After forming strategies and tactics, networks conduct specific advocacy activities or events, such as meeting a particular official over tea or posting an open letter online. Often, repertoires take shape organically through trial and error or 'venue shopping' as networks seek appropriate frames and audiences for their advocacy messages (Keck and Sikkink 1998: 18).[12] Few observed networks have formal advocacy strategies with position papers, objectives and definitions of success. Instead, strategies are understood inductively through the statements and actions of network members.

Advocacy is a key defining feature that distinguishes civil society networks from personal networks. As one Vietnamese activist states, 'networks are most effective and achieve their greatest power when presenting advocacy messages' (Vu T 2008: 31). Networks are necessary for local groups to advocate with a common voice. Chinese NGOs, similarly, are 'increasingly aware of the need for joint actions', since most NGOs are not large enough to carry out advocacy on their own (Lu 2008: 135). The focus on advocacy strategies does not mean that other network functions are less valid or important, or advocacy is a higher function than others. Korten (1990a: 127–8) describes four 'generations' of voluntary action, beginning with charity and moving to community development, advocacy, and alliance-building, stressing that all these components are necessary, and mature organisations may engage in all of them. Advocacy is not limited to civil society networks: business interests also invest heavily in advocacy campaigns for their own benefit (Vu T 2008: 25), using some of the same strategies and tactics as civil society.[13]

The term 'advocacy' has entered theoretical vocabularies relatively recently in China and Vietnam, but the practice has long existed in reality (Asia Foundation 2008: 6). A study of Chinese NGOs conducted by *China Development Brief* found that most conduct some form of advocacy, favouring non-adversarial tactics (Wexler et al 2006: 9). Over two-thirds of 79 Vietnamese NGOs report an interest in advocacy, but most have little capacity or strategies in place (Asia Foundation 2008: 32–7). Kerkvliet, Nguyen and Bach describe cases of advocacy in which authorities resisted or showed suspicion at first, but 'over time, the relationship improved' (2008: 27). This suggests that organisations or networks that have been established for a longer time will have better results from advocacy than newly-formed groups, a hypothesis that the Vietnamese study did not test, since they only selected organisations with 'some years of experience' (9).

Existing research on advocacy in China and Vietnam emphasises its supposedly 'non-political' orientation (Wexler et al 2006: 37). Ho (2008b: 29) sees de-politicisation as a conscious strategy of Chinese environmental organisations seeking to avoid state repression. Hannah depicts leaders of several Vietnamese organisations as 'non-political professionals' who work through partnership, not confrontation, a choice based on their personal working styles (2007: 186–210). One interview respondent presents this approach as an immutable aspect of cultural heritage:

> Just saying no to things is effective advocacy in some countries, but not in Chinese culture. It makes you look like an extremist going against the 'golden mean'. To be mainstream, you need public support and for that, you can't just be opposed to things.

This exceptionalist view is based on an assumption that all Euro-American advocacy is confrontational all of the time. To be fair, one could easily get this impression from reading the contentious politics and social movement literature: at times, 'contention' seems to mean confrontation or illegal protests only. Applied too strictly, the theory could lead to the conclusion that China has no environmental movement because environmental advocacy is not 'contentious' enough (Stalley and Yang 2006). Actually, thousands of annual environmental disputes become confrontational; the questions are how civil society networks do or do not link with protestors and what strategies they employ at different times.

Hannah (2005: 106) theorises a continuum of possible civil society roles stretching from implementation of state policy to 'public resistance', with intermediary steps of advocacy, lobbying, watchdog and opposition.[14] At the time of his field research, he found that the Vietnamese state sanctions only advocacy for better implementation of existing policies, not calls for policy change or public opposition (2007: 249). In fact, the state is not a monolithic unit, and the lines of what is possible have shifted significantly over time. In 2008, a Vietnamese NGO presenter at a conference in Hanoi cited four different advocacy techniques – lobbying, social mobilisation, demonstrations, and public pressure – then added, 'in Vietnam, we don't use these last two'. By 2009–10, activists publicly described their role as 'watchdogs to ensure that rights of affected people are safeguarded'. Some networks have made selective use of both demonstrations and public pressure, even though these tactics are potentially 'sensitive'.

On paper, to be sure, the space for contentious advocacy tactics is highly restricted. Vietnamese regulations issued in 2009 limit the approved advocacy activities of associations and other social organisations to a long, but far from exhaustive, list of scientific and professional topics (Sidel 2010). Furthermore, policy recommendations must be communicated privately to the state, not shared with the public.[15] International observers worry that the decree is having a dampening effect on advocacy, while informal network activists interviewed are not overly concerned that it applies to them, as long as they do not take legal steps to formalise their network. In practice, the sensitivity of a topic or sector in China or Vietnam is conditioned by social context, framing, timing and location (Shi 1997: 252), with a shifting 'zone of tolerance' (Shi and Cai 2006: 331). Although gender equity may be less sensitive on the whole than labour rights, one interviewee stated 'it's easier to talk about labour in an informal closed meeting [with government officials] than to talk about women's rights on June Fourth'. As a Yunnan association member told Howell, 'You can do difficult things but you have to be careful. You need the government's approval, so there is a limit. It depends on timing'. Howell concludes that activists tread a 'precarious line...in a terrain where the boundaries of the possible [are] fluid and unpredictable' (2004a: 159).

Thus, the argument that advocacy has been 'depoliticised' depends on one's perspective and definition of politics. In the narrow senses of politics as internal affairs of the state or opposition to the regime, there is very little space for networks to engage. But most network members have no such aims. Instead, they wish to change certain policies and practices of the state and social elites. These goals are indeed political in a broader sense, whether activists choose to describe their advocacy in these terms or not, and regardless of how contentious or 'sensitive' a particular tactic or action might be perceived to be. Given the shifting and contingent nature of sensitivity and the fuzzy boundaries between contained and transgressive contention, it is inadvisable to define advocacy by how the state (or part of a state) reacts to it. A viable alternative, in keeping with an actor-centred approach, is to conceptualise advocacy based on the goals and methods used by advocates themselves. The selection of advocacy strategies and tactics is structured in part by limits imposed by state agencies, by the fragmented nature of the state, and by complex and incomplete legal systems, yet successful activists find room to manoeuvre within, or around, structural limitations.

The advocacy strategies of Chinese and Vietnamese networks can be summarised in three inductive categories: embedded, media, and community.[16] Embedded advocacy, which has been described most thoroughly in the literature on China, consists of working within the system and making direct contact with parts of the state using personal and institutional ties. Media strategies work through state-owned newspapers, online media, blogs and international media to reach advocacy objects indirectly. Community advocacy seeks to put public pressure on advocacy objects by involving more people and building links between local residents and elites. Figure 2.3 presents an illustration of the three strategies, associated tactics, and objects of advocacy.

In a broader definition of contention as non-institutionalised politics, almost everything in Figure 2.3 qualifies, except for the internal policy channels at the top of the tactics column. Much of the literature on contentious politics privileges protest narratives, with even embedded tactics such as petitioning described as a form of protest (O'Brien 2008). Repertoires of collective action are really collections of tactics, with less attention to underlying strategies. In practice, activists choose advocacy tactics to be more 'radical' or 'moderate' depending on the object, location and other factors (Chen 2007, Lin 2007). Even institutional tactics can be applied in a confrontational way, for instance using government workshops to criticise policies in an 'impolite' way (as some people with disabilities and people living with HIV have done). Conversely, protest can be carried out in a more or less confrontational style.

Embedded advocacy

Embeddedness is a central concept in social theory, describing relations between the state, economy and society (Granovetter 1985, Evans 1996). In a narrower sense, embeddedness refers to mutually co-opted relations between an individual, organisation, or network and elites, and is closely linked conceptually with *guanxi*, vertical social capital, and corporatism. Embedded advocacy is based on reciprocal relationships with authorities. In China and Vietnam, all social organisations need permission from some level of authority, which in turn can exercise oversight and control over the organisation. Yet the same relationship can also form an entry point for advocacy, as networks leverage access and connections with other parts of the state. A network member who is a current or former state employee may use this position to collect information or influence others.[17] Embeddedness carries positive connotations of state-society synergy (Fox 1996), but it also suggests a lack of objectivity and independence, as

Figure 2.3 Overview of civil society networks' advocacy strategies and tactics

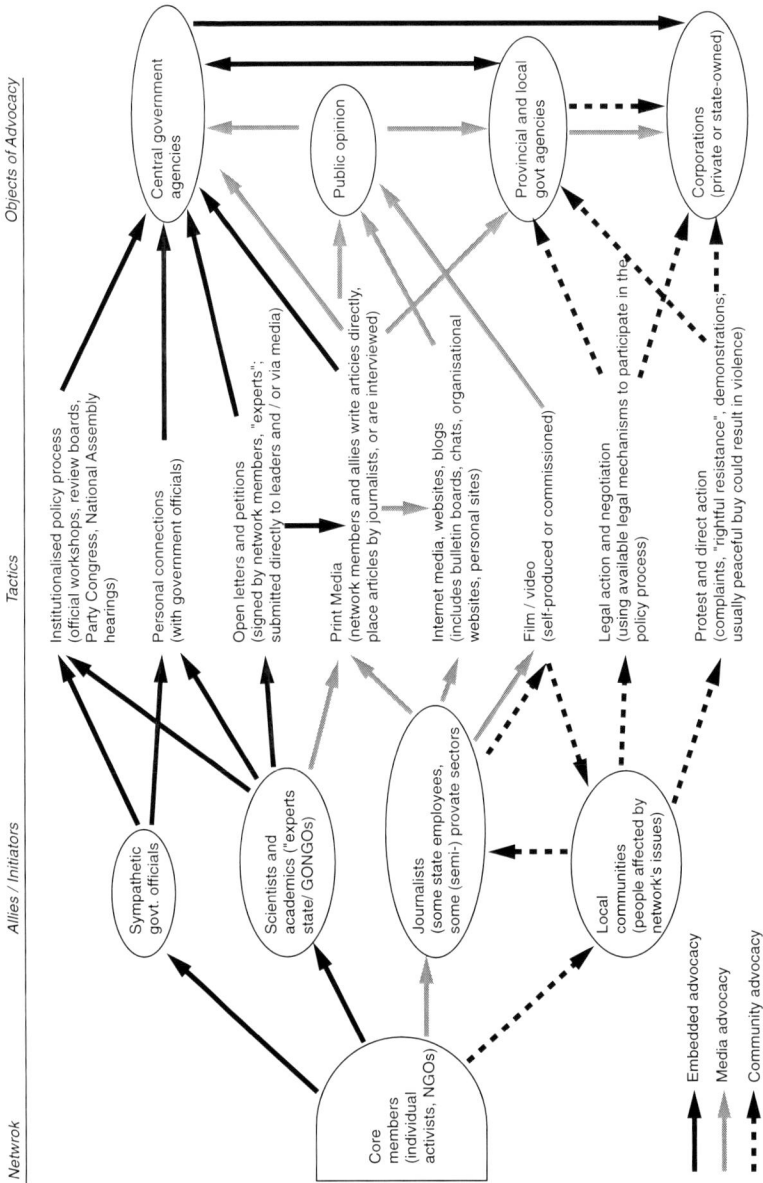

in journalists embedded with military units who lose sight of the broader context of the conflict. How can civil society networks take advantage of connections without 'getting in bed with' the authorities they seek to influence?

Interview informants routinely confirm that they need good personal relationships with government officials in order to carry out advocacy. 'We deal with people [as individuals], not with the authorities as an institution'. In return, most informants feel that authorities welcome their participation, although there is a range of views within both the Chinese and Vietnamese states. A network leader observes, 'Government agencies have their own social development strategies. They don't pay too much attention to us. Their attitude is, if you have money you can do something, if not what's the point of it?'

'The government does some things well, other things less well', says a Chinese NGO director. 'Many of its social policies are good, but the government doesn't know how to apply them. NGOs can give them advice on this'. The same applies for advocacy towards GONGOs, says another activist: 'they are not progressive, but we bring our agenda to them. They want to involve young people, because there is lots of funding, but they don't know how... When I tell them, "This is what we want," they usually say yes'. Effective engagement requires knowing where to engage in an immense, fragmented bureaucracy with its own agendas.

These views are supported in the NGO/development literature in general and studies on China and Vietnam in particular. To be effective advocates, writes Bratton, organisations need to 'identify openings in the administrative system' and 'cultivate non-adversarial working relationships with the politically powerful' (1990: 95–6). Chinese NGOs prioritise finding ways to agree and communicate with government (Wexler et al 2006: 34). Rather than compromising activists' independence, state connections are desirable and necessary for achieving grassroots impact and policy objectives, making activists more effective communicators and advocates, as well as shielding them from potential criticism or reprisals (White et al 1996, O'Rourke 2002, Heng 2004, Bentley 2004, Ho 2008b, Lu 2008: 116–17).

As outlined in Figure 2.3, tactics of embedded advocacy include both personal lobbying and the use of expert intermediaries. Howell summarises major activities of NGO advocacy in China as 'research dissemination, the demonstration of alternative models, and conducting training courses for government leaders' (2004a: 160).[18] In addition, networks as well as communities make heavy use of open letters and petitions to higher-level authorities, a 'new norm' that is encouraged by the state to some degree (Zweig 2003, Minzner 2006). The prevalence of petitions may be new, but the processes are not, as Ding's (1994) discussion of 'amphibiousness' shows. Marr (1994) described Vietnamese civil society 'infiltrating the state, finding informal allies and building networks' (cited in Hannah 2007: 116). Even during pre-reform days, advocates could attempt 'the Zhou Enlai end run': appealing to an apparently sympathetic official at a higher level in hopes of personal intervention (Meyer 2008: 182).

A Vietnamese activist notices improved state responsiveness to advocacy efforts:

> Five years ago, if you wrote to the Prime Minister's office, there would be no chance of a response. Now if you put in the correct language, pick the right issue and send the letter at the right time, you can get a response. It's possible to know where the line is if you keep contact with people in high positions.

By keeping contact, this respondent means sharing drafts of a letter first and listening to allies' advice on when it's 'safe' to send. In addition to phone and e-mail, contact is maintained through informal meetings and 'occasionally having a dinner to talk about the issue, but not too often'. A Chinese blogger notes,

> There seem to be two common ways of lobbying the Chinese government or corporations. One is taking officials or researchers on study trips to the affected sites; this is expensive and...counts too much on the emotional impact of what they witness. What if they don't change their minds? The other is working with Chinese academics who are positioned near official ears. (MqVU 2010)

Effective embedded advocacy requires having something to say that elites will listen to and take seriously: not only arguments, but also 'scientific' evidence. Actions can speak louder than words: 'We don't push [authorities] and tell them what to do; we do our own thing, and if it's good they'll take it on. We can afford to make mistakes, but the government thinks they can't'. However, evidence can be hard to obtain if state or corporate actors restrict access; control of information can then be used as an excuse to deny activists standing to comment on policy issues. If networks cannot provide evidence on their own, one alternative is to circulate information on a related subject written by others. According to one research institute expert, the most success-ful advocacy is carried out by 'famous scholars' – individuals who are well-connected, rather than NGOs who often are not (Wexler et al 2006: 70). Translations from foreign sources demonstrate international links, therefore credibility, and also show that an issue is not limited to the local context. A Vietnamese environmental network might dissem-inate information about Thai dams, for instance, or renewable energy in China, sending an indirect critique of Vietnamese policy.

Embedded advocacy in the Chinese and Vietnamese contexts is limited by the gap between policy and practice: just because activists succeed in including a provision in a law or policy does not mean that other parts of the state will implement it. A second limitation is that the topics that can be selected for advocacy must not be interpreted as a threat to existing elites (Gamson 1990: 41) or to networks' broader constituencies. 'If we go slowly and gradually, according to the appro-priate way, we can still get many things done', says a Vietnamese network coordinator. 'We need to be flexible and not too strong [in advocacy messages]; if we were, it would make it hard for many of our members to take part'.

In a recent book on Chinese environmentalism, Ho and Edmonds (2008) describe 'embedded activism' as a China-specific phenomenon resulting from a mixed political context that is 'restrictive but con-ducive' (Ho 2008b: 21). This results in a 'fragmentary, highly localized, and non-confrontational form of environmentalism' that nevertheless can be highly effective within China's political system (2008a: 14). Using an approach based on social movement literature, Ho brilliantly captures the 'negotiated symbiosis' of state-society relations (2008b: 36) that have moved beyond corporatism but not (yet) approached pluralism. However, in so doing he misinterprets the nature of some of the advocacy he describes. Ho sees embeddedness as central to the identity of Chinese NGOs: 'civil organizations find themselves embed-ded in a Party-statist structure of control, as well as an intricate web of personalized relations and informal politics.' Based on a 2000 interview with the leader of one NGO who disavows 'political aims' and 'extrem-ist methods',[19] he claims that environmental activists 'de-politicise politics' and engage in 'self-imposed censorship' (2008a: 8, 2008b: 29, see also Jiang 2005). This picture assumes that activists really desire to engage in oppositional political action but are constrained from doing so by the state: if these activists then claim they have no such goals but just want to protect the environment, this must be a sign of their own false consciousness or colonised minds.

My interviews and data collection with leaders and members of many of the same environmental groups that Ho studied result in different findings. Regardless of their particular political views, these respondents have definite policy and organisational objectives in mind and pragmatic strategies to achieve them. While Ho is correct that Chinese activists face a mixed and sometimes contradictory set of political opportunities and constraints, this does not 'force' them into 'de-politicized spaces' where they can only carry out 'media-attractive yet politically innocent activities' (2008b: 29). Instead, activists engage in strategic framing (Gamson and Meyer 1996, Keech-Marx 2008) and consciously select strategies and tactics that they believe will be effective (Lin 2007). At times, these are embedded strategies. At other times, the same networks engage in 'boundary-spanning' or 'transgressive' actions (O'Brien 2004, McAdam et al 2001) that extend well beyond the tame, constrained activism described by Ho.[20] Thus, embeddedness is best understood as one among several advocacy strategies, not as an essential characteristic of Chinese (or Vietnamese) activism. Choosing an embedded strategy does not require censoring oneself.

Along similar lines, Lu Yiyi argues that Chinese NGOs take a pragmatic or opportunistic approach to relations with the government, seeking to advance their own interests, not mount a political challenge (2008: 144). Their 'multiple dependence on the state has led many NGOs [directors] to view their relationships with government agencies and officials as the most important of all' (117). While perhaps accurate for some NGOs, I did not find evidence of such displaced accountability among civil society network members in China or Vietnam. Working with (parts of) the state, such as (in Lu's example) inviting officials to write blurbs for an organisation's promotional materials, does not automatically indicate dependence: it could also be a conscious strategy to form alliances and protect one's interests against opponents. There may be some truth to Lu's arguments in the case of small NGOs who face difficulties in registration and inadequate funding, and thus need good relations with government, while large organisations can act more strategically. Lu, however, actually argues the opposite: larger organisations may receive outside funding, but then need official cooperation in order to carry out programmes, while small groups can afford to act without government support. 'The bigger you are, the more you need the state!' (Lu 2008: 45). Both have a point, but need to specify their arguments. Different organisations need different parts of the state for different things. Close ties with a government agency do not equal dependence; conversely, a lack of connections does not necessarily result in autonomy, but might lead to isolation.

When organisations use tropes of state discourse, such as a 'harmonious society' (和谐社会, *héxié shèhùi*), they creatively hold the state accountable to its own laws and rhetoric, pointing out the gap between rights promised and delivered (O'Brien 1996: 55).[21] This is a key technique of network advocacy (Keck and Sikkink 1998: 25). Chu shows, for instance, how Vietnamese Catholics are skilled at maintaining the 'illusion of state control' within existing rules of the game, finding ways to use the state against itself (or parts of the state against other parts) and express criticism in subtle ways (2006: 28–35). Shi Tianjian (1997: xii) describes ways that Beijing residents play politics: 'Rather than trying to influence or change bureaucratic decisions, people usually manage to circumvent them' by looking for new sponsors or allies. 'Since government policy is hardly monopolistic, there is always space for citizens to maneuver' through patron-client exchange transactions, 'borrowing' power from others using connections, or exploiting state fragmentation by asking government to 'faithfully' implement existing policies, using a higher level of authority against a lower one (1997: 17). Such advocacy remains within the system, but pushes at the boundaries of embeddedness.

Media advocacy

The second major advocacy strategy of Chinese and Vietnamese networks involves information technologies of all types: print and online newspapers and magazines, blogs, e-mail list-serves, chat groups, even mobile phones and texting. Internet and other communications technologies are crucial advocacy tools. Media strategies differ from embedded advocacy in their public nature and use of channels both within and outside the fuzzy boundaries of the state. The purpose of media advocacy is both to reach leaders and to influence public opinion. If activists use connections with officials or other prominent people to place an article in state-controlled media, this would qualify as an embedded tactic (see Figure 2.3). Most of the time, however, this is not the case. Journalists for state-owned media outlets report the news (Yan 2009). Most of them are contract employees, not government staff. Some go beyond neutrality to be explicitly sympathetic with networks they are covering. In this way, media have become 'the natural ally of civil society' (Baum 2008: 176), at a minimum 'useful intermediaries, even the "people's friend" on certain occasions' (Marr 2003: 284).

State-owned media can be colonised by civil society networks, and state control over the Internet is often partial at most. In cases such as the Reunification Park and China rivers networks (Chapters 5–6), journalists are not only allies of civil society networks, but active participants in them. Journalists publish their own articles and interviews with other network members, and facilitate public comment through web interfaces. Prominent journalists are public figures or experts in their own right and can lend their clout to a campaign through coverage (O'Brien 1996: 44). Two network participants, an architect and a journalist, describe the media as

> a system of public information [that] plays an extremely important role… It is *just about the only* information source for the community to understand about the situation, its changes and structure… Journalists always gather the opinion of people living in the surrounding areas. This is almost the only channel that people have to present their opinions. (Tran and Linh 2010, emphasis in original)

In particular, these analysts continue, the media plays three roles in an advocacy campaign: first, providing information by bringing issues to light; second, using interviews as a way to force leaders to speak and respond to criticism. This can increase the sensitivity of an issue, but also help to suggest solutions; however, leaders' statements alone are not enough to solve a problem, as verbal remarks do not have the official weight of a signed, stamped document. Third, the media can facilitate the formation of a discussion forum that includes both experts and community opinion, becoming spontaneous voices of the people (Tran and Linh 2010).

One Vietnamese activist says that 'if you have your own funding source, sometimes it's so easy to put something in the news'. Technically, printing materials and circulating them publicly (or to government officials such as National Assembly members) requires prior permission from the Ministry of Information and Communications. But in reality, 'as long as we don't ask for permission, it's no problem. If we did ask for permission, it could take two or three months'. This network's media strategy is to say nothing at all about themselves. 'Occasionally one of us will give a personal interview if requested, but in that case he will appear as a neutral expert, not as an NGO activist. If it looks like organisational public relations or fundraising, everyone will dismiss what you say'. Media can also be used for direct criticism of government actions or policies, as in Hannah's categories of watchdog or opposition. 'When we have to do more confrontational advocacy, we don't do this ourselves but leverage the media. But this is not our first option'.

The *China Development Brief* advocacy study found that environmental organisations and networks were the most likely to seek out and use media as allies (Wexler et al 2006: 30). Their strategy is to raise public awareness of an issue through the media, then use media articles to advocate with the government. Media are both objects and means of network advocacy. Journalists and NGOs work together: 'NGOs can better motivate the public, and media can disseminate information. This [combination] is an effective way to reach the government. But the media [alone] has many limitations; NGOs can reach a broader public and get more people to participate'.

This portrayal of what one Chinese network activist terms 'smart, idealistic and risk-taking' journalists clashes sharply with 'the standard international presentation', which focuses on violations of press freedom in both countries. Vietnamese journalists have been jailed for reporting on anti-corruption cases; blogs have been shut down for airing what regimes see as anti-government views; websites containing sensitive information are blocked, especially by China's 'Great Firewall', while other websites have been attacked by hackers believed to be linked to government agencies.[22] When journalists receive information, they need to receive approval from their editors before publishing. Although articles are not subject to pre-censorship, editors are responsible for the political content of everything they print (Heng 2003: 569). Networks have also been the subject of Internet censorship and cyber-attacks, as in the case of one unregistered regional network in south-west China whose website has been blocked on several occasions; the network responded by setting up a new web address in the info domain that is registered outside China and thus not subject to state controls.

Despite these limits, the media environment is not as closed as the legal structures make it appear, or as many external analysts suggest (London 2009: 392, Hayton 2010: 140–58). Censorship affects only a small fraction of websites, and Internet use continues to increase geometrically in China (Rawnsley 2008: 126–33, Wang 2009) and Vietnam (Cullum 2010). Media roles are relatively less restricted by the state than other civil society roles. A social organisation that crosses a political line can in extreme cases be shut down, while a newspaper may have its editorial board replaced, but remains owned by its managing agency. For individual participants, there is little to no risk from posting a comment online, compared with the potentially substantial risk from joining a demonstration. In this way, media act as 'insider-dissenters', using their connections with the state to limit risk (Heng 2004: 154–6).

With the proliferation of blogs and websites, it is no longer the case that all media in China and Vietnam are state-controlled. Blogs can be blocked and their authors intimidated or arrested, but most activists know how to thrive despite these limits (Yang 2008: 129, 2009: 35), and new blogs keep arising (Esarey and Xiao 2008). Of course, all media are not equally powerful, and not all blogs are widely read, but some have gone viral and attracted wider notice than any print media article. Although authorities are still controlling media and the Internet, a 'quiet revolution is underway' (Baum 2008: 162). As long as articles avoid perceived anti-government topics, blockage is unlikely. If one blog site or social messaging service is blocked, Internet users move to another. Even when a site is removed, 'the Great Firewall has numerous leaks, and many netizens have become adept at navigating around it' (173). Once Chinese or Vietnamese print media articles are published on newspaper websites, they are then uploaded onto international sites where they remain in the public domain, in theory forever. Conversely, when a user posts a comment on a Chinese- or Vietnamese-language website, it is generally not possible to identify whether the post originates from within the country or outside. When advocacy messages are circulated by mobile phone texting, as in the case of the SARS epidemic (Baum 2008: 173) or the Xiamen chemical plant 'flash mob' (Li 2007), official control is virtually impossible.

Thus, civil society network members generally experience enough freedom to meet their purposes for communication and advocacy. 'If the media were afraid of the authorities, we wouldn't have any place to do advocacy', says a Vietnamese activist. 'They give me a forum and are open to balanced views'. However, the potential of the media and Internet should not be overstated. Communication technology can be an empowering force challenging state control of information, but does not change the underlying reality of state power or lead to 'the development of democratic politics' (Wang 2009). Although there are clear links between the Internet and network formation, this should not be equated with democratic political potential (Rawnsley 2008: 132).

Community advocacy

Both embedded and media advocacy are basically elite strategies that can be carried out by small groups of urban activists with connections to government or journalists. The third network strategy, community-based advocacy, instead requires building larger and broader-based networks with communities affected by an issue: in short, community organising. Both China and Vietnam have indigenous traditions of such advocacy, including James Yen's Rural Reconstruction Movement in the 1930s and Thich Nhat Hanh's engaged Buddhism and School of Youth for Social Service in the 1960s, not to mention the origins of the Chinese and Vietnamese Communist Parties themselves. Perhaps because of these historical connections, community advocacy often faces restrictions from security forces in both countries. This does not mean that local protests and legal disputes are rare. Environmental pollution, corruption and land expropriation, among other issues, result in thousands of disputes each year, particularly in rural areas (O'Brien and Li 2006, Cai 2008, Bernstein and Lu 2003).[23] In Vietnam, spontaneous demonstrations over land rights and compensation have occurred in Hanoi and Ho Chi Minh City on a near-daily basis in recent years (London 2009: 394, Wells-Dang 2010).

Most community protests take place with no links to networks or NGOs. A common finding from research on rural protest in China is that networks among protestors from different communities, or different factories, are the first to be suppressed. There are many outspoken individual 'rights defenders' in rural areas, but they have not formed networks among themselves or set up NGOs (Johnson 2004, Brettell 2008: 132–3). Ho and Edmonds claim that 'activists are forced…to abandon any radical, confrontational, and mass mobilisation tactics to achieve political objectives' (2008: 221), assuming that they had these aims in the first place, and that confrontational tactics are desirable and effective. In reality, community-based protests have used all of these tactics as well as others, sometimes effectively and other times not (Cai 2008, Shi and Cai 2006).

An alternative strategy is to address injustice through legal means. Several Vietnamese networks have undertaken education campaigns to inform local residents of the rights they already enjoy, at least on paper, in Vietnamese law. Once people know their rights, they can then advocate with local and sometimes national government to address their grievances. This type of organising can be paternalistic if networks simply tell communities what to do, but in a more activist version, network members are able to directly implement laws in the community, as long as they act 'sensitively and according to the law'. In China, a 'rule of law' network of environmental lawyers has formed in recent years alongside a broader 'rights defence' community (van Rooij 2010, Béja 2009: 13–14). Chinese NGOs do not have standing to sue on behalf of communities, only acting as legal aid intermediaries for class action suits. Up to now, there have not been any successful cases of legal action for people threatened by resettlement, while collective action and protest have been successful in some cases (Zweig 2003, Chen 2007, Cai 2008). Facing such mixed opportunities and constraints, network members are pushing at the boundaries of the legal system. Community-based legal advocacy may be expected to increase in China in coming years, alongside the established repertoire of embedded and media strategies.

Incidents of community environmental activism have attracted media attention within and outside China: the Xiamen chemical plant protests (Li 2007, Watts 2007), Shanghai homeowners' protests against a high-speed train (Wasserstrom 2009), and a Beijing community, Liulitun, organising to oppose construction of a solid waste incinerator on the site of an existing landfill (Kuhn 2009). In 2007 on 5 June, which is World Environment Day and also a sensitive day in the Chinese political calendar, more than 1,000 Liulitun residents in matching T-shirts held a protest in front of the Ministry of Environmental Protection's office in downtown Beijing (Feng 2008). The project had already been approved by the municipal government (Yu and Zhu 2007), and protest appeared fruitless given MEP's limited power (Liu 2007b). However, city authorities put the project on hold, citing residents' opposition, and in January 2011 announced that the Liulitun project was cancelled and the incinerator would be built instead in a distant Beijing suburb (Cui 2010, *Global Times* 2011).

Most cases of community activism are not connected with NGOs, leading some to wonder if Chinese NGOs are losing relevance (Lo 2007). Local governments do not always welcome NGO presence, and NGOs are hesitant to take sides in disputes. In Liulitun, residents faced threats and intimidation from police to keep them from forming a formal organisation or linking with other communities (Kuhn 2009). Given these barriers, NGOs and networks need to tread carefully. Because of its existing community activism, Liulitun was selected by the environmental NGO Friends of Nature as a location for a community education project to reduce solid waste production, but FON was not able to work directly on the incinerator campaign. Community advocacy is thus highly sensitive even in major cities, and there are few cases where government has responded positively to outside facilitation. Network members can share information, but not encourage people to take action, which would be viewed as political instigation. These pragmatic considerations keep most networks using elite advocacy strategies and prevent them from too close identification with communities.

Many community activists start out with embedded tactics, such as petitions to higher levels of government, seeking to stay within the law in the tradition of 'rightful resistance' (O'Brien 1996, O'Brien and Li 2006).

In the view of one Vietnamese network member, a retired official now leading a professional association,

> The demonstrators have justice on their side. The problem is that the laws [on land compensation] are not clear or well applied. No social organisation is able to protect people's land rights in a situation like this... Demonstrations are risky and often ineffective, but what other choice do people have? There should be a clearer system of complaints and comments, and if that fails, access to the courts. But we don't have a system like that yet.

When petitioners cannot obtain satisfactory results from local or provincial officials, who may be corrupt or the cause of the problem, they 'scale shift' to the national level (della Porta and Tarrow 2005: 126, O'Brien 2004: 110). In both China and Vietnam, well-connected urban residents, such as intellectuals, artists and retired officials, feel greater freedom to speak out on public issues. Poor and rural citizens have fewer chances to raise their voices through the Party-government system and resort to public protest after they have 'exhausted approved but ineffective channels of participation' (Cai 2008: 164, Brettell 2007: 156–9, Liu 2007, Yang 2010: 112). In many cases, a combination of embedded and community-based strategies may offer the best chances of success (Zweig 2003). In Vietnam, successful strategies combine local-level networks with state connections, mustering political resources through both vertical and horizontal networking (O'Rourke 2002: 97, Vasavakul 2003: 26).

Hypotheses on network effectiveness

Based on the observed variety in network types in China and Vietnam, it is possible to pose general hypotheses concerning advocacy and effectiveness of civil society networks:

Denser ties: Networks with closer cooperative ties (social capital) will be more effective.[24]

Size and structure: Larger networks with more formal structures will be more effective.

Change over time: The three network advocacy strategies are a cumulative, chronological process.

Research findings broadly support the dense ties and change over time hypotheses, but not the importance of size and structure (see Chapter 7).

In the 1990s, embedded advocacy was the only option available. By around the middle of the past decade, this situation had shifted: as media became relatively freer and Internet technologies more available, media advocacy became more prominent, though not replacing embedded strategies. However, the availability of media access makes connections with state agencies less crucial for advocacy than previously. In theory, an individual with no links to officials can now engage in advocacy through a computer and an Internet connection, even if based in a rural area.

The last decade has also seen an increase in community advocacy in China and Vietnam, though mostly not yet networked with each other. Network linkages are hypothesised to increase over time to the extent that authorities do not repress them. As nodes mature and personal network ties develop, urban NGOs and networks will seek to develop and deepen advocacy links with rural as well as urban poor communities, and disadvantaged groups will increasingly link with each other.

This hypothesis does not imply linear movement towards progress. Once a strategy is widely used in activists' repertoires, it is assumed that it will not be given up. But strategies alone do not equal success, and the availability of more strategies does not automatically result in better outcomes. Effective advocacy will result in political change in terms of policies, implementation mechanisms, and public participation, but these changes are expected to take place within the existing political system. As strategic options increase, opponents of civil society networks also have increased opportunities: for instance, media and the Internet can be used by all, as can techniques of community organising. If activists do not use available strategies effectively, or are unable to due to state restrictions, the tables can be turned against them, as occurred to Catholic land protestors in Hanoi (*VietNamNet* 2008, AsiaNews 2008).

Most networks use a varied collective action repertoire, on the basis that they want to reach an objective and will try all feasible means to get there. Such advocacy has some elements in common with O'Brien and Li's (2006: 2) model of 'rightful resistance', which 'hinges on locating and exploiting divisions within the state, and relies on mobilizing support from the wider public'.[25] Based on perceived state fragmentation and gaps between the central and local levels, activists identify 'local targets who can be blamed and elite advocates who can be trusted' (2006: 42).

Given the limited institutionalization of Chinese politics and because their opponents usually have protectors among the local notables who matter most, rightful resisters typically find it advantageous to press their claims wherever they can. They recognize that state power nowadays is both fragmented and divided against itself, and they know that if they search diligently, they can often locate pressure points where elite unity crumbles. (O'Brien 1996: 44–5)

This experience leads to three further hypotheses:

Elite allies: Networks select strategies based on the presence of allies at different locations within the elite.

Multiple strategies. Networks that use multiple advocacy strategies and tactics will be more effective than those that use only one.

Diverse membership: Effective networks include diverse members who specialise in different advocacy strategies and tactics.

According to the elite allies hypothesis, if networks identify partners in a local government or department that can easily be accessed, they will likely choose embedded strategies. If local government or corporate elites are opponents, but allies can be located at a higher level, then media or combined strategies will be more effective. The most common combined strategy is an 'inside-outside' model that balances allies within part of the elite with external allies in the media, public opinion, or international links (Büsgen 2006: 28, Chapman and Fisher 2000: 158).[26] In particular, the combination of embedded and one or both of media and community strategies forms an effective combination that can put pressure on power-holders from several directions at once. In some networks, members specialise in different strategies, using diversity as a strength; in other cases, says a Chinese activist, individuals 'wear different hats – journalist, researcher, and so on. They use these multiple identities as assets to their advantage'. With one foot in the system and another outside of it, or some members in and others out, networks can obtain leverage that a single approach would be unable to accomplish, using external means to support internal allies to gain the upper hand against opponents. Research findings support all three of these strategy hypotheses.

An inside-outside strategy gives civil society networks the possibility of influencing political decisions even when they are much weaker than their opponents. The strategy's success depends on fragmentation of state authorities into multiple levels and components, some of which are aligned with, or themselves members of, the network. It does not require that the network's allies be the most powerful components, which is unlikely in any case, as the power-holders would then have little incentive to cooperate with civil society. As one of Büsgen's informants describes, 'We never directly confront the state, but we support one department to oppose another' (2006: 30). Using the image of a balance scale or a see-saw, even a small weight placed at a point of high leverage can tip the balance against a heavy force on the opposite side. This technique is reminiscent of martial arts such as jujitsu and aikido, through which a lighter contestant can use positioning and the opponent's own momentum to throw a stronger contender off balance (Fowler 1997: 227).[27] To some extent, each of the civil society networks profiled in this book have used jujitsu advocacy, with differing levels of skill and effectiveness. This is implicit in Büsgen's description of Chinese environmentalists as 'the weakest part, but the strongest link' (2006: 36) in tipping the balance against the Nu River dam projects (see Chapter 6).

The balancing metaphor also contains the concept of a tipping point, a point at which accumulated pressure builds up until an irreversible change takes place, like the proverbial last straw that breaks the camel's back. Networks may face seemingly impossible odds of success against powerful opponents and engage in activity after activity with little apparent result until, sometimes quite suddenly, the political equation shifts and a decision comes in their favour. Authorities may, of course, postpone or prevent a tipping point through repression, and some advocacy efforts never produce results regardless of effort. Yet repeated failure can also result in increased pressure during subsequent advocacy cycles. Power-holders who avoid responding to civil society concerns may inadvertently sow the seeds of increased contention in the future. As some critics warn, long-term regime interests might be better served by promoting state-society cooperation and allowing smaller, more gradual tipping points to occur naturally (Yu 2009: 78, 90, Mertha 2008: 157).

Tightrope acts

Networks, organisations and individual activists also need to keep their balance while engaging in advocacy, as opponents attempt to destabilise them. One interview respondent describes her advocacy efforts 'like walking on a tightrope'. Tightrope walkers typically carry a long pole, carefully balanced with an equal weight on both sides.[28] If the acrobat keeps focused on the end goal, she will move forward, but if one weight is heavier than the other, she will fall off.

Many network activists have done a remarkable job of staying on a tightrope despite pressures from many sides. Not all have been so lucky. Several Chinese HIV activists, for instance, could be said to have fallen off, or been pushed off, ending up in prison or in self-imposed exile. In 2009, one network leader, referred to by some as 'China's foremost activist' (Gallagher 2004: 445), faced a financial crisis due to a cut in donor funding. Without funds, the activist couldn't 'keep friendship relations' with the over 30 other network members that had been supported financially for four years. External funding gave the network coordinator position and balance, and the network was able to access support from potentially controversial donors without government blockage. When the activist's host organisation lost these funds, he became an easier target for his enemies in the government, who saw his situation of weakness and found regulations they could use against him. 'The pressure is always there', another activist commented afterwards. 'The government can act against people at any time and implement the law on a selective basis'. After moving to the USA, the activist told a reporter that 'there's no clear boundary between a political and a non-political organization', since the line is always moving (Richburg 2010).

A typical balancing act, as in the above case, is between government minders and international donors (Lu 2005: 7). Organisations need to negotiate political space and keep good relations with the state, while satisfying foreign donors that they are autonomous enough (Chan 2005: 37). Bratton (1990) found that among other factors, effective advocacy relies on a domestic funding base, rather than dependency on foreign sources (cited in Lewis 2001: 124). Domestic funding is just beginning to be an option for organisations and networks in China and Vietnam, and could provide a defence against nationalist criticism. Yet domestic foundations and corporations may also have their own balancing acts with government to consider and prove unwilling to fund advocacy initiatives. Along with multiple advocacy strategies, networks will also keep their balance better with multiple funding sources.

The first two chapters of this book have introduced civil society networks and advocacy strategies in China and Vietnam. The succeeding chapters explore network structures, history, strategies and effectiveness in four in-depth case studies, alternating between the two countries.

3
The Bright Future Group of People with Disabilities

On 16 November 2008, a network of disability activists in Hanoi called the Bright Future Group celebrated its 20th anniversary with a review workshop 'to share experience in working for advocacy' for the rights of people with disabilities (Bright Future Group 2008). The event was held at a government-owned hotel in Hanoi that is known as a centre of NGO activity and is one of the few affordable workshop venues in the city that is accessible to people with mobility impairments. Network members showed a video of their history that was produced for the occasion, sang songs, and gave emotion-filled testimony of how much the network has meant in their lives.

A diverse group attended the celebration, including government staff from the National Coordinating Council on Disability (NCCD)[1] and its parent Ministry of Labour, Invalids and Social Affairs (MOLISA); international and Vietnamese NGOs who have been key partners of the network, other groups of people with disabilities in Hanoi and neighbouring provinces, such as the Hanoi Club of Disabled Women and the Hai Duong province association of people with disabilities (PWD); and three reporters from the local and national print media. One international guest came from the Hong Kong Society of Rehabilitation who also serves as Vice-Chair of the Asia Pacific Disability Forum (APDF). In the discussion and question-and-answer sections of the workshop, participants suggested how Bright Future's experience is relevant to other self-help groups of people with disabilities that have formed more recently. The workshop and celebration that followed were funded by small donations from three international NGOs, a private Vietnamese company whose director is a network member, and an individual contribution from the network's then-vice-chair (BFG 2008).[2]

Bright Future Group of People with Disabilities (*Nhóm Vì tương lai tươi sang của Người khuyết tật*)[3] describes itself as 'the first organisation of people with disabilities in Vietnam' (BFG 2008). Bright Future has never operated as a formal organisation, but is rather a membership network of individual activists. BFG members have been present at almost every important event and policy decision relating to people with disabilities in Vietnam over the past 20 years; in the view of one international NGO leader, they have been 'the most sophisticated in terms of advocacy, with the closest links to policy-makers over many years'. BFG members have become the core of the Hanoi Association of People with Disabilities (DPO Hanoi), founded in 2006. As I will show, the network has passed through distinct stages of group formation and has pursued varied advocacy strategies: primarily embedded advocacy within existing state structures, at times combined with more confrontational, community outreach-based strategies.

Little has been written about disabled people's organisations (DPOs) in literature on civil society worldwide, perhaps because their members are socially marginalised, or because disability activism does not fit a 'romantic vision of civil society as a democratic surge that would bring political change' (Young 2008). The number of academic studies of disability issues in Vietnam and China can be counted on one hand (Vasiljev 2003, Chen 2007). DPOs are membership-based self-help groups (*nhóm tự lực*), which most other groups calling themselves NGOs are not; in a way, this makes them more akin to the Philippine category of 'people's organisations' (Kerkvliet 2003: 8, Silliman and Noble 1998: 29) or what are usually termed 'community-based organisations' in Vietnam. While the idea of 'self-help' or 'self-reliance' is broadly compatible with socialist ideology, the number of such local groups has not historically been large (Vasiljev 2003: 138–9). Vasiljev (2003) stresses links between people with disabilities and Vietnam's war-torn history. As time elapses, the effects of war are less salient, and although landmine injuries make up a small proportion of physical disabilities, the majority of disabled Vietnamese have no direct connection to the war. The symbolic link, however, remains politically important.[4] Vasiljev focuses on a self-help group in Hoi An in central Vietnam and the Disability Forum in Hanoi;[5] including one brief, accurate mention of BFG (2003: 140), the only published reference to the group in English.[6]

The Bright Future anniversary event was an exemplar of the network's advocacy strategy to embed itself in existing structures of state and society in order that PWD are fully included in these structures, while also linking horizontally with other disability organisations and networks with varying degrees of connection to the Party-state. The group's own internally circulated report on the anniversary noted that one outcome was 'a good opportunity for the community and authorities to recognise the abilities of people with disabilities' and garner increased media attention (BFG 2008: 3). As one Vietnamese journalist summarises, the status of people with disabilities has improved over the past decades for a variety of reasons, but crucially through the efforts of PWD to organise themselves into self-help groups, of which the Bright Future Group was the first (Thanh 2010). In this way, the experiences of Bright Future members and other disability activists are emblematic of larger social and political changes and shifts in state-society relations in Vietnam (Vasiljev 2003: 134).

Network formation and history

The Bright Future Group was formed in Hanoi in the mid-1980s by seven people with mobility impairments (four men, three women) who met while attending university in Hanoi. Five of the seven are still active; one has passed away. Some members had known each other previously, even since childhood; for instance, the second chair went to school with the wife of the first chair, and two other members were neighbours growing up. As one of the seven founding members writes on the group's website:

> I still remember like it was yesterday what it was like when we all first met each other. At that time, the spirit of renewal [*đổi mới*] was beginning to spread throughout the country, and international organisations began to enter Vietnam, among them Bread for the World [from then-West Germany]. They had a project with the National Economics University, and suggested that they might take a small part of the project funding to support an organisation of people with disabilities. So the school sent someone to look for one. They asked MOLISA, but received the response that there was no such organisation. They then went themselves to look for people with disabilities in Hanoi to gather together, and through contacts with a few friends who knew each other, we were all introduced to each other. The first meeting was at Mr. H.'s house, there were five of us... (BFG 2010a)

Initially, members supported each other to find work and earn income, a difficult task for all Hanoians in the 1980s, especially for people with disabilities who faced many social barriers to inclusion. In 1988, the seven original members decided to form a club and elected one member as chair.

> The idea to form an association of people with disabilities was H.'s. Everybody supported it. We wrote up by-laws and submitted a letter to the Hanoi People's Committee [city government] and MOLISA. With the enthusiasm of youth, we even thought we could 'pressure' the ministry into forming a national association, as Mr. T. [another of the group] put it! The ministry sent one person down to meet us. Because the conditions in Vietnam were not yet ripe, they didn't agree with our request. After that H. sent a letter to the People's Committee asking to set up a Hanoi Association of Disabled Intellectuals. They also refused and said we could only form a group or a club among ourselves.
>
> We were all disappointed by this. But then Ms. T. said, 'Well, we've already formed a club, haven't we? Let's just go ahead and keep meeting at H.'s house!' Every holiday or special occasion we all got together and shared among ourselves, anyone who had difficulties got support and advice from the others. The name 'Bright Future Group' didn't appear until 1995...[when] we applied to register with the Hanoi Support Association for Handicapped and Orphans [a government-organised NGO].[7] The leadership board of the Association helped us heartily, especially the chair, Ms. C...
>
> [From that point on,] the main activities of the group aimed at influencing the legal documents and policies of the state about disability issues, among them the Ordinance on Disabled Persons [1998] issued by the National Assembly Committee on Social Affairs, the construction standards of the Ministry of Construction relating to accessibility, and other policies to improve awareness and inclusion of the disabled. (BFG 2010a)

From 1995 onwards, BFG transformed from a personal network of people with disabilities to a civil society network advocating for disability rights. This intent was present in the group at its founding, but an expanded role only became possible in the mid-1990s due to established trust among members, support from government agencies, and international exposure. A key indicator of this change was the naming of the network as 'Bright Future Group', which happened in response to external opportunities: 'Other people wanted to work with us, and we needed our own identity for that'. When opportunities became available, members had already been meeting together regularly for at least seven years, forming a reserve of social capital. As a result, funding and international travel were not viewed primarily as means for individual advancement, but rather were shared as a contribution to the whole group.

Network membership and structure

Bright Future's membership has varied somewhat over time, but remained small: about 20 members at any given time, with a core group of ten who are most active; the current membership of 30 includes a number of new, younger people. All membership is on an individual, voluntary basis, and almost all members have full-time, outside jobs; BFG has never employed staff, and there is no permanent office. At one point in the 1990s, many members lived together in a rented house, but this ended when external funding for the facility ran out. Some members are government employees, including teachers; others are in business, others staff of local or international NGOs. The group appreciates this diversity and uses it consciously. The level of joint decision making is high, even about members' jobs: members talk about 'assigning' or 'seconding' members to work in different organisations. BF members are represented in most of the key local and international NGOs working on disability issues in Hanoi, as well as within several government ministries.

Members and outsiders alike agree that the main characteristic of Bright Future, compared to other disability groups, is that its members are educated intellectuals, an exception in a society in which most PWD have had limited opportunities for education. Almost without exception, BF members have mild to moderate mobility impairments: paraplegics, polio victims, amputees, and people with cerebral palsy. Most get around using wheelchairs, adapted three-wheeled motorbikes or motorbike taxis. Compared with most PWD in Vietnam, BF members could be considered an elite, relatively advantaged group, though none is rich by local standards. All members have engaged in national and international disability advocacy, and each is 'an example of special effort to integrate into mainstream society' (BFG 2008). It is this combination of success, commitment and vision among the core group that has attracted new members to join the network.

Membership in Bright Future is a core part of members' identities, even a life-changing event: 'My life used to be concentrated only on my family and relatives', says one member who joined around 2000.

> Since I've participated in the group, I feel like I have a new life. I consider the group is my second home. I love participating in

group activities and do everything to the utmost of my effort. The first time I came to a meeting, I just sat there and didn't say anything, but I still really liked it.... [Now] when I conduct training on forming self-help groups, I always share my own personal experience: from a person confined to my family, I've become a specialist in my work. Through the group's activities, I am more aware of my rights and more self-confident.

The network's structure is horizontal and democratic, with key decisions voted on by all members at quarterly business meetings. These gatherings are usually held at members' houses or in a meeting room borrowed from another organisation. An Executive Committee is elected every two years in accordance with the network's by-laws, consisting of a chair, two deputies, a secretary and an accountant. There have been three chairs over time: one man and two women. The current chair, serving since 2006, is in her 30s. The first two chairs, both original founding members, are now serving as president and vice-president of DPO Hanoi. In February 2010, Bright Future elected a new Executive Committee, with only the chair continuing from the previous committee.

Some significant differences exist between older and younger members, a reflection of social and economic changes in Vietnam since the 1980s. Members identify three generations in all: the original founding members are the first generation, now in their 50s and 60s; a second generation joined in the mid-1990s and are now mostly in their 30s; and the third generation in their 20s has joined recently. All of the new Executive Committee officers come from the younger generation (BFG 2010c), a shift that older members have supported. As the first chair stated in an online interview, 'the contribution from the younger generation is always present in all periods; some even are better than the senior members. I believe that it is time for the younger generation to grow up and replace their predecessors' (Thanh 2010).

While younger members consider themselves part of a network, older members refer to themselves as a 'group' or a 'club'. This is largely a linguistic issue: the term 'network' has only been widely applied to social groups in Vietnam for the last five years or so; BFG's existence far predates this. Over time, the network's structure has evolved from a tight personal network (at left in Figure 3.1) to a more expanded structure (centre and right).[8]

Communication among network members is mostly by e-mail and via a phone tree structure. As the network is in a large city, access to computers and phones is not a difficulty, but transportation for PWD can

Figure 3.1　Bright Future network stuctures over time

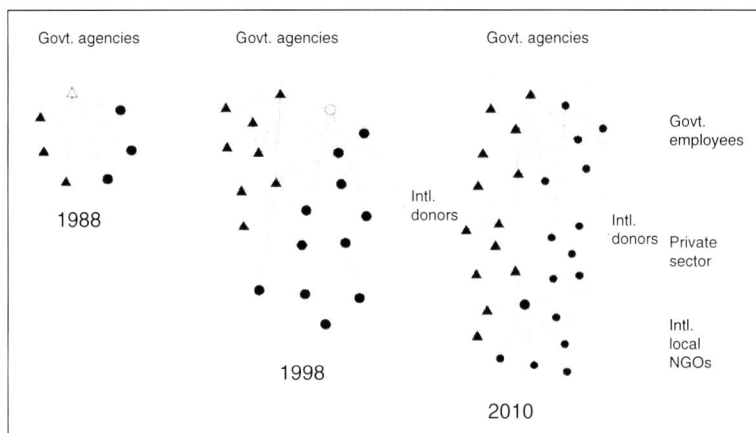

be a challenge, and face-to-face meetings have become less frequent as members have busier schedules. The executive committee is in touch on a daily basis. Members are expected to attend quarterly meetings and contribute small monthly dues according to the network's financial regulations. Dues have been collected since the start of the network, beginning at 10,000 dong per month (about 75p at 1990s' exchange rates) and now increased slightly to 150,000 dong per year. This is easily within members' ability to pay. Several members who have been 'assigned' or 'seconded' to jobs contributed 10 per cent of salaries they earn to the network, a unique practice among Vietnamese civil society groups.

The network has faced challenges in recruiting new members. Some members feel the younger generation of PWD, having grown up in a period of rapid socio-economic development and expanding opportunities, is less committed to the cause of disability rights:

> For several years now we have tried to invite more young people with disabilities to participate, but this is very hard... Before, there were some people who applied to join the group but thought that as members they would get benefits for themselves. When they realised that they had to pay their own motorbike taxi fares to come to meetings, they got bored and left the group.

Others were invited to join, but declined because they were not interested in a group that was made up only of other people with disabilities.

Naturally, when the group looked for new members, they tended to identify people similar to themselves – well-educated and mobility-impaired – which also may have limited their success. Some younger people are hesitant to join a group with many mature members, especially as more student groups of PWD have now formed. To address these issues, BFG is working to build links with younger groups and improve its media outreach to attract broad participation from PWD in the city. Bright Future is also implementing a new project to operate an Independent Living Centre for PWD in Hanoi.[9] Unlike previous BF initiatives, the Centre emphasises the needs of people with severe disabilities who are not able to take care of themselves (BFG 2008).

Advocacy strategies

Bright Future's public description on its Vietnamese-language website presents the group's mission and objectives as follows (BFG 2010b):

(1) Encouraging people with disabilities to live independently, and removing social barriers and prejudice against PWD;
(2) Creating opportunities for vocational training for PWD in information technology, foreign languages and other areas, and encouraging PWD to contribute to soc
ial action;
(3) Exchange information and promote social awareness for PWD to integrate into their communities.

In an interview, one of the founding members gives a slightly different, more advocacy-centred version of these three main objectives:

(1) Raise awareness of PWD and of society on disability issues;
(2) PWD help each other to share information and educate themselves;
(3) Build an accessible society that eliminates obstacles for PWD.

Of eight main activities listed in the network's public materials (BFG 2010b), six include advocacy components: lobbying for policy change, advocacy on behalf of constituents for better policy implementation, and support to implementing state services. Bright Future members and other disability activists frequently use the term 'awareness raising'[10] as a synonym for a form of advocacy towards both authorities and public attitudes. Activities to 'disseminate' information and policies can be interpreted in the same fashion.

In interviews, BFG members use terms such as 'policy advocacy' (*vận động chính sách*), 'movement' and 'civil society' that do not appear on their website. They express more clearly that policy advocacy is their priority and main contribution, while projects and direct support come second. 'Our group members are educated people with access to information, so we are able to contribute to policy. All important legal documents like the Ordinance on Disability include opinions from our group.' As with the differing versions of the group's objectives cited above, this should be understood as a deliberate decision to adjust wording to suit different audiences. Nothing is left out or changed in public materials, only presented in different terms or in a different order.

The denial of legal recognition from state authorities in 1988 forced BF members to postpone their plans for expanding into a larger association. By the mid-1990s, official attitudes had loosened, and BFG was allowed to register as a subsidiary of a GONGO. Advocacy and cultivation of important relationships, as with Ms. C. at the Association of Support for Vietnamese Handicapped and Orphans (ASVHO)[11] cited above, also contributed to changed government responses. Registration gave the network standing to participate in policy discussions:

> The drawback was that we didn't have our own stamp or legal identity and had to go through the Support Association for everything. But the good part was that as members of the association, we got invited to meetings, conferences and workshops. If we hadn't [registered], there's no way the authorities would have paid attention to us. When we went to meetings, we spoke out about the needs of people with disabilities, such as going to school and getting a job. The officials may not have liked it, but they had to listen to us. Even if they didn't listen a lot, they had to listen a little. Our voice was weak at first, but over time we had more quality. Our understanding kept improving, and our analysis got better too.

Close connections with authorities are a prerequisite to engage in this form of advocacy. The Bright Future Group is embedded in the state system in two ways: first, it is registered as part of an official association, and second, some of its members are themselves current or former state employees. One BF member has also participated as a member of the NCCD executive committee since 2001 (BFG 2010a). Yet the network as a whole, and its members as individuals, make their own decisions and express their views without state control. Despite their close connection with ASVHO over the years, for instance, BF members have no hesitation in criticising the group in print for focusing too much on individual charity, rather than support to disabled people's organisations and collective efforts (Thanh 2010). Advocacy has taken place through three main channels: direct contact with government officials, complaints and petitions, and through workshops and events held together with international partners.

All three channels were applied in a multi-year advocacy effort on national construction standards, first to include disability-related language in the standards, then to support their enforcement. One group member, who is an amputee, describes the beginning of this effort:

> Many of our group members are working in state agencies, even at the ministry level. We always talk about disability issues to everyone at every opportunity... The group makes copies of international documents, translates them and distributes to all participants at ministerial meetings... Since I work at the Ministry of Construction, I pay a lot of attention to [physical] accessibility. I've translated a lot of material from English to Vietnamese about this and written articles in specialised journals. At the ministry I often have the chance to meet leaders. One day [in 2000] I met Mr. L. who was Vice-Minister of Construction at the time. He told me that he was cooperating with Australia to develop national construction standards for Vietnam... I immediately said that there need to be standards relating to disabled accessibility in construction projects, and that this was a common international practice. He agreed and told me to get in touch with the drafting committee and research institutes.

She introduced information provided by existing BF project partners in Hong Kong, Japan and the US, and was then invited to participate in a ministry delegation for one month to study US construction standards. This advocacy led to accessibility being included in construction standards issued in 2002, although enforcement remains a problem.

Bright Future members and other groups of PWD in Vietnam also made substantial contributions to the 2010 Law on People with Disabilities. BF members participated actively in online discussions and workshops leading up to the drafting of the law and commenting on MOLISA's drafts, including events sponsored by NCCD, international NGOs, and United Nations agencies.[12] The Bright Future Group never sent coordinated comments as a network, but members submitted individual comments and suggested additions and revisions to the draft law to DPO Hanoi, who collected their comments and sent them to the Drafting Committee. Not every comment was accepted, and the final law text omitted several points that BF members thought important and covered others in general language only. However, feedback from PWD, including Bright Future members, verified that the law followed a rights-based approach and reflected priorities of people with disabilities, particularly on accessibility issues. One result was that the name of the law was changed from *tàn tật* ('handicapped, crippled') to *khuyết tật* ('disabled'), the term used by PWD themselves; earlier legal documents used the older phrase even though many PWD found this offensive. The law includes sections on independent living and on associations of the disabled, which have a specific function in 'developing, monitoring and implementing policies and laws relating to people with disabilities' (National Assembly 2010, Article 9.1). PWD advocacy efforts also resulted in social welfare policies in the law being open to all PWD, not only those living beneath the poverty line (Article 44).

Bright Future members work both as individual activists and as part of a team. The network realises that some members have strengths in different areas of advocacy and seeks to bring all of these into play: 'in order to influence a policy, many different sides need to join in, and every side will have its own way to make an impact'. Some members speak in ways that officials want to hear, while others are more confrontational. 'Within the group we have a division of labour. Some people who do not work for state agencies can speak out more strongly, while [those who do] have an advisory role.' There are sometimes differences of opinion within the network, which tend to break down along generational lines and according to degrees of closeness or distance from the state. The Ministry of Construction employee, for instance, prefers face-to-face contacts with officials: advocacy requires knowing the right person and speaking at the right time. 'Our group's experience in policy advocacy is that we need to take advantage of access to state officials whenever we can, and need to build relationships (*quan hệ* = guanxi) with them. We also involve them in our project activities so that they understand more about the issues we want to affect.' The head of the government's drafting committee for the Disability Law appreciates this approach: 'We are developing a legal system on the basis of rights, so people with disabilities have the right to speak up... If people speak strongly, I think that's a good thing, as it shows our society is developing.'

Not everyone in the Bright Future Group agrees. As a second-generation member states,

The brothers and sisters in the first generation have a state mentality. Anything they do has to link to state agencies and seek permission in order to do anything. Those of us in the younger group have newer thinking and want to operate more independently. We think the state system works very slowly, asking permission for everything but taking a long time to make decisions, and this affects the quality of work.

Yet this same member sees the value of varying roles within the group:

The members of our group have different impact on policy depending on the strengths of each person. Mr. T. is an excellent speaker, so he always gets up to give speeches at public events. He used to work as a journalist so he has a lot of friends in the media... Ms. V. works for a ministry, so she has a lot of connections with other state agencies. I speak foreign languages so I am often in contact with foreign organisations. To impact policy, we need a lot of different paths. Our group doesn't advocate only as a collective, but each member finds many ways and channels according to our own strengths.

All of these tactics fit within the overall framework of embedded advocacy, summarised in Table 3.1:

Table 3.1   Advocacy tactics – Bright Future network

Advocacy tactics	Notes
• Direct lobbying to officials • Letters, petitions, complaints • Speak at workshops, conferences • International travel • Form and register a membership association • Community advocacy: organise groups of PWD, support demonstrations	– Build a reputation as experts with access to specialised information, such as international contacts – Division of labour among group members according to comparative strengths – Use multiple methods to advocate on a single issue – BF network plays supporting role to community-based groups

Bright Future members realise that successful advocacy requires extending beyond their small membership. As one member describes,

When we engage in policy advocacy, my view is that we should select issues that relate to many people with disabilities, [issues where] we can have an impact, that don't create large social conflicts and that can be accepted by the society. For instance, accessibility is a problem

that affects many people with disabilities and doesn't cause social conflict. While the problem of southern disabled veterans [not being recognised by the communist government] could easily lead to disputes, so
we don't advocate about that. We have to reach out to people with
disabilities in the community and create a strong collective voice.

This awareness has led Bright Future members in several directions.
International linkages have been an important aspect of the network
since the mid-1990s and have continued to strengthen. At the same
time, the founding members have been able to achieve their long-held
goal of establishing a membership association, diffusing the Bright Future
model throughout Vietnam. Meanwhile, some younger members have
begun community organising among PWD, including on some controversial issues. In this way, they have taken steps away from embeddedness and towards a more community-based strategy. These activities have
contributed to network effectiveness in the three senses of achieving
policy objectives, growth and sustainability of the network, and affecting
political space.

International linkages

Bright Future's advocacy is supported and enabled by connections with
international NGOs and organisations, as well as with regional and global
disability networks. INGOs frequently invite BFG members to lead training courses and speak at conferences, which gives them credibility and
face with Vietnamese authorities. 'When there are conferences and workshops organised with government partners, the foreign organisations often
demand that PWD are present, and this gives us an opportunity to speak.'
Through international projects, PWD and government policy-makers have
multiple chances to interact, and this helps to increase knowledge and
awareness among both groups.

   Travel to international conferences has been a significant advocacy
opportunity for BFG members not only to meet foreign partners, but
also, ironically, to engage with Vietnamese government officials on a
more equal basis.

   The Ministry of Health had been implementing a community-based
   rehabilitation programme since the 1990s, but hadn't invited our
   group to participate. However, on one international trip to attend a
   conference, Ministry of Health staff and Bright Future Group members
   both attended, and we met each other there and got to know each

other. After that, the Ministry staff invited our group to participate...so we could raise the voices of people with disabilities.

Another member adds,

> Since we've been able to go to international and regional conferences... we've learned more about disability movements in other countries, and gradually we've also learned how to write proposals, manage projects, and about the rights of people with disabilities. We've also studied books and documents so we know more information about disability and international experience. That way, when we go to meetings we can speak up strongly, and people will listen to us.

Bright Future members view their links with regional disability networks and international NGOs as important primarily for exposure and contacts. Funding is a secondary benefit, in many cases small: several hundred dollars to attend a workshop, a few thousand for a training programme. BFG has received international funding on numerous occasions since the mid-1990s and has relied on these grants to carry out most of the activities listed above, as membership dues and other local contributions are hardly sufficient for the network to operate. But this funding has not been essential to forming or sustaining the network, which has remained internally driven. Instead, international organisations served as instigators, bridges and brokers, even unwittingly, as in the first effort from Bread for the World. In one case, funding from one organisation was used to leverage additional funds from other sources:

> In 1995, with the permission of MOLISA, we received support from an American NGO, CRS to send two members, Ms. V. and Ms. H., to attend a conference on women with disabilities in the Asia Pacific [in Thailand]... It was at that conference that we raised funds from Hong Kong and Japan for language and computer teaching. This project contributed a lot to the development of our group. (BFG 2010a)

Many donors explicitly do not fund international conference attendance and study tours, preferring to support discrete projects that can be measured and have set outcomes; but Bright Future's experience shows that this can be short-sighted. The UN conference trip

> was very meaningful for me... It was the first time that I knew there was a UN Decade of the Disabled, that there were self-help groups of

people with disabilities [in other countries], that there were so many international conventions and documents about the rights of persons with disabilities, and that there was an international and regional disability movement... It was also the first time I met funders and heard about regional NGO networks.

In such ways, diffusion from disability movements in Asia, Europe and the USA has had significant influence on Vietnamese organisations and networks (Vasiljev 2003: 141). But in BFG's experience, the impact of international funding has been mixed, presenting opportunities for advocacy and mobilisation of new members, but also management challenges. Most donors will only fund projects to provide services, not general support funds for advocacy. Some BF members' ability to speak foreign languages and communicate well with donors enabled them to attract exposure and funding, but without a strong organisational structure, their actual project activities were not sustainable and ended after the funding ran out. Speaking about disability self-help groups generally, one BF member notes,

> People start participating for the personal, non-material benefits it brings them. But many people also want a little material benefit. When there is a project that supports a little of these costs, then everybody is motivated, but when the project ends members are no longer very interested. Almost all groups face these difficulties with funding, and no one has found a way out yet.

Network effectiveness: Policy change

In the examples of accessible construction standards and development of the Disability Law cited above, Bright Future members leveraged their links with government ministries and diplomatic skills to promote policy change through an embedded strategy. The benefits and limitations of this strategy appear in sharper relief in a contentious episode in 2007. On 29 June, the Vietnamese government issued a regulation (SRV 2007b) restricting the registration and circulation of certain motorised vehicles under the pretext of 'controlling transport accidents and traffic jams.' Previously, three-wheeled carts (*xe ba bánh*), similar to tuk-tuks or samlors in other Southeast Asian countries, had been exempt from licensing requirements; many are driven by disabled veterans who proudly note their status on the back of their vehicles. As traffic problems have increased in Vietnamese cities, however, these slow vehicles, including more than 2,000 in Hanoi alone, became a target for regulators.[13] Under the new rules, all vehicles self-assembled by PWD were to be banned by 1 January 2008. PWD were also required to obtain driving licences, show evidence of 'health', register their vehicles (including motorised wheelchairs) and pass inspection 'to assure sufficient quality, technical safety and environmental protection' (IDEA 2008). These requirements were perceived by PWD as highly burdensome and discriminatory.

The regulations were issued in spite of earlier protests by disabled veterans. In March 2007, the Ministry of Transport issued a letter requesting the Ministry of Public Security to ban three-wheeled vehicles. This led to an immediate response from members of the Association of Disabled Veteran Drivers (*Hội Anh em Thu'o'ng Binh vận hành xe ba bánh*), who drove their vehicles to block the entrance of the Ministry on 7 March (Thuy and Anh 2007). Facing a lack of response from authorities, the frustration and anger in the disability network grew.

In a letter to Prime Minister Nguyen Tan Dung, Bright Future members used reason and persuasion. Three-wheeled drivers were mostly veterans and PWD over the age of 50. If the state forced them to stop using their own vehicles to carry goods, it was not realistic that they could get another job. The letter went unanswered. '[The authorities] are really hesitant to answer in writing', said a BFG member. 'Then they have to assume responsibility.' When it looked like the ban would proceed, the Hanoi Association of PWD compiled statements and views into a packet that was shared with the Hanoi People's Committee and other authorities, along with recommendations.

However, the leading role in the contentious episode was not played by BF members but by a group of 200 veterans who were drivers of three-wheeled vehicles. As one activist describes,

> In an NCCD meeting, the Ministry of Transport spokesperson... didn't pay attention to people with disabilities and reaffirmed the decision [to ban three-wheeled vehicles]. In Vietnam, debating legislation doesn't get you anywhere. But when the group of drivers decided to get together, they circled their vehicles to block streets in several locations; the largest was several hundred vehicles in front of the National Assembly's public reception office near the Ho Chi Minh Mausoleum.[14] When they took strong steps like that, then the Ministry of Transport had to listen to them. They really knew how to struggle! When [the drivers] got up to speak, they didn't say they opposed the law, but said they need support in order to work.

Three-wheeled vehicles are our means to earn a living! If you ban them, then arrange some other jobs for us to do. So for more than a year now, the law has been suspended and people are still using three-wheeled vehicles to make a living.

Through this case, we can see that the self-initiating character of the masses is still stronger. This is their life, no one was able to help them, so they had to organise themselves to help each other. All the three-wheeled drivers know each other and they agreed to park their vehicles in certain places. Then they met and discussed what they would do. They were even prepared to take more drastic measures. If after this episode, their vehicles were still banned, they were ready to keep opposing until the end. The people in the Association of PWD just talked about it, they didn't do anything strong like that.

Bright Future members confirmed this account:

IDEA [Inclusive Development Action, a Vietnamese NGO] and the Disability Forum organised a meeting and invited many groups to participate, including three-wheeled drivers. After this meeting, we drafted a petition that many people signed.… It was the drivers themselves who were the most heavily involved. They organised a demonstration with a lot of people and generated a lot of pressure [on the Ministry of Transport]. At the end, the state had to cancel their plans to carry out this unjust regulation. In addition the media was also very active.

The DPO Hanoi vice-chair, by contrast, supports 'policy advocacy through constructive means', defending the use of a written petition to the Ministry of Transport 'even though there were some groups who were organising in the style of a demonstration. The Association's view is to work together with government and local mass organisations [to solve problems].' Other Bright Future members, however, did not find this convincing, saying the DPO leaders were 'thinking like officials' and 'didn't have much of a voice' about the issue.

Bright Future members went ahead with a multiple-channel strategy. In addition to letter-writing, one member spoke out in an NCCD meeting on 21 December 2007 that included participation from the Ministry of Public Security. Another member worked on a small World Bank-funded project on traffic safety for PWD that included a television programme, which she used to engage a Ministry of Transport official in dialogue about the three-wheeled vehicle issue. A third member was working at IDEA and organised a forum of PWD about the issue. Many PWD learned about the case online; information got out to people on time, and activists used media effectively. At the last minute, the government compromised, issuing a joint circular on 31 December 2007 postponing the ban, initially for a one-year period. Furthermore, owners of three-wheeled vehicles were awarded cash support of up to five million dong (£160) to upgrade their vehicles to meet the standards.[15]

The successful reversal of the ban on three-wheeled vehicles came about through a mixture of push and pull factors, with various actors stressing different approaches. According to one BF member, meetings were more important than demonstrations overall: the protest actions forced the government to pay attention, but didn't explain the positions of PWD. An outside observer, however, believes the drivers' demonstration was the critical turning point, since it was led by war veterans, a group the government was afraid to offend. The drivers also had sympathetic allies within NCCD and the Ministry of Transport, which helped to prevent any negative consequences from their protest actions. Either community-based or embedded advocacy alone might have been insufficient to reverse the outcome, but the combined pressure from institutional and extra-institutional sources proved effective.

One BF member reflected afterwards, 'We didn't discuss any of this in advance, but everyone used his or her own position to engage in policy advocacy'. Although members stress their unity and high level of internal agreement, outsiders see less coordination of messages and perceive that most activism is carried out by individuals, not in the name of the Bright Future Group. This may be due to the fact that some members have strong individual voices and also due to differences in opinion and strategy within the network. 'Through this incident, the network also learned some experiences that we need to gather opinions from everyone in the [disability] community first, then need to outline who will meet whom and what they should say. At the moment, we're still acting too separately.'

Network effectiveness: Sustainability

Expanding their group to form an association of PWD was a Bright Future objective from the beginning. BF members, especially the more government-connected of them, reasoned that if women, veterans, and other social groups could have associations to represent them, then people with disabilities should also be able to register. The formation of self-help groups into a national association, says the first BFG chair, enables outreach and support to PWD in all provinces who are interested in learning from BFG's model. 'When people with disabilities recognise their benefits in joining activities...the disability movement [will] spread widely' (Thanh 2010). There were also possible sensitivities in organising an association. Other social groups had mass organisations set up for them by the Party; would people with disabilities be thought 'too self-important' for organising their own? And, keeping the Veterans Association in mind, what about Southern veterans? They fought for the other side, but many of them were disabled too; should they be included in a disabled people's association? 'In the past, people would have said no. But now the situation had changed. We didn't hear anyone mention these sensitive issues anymore.'

Bright Future activists learned from their international exposure that all other ASEAN member states, plus China, South Korea and Japan already had national associations of the disabled, more or less autonomous depending on each country's political situation (United Nations 2006).[16] Vietnam had no such association, despite a robust system of government-organised associations and Vietnamese people's high level of participation in social groups (Dalton and Ong 2004: 3–4). BF members also realised that international funding would one day end and thought it desirable to attract Vietnamese government funding at least for certain core activities. The fact that by registering as a social organisation, the Hanoi Association of PWD would also be subject to heightened government regulation did not bother the organisers greatly, although some realised that by accepting city subsidies for their office, it did affect their ability to oppose city policies. They focused instead on the increased opportunities for advocacy, 'to be an intermediary between the government and people with disabilities. If there is a new policy, the government will ask the Association to consult and submit opinions, or we will provide recommendations on our own.'

In 2005, recognising that political opportunities had shifted in their favour, BFG members worked with other self-help groups of PWD and city authorities to initiate the establishment of a Hanoi Association of PWD. They succeeded in raising funds from the Danish Society of Polio and Accident Victims (PTU) to set up the association. Their application to the Hanoi People's Committee was approved, and the Hanoi Association of PWD held its founding conference in April 2006. BFG became the core of DPO Hanoi, owing to their recognised status in the disability community, as well as their levels of education, communication skills and connections with government and international organisations. One could say this was pre-ordained, as BFG managed the funding that was used to set up the Association.[17] The first chair of BFG was elected president, and four other BF members were elected as vice-chair and executive committee members (BFG 2010a). Leadership positions are unsalaried, as is required by law (SRV 2003), but the Association has recruited two full-time and at least one part-time staff for projects funded by PTU and the International Labour Organisation. The Association has set up branches in 17 of Hanoi's 29 urban and peri-urban districts. In all, the association's members include 3,000 out of an estimated 28,000 PWD in Hanoi (Trung 2010). Increasing membership is a key priority, among other reasons for stronger advocacy with local authorities, although the president states '[we are] not running after quantity [alone], because our first and the most important principle is that everyone should be voluntary' (Thanh 2010).

As of April 2010, Bright Future is one of 37 organisational members of DPO Hanoi, each with one seat on the executive committee. In an intriguing symbiotic relationship, BF is now legally part of the Association, while the Association is itself a product of BF, is led by BF members and constitutes one of the advocacy channels that BF members use. Rather than being subject to the tight management of its parent association, as Vietnamese regulations stipulate (Sidel 2010), Bright Future has effectively set up and colonised its own GONGO, while continuing to operate independently in other areas. As one member describes, 'The Association and Bright Future are almost like one entity... The association is a big tree, and our group is its largest root.' A writer in the Association's magazine argues that DPO Hanoi, with its multiple sub-associations, 'has been established in a systematic way' and meets the 'three deciding factors for the success of a network': legitimacy, a strategic plan and fixed leadership (Trung 2010: 34–6).

From their new position in the Hanoi Association, BF members next began advocating for the establishment of a national disabled people's organisation. Local networks and self-help groups of PWD have formed in many, though not all, Vietnamese cities and provinces over the past decade. Some of these groups exist informally, while others are registered with local governments or mass organisations. BF members drew on their own experiences of empowerment and personal change to mobilise others to join DPOs (Trung 2009), particularly in the north, through an earlier INGO-funded project, as individual consultants and staff of local and international NGOs and more recently as part of the Hanoi Association of PWD. Dense network activity has also taken place in Ho Chi Minh City around two major nodes, Disability Resource and

Development (DRD) linked to the Open University, and the HCMC Club of Disabled Youth, linked to the Youth Union (IDEA 2009). The spreading of the network to other provinces also contributes toward resolving a perceived urban bias in organising among the disabled in Vietnam (Vasiljev 2003: 146). As of July 2010, 15 provinces and cities have DPOs, and more will be formed after the formation of the national association, which is currently in process awaiting final approval by the government and the confirmation of a suitable president.

Efforts to set up DPO Hanoi and a national association have never faced serious opposition. However, bureaucratic procedures take significant amounts of time, and many different ministries and branches of government need to sign off on the plan. The longest-running disability-related association, the Vietnam Blind Association,[18] showed little enthusiasm for a national disability association. Other groups of PWD, such as the Hanoi Deaf Club, have participated actively. Financing of a national association is also a consideration, as the Vietnamese government appears to have neither the funds nor the inclination to provide direct funding for the Association in the long run. DPO leaders differentiate themselves from GONGOs, stating that their salaries are not paid by the government and that they are therefore able to represent their membership constituency more independently. The Bright Future Group has been remarkably able to contain different approaches to organising within its own membership, and has thus contributed to cooperation and conflict reduction among different strands of the disability movement.

Over time, the example of Bright Future has spread by diffusion to other parts of Vietnam:

> At first there was just our group up north and the Disabled Youth Club down in the south. Gradually other people with disabilities heard information about us, then held meetings of the disabled in all parts of the country, so people with disabilities in the provinces also formed groups. Then there were international projects that helped support them too. When you add it all up, awareness in society has really changed, and the awareness of people with disabilities ourselves has changed too.

The Bright Future model has been replicated widely, including to student groups and local NGOs. BFG members are optimistic about their network's continuity. 'I think in the future the Bright Future Group will continue to exist. We will continue to contribute many voices.' Another member adds:

> In the future, we still have to continue policy advocacy and aware-ness raising towards the society and authorities. Many people ask why we have to keep on raising awareness for such a long time! I reply 'because awareness sometimes rises but sometimes falls'! One important contribution of the Bright Future Group is to help change the image of people with disabilities and change social attitudes about people with disabilities.

The same activist also adds a cautionary note: 'If group members lack commitment, then it will be hard to preserve the reputation of the Bright Future Group. For many years, we have been considered pio-neers in the disability movement, but now we don't yet have a new direction.'

Network effectiveness: Political space

While Bright Future members have made conscious decisions to engage in advocacy, they rarely speak of their work as political. 'We don't do politics', says one member. 'In other countries, where there may be many parties, what we do might be political, but in Vietnam the idea of politics is different.' One donor representative with long experience in the sector notes that the fact that disability issues are generally not considered 'sensitive' makes advocacy on these issues acceptable while other rights-based claims might be restricted by the state. A BF member says, 'we pay attention to anything that is relevant to us. But if the question is who becomes prime minister, then we don't care much about that, since we can't affect this anyway.'

If 'political civil society' is equated with dissidence and political opposition (Thayer 2009), then disability rights advocacy does not qualify. But in a broader definition of politics as a process of public deliberation, shared by most international disability activists, Bright Future's advocacy activities certainly do qualify. Given that BFG members seek equal rights and inclusion for PWD, their choices of embedded and community-based advocacy strategies are appro-priate for the network's goals. Even if some individual BFG mem-bers might like to see larger changes in their political system, the main goal of their advocacy is not to replace the system, but rather to join it.

Aware of the political context, Bright Future members have generally chosen low profile tactics, keeping their distance from transgressive actions such as the 2007 three-wheeled protests as well as from the large public rallies (*mít-tinh*)[19] organised by ASVHO and other mass organisations on International Disability Day (3 December) and Vietnamese Disability Day (18 April). The Bright Future name is not frequently used in advocacy efforts, with many members acting under the auspices of DPO Hanoi, NCCD or the Disability Forum. After the formation of DPO Hanoi, the status of BFG appeared 'smaller by comparison', and it was often more advantageous to use the name of the Association. As noted with previous public statements by the group, there is no evidence here of 'self-censorship', but rather smart strategising.

Conclusion

BFG considers that 'its contribution to the disability movement in Vietnam has been very large nationwide' (BFG 2008). Indeed, in large measure due to the efforts of Bright Future, it is now possible to speak of a 'movement' (*phong trào*), a term increasingly used by BF members and other activists to describe their activities.[20] Defined in ecological terms, the disability movement comprises numerous networks, non-governmental and government-linked organisations, many of which were present at Bright Future's 20th anniversary celebration. Membership among the various networks that make up the disability movement is overlapping, and members both advance their own interests, for instance through education and income generation projects, as well as advocate for policy change. However, the degree of coordination among various disability networks remains limited.

Although its public statements are equivocal, in practice the Bright Future Group has prioritised advocacy over its own fundraising and organisational development, which could be characterised as ad hoc and opportunistic. A blind activist in Hanoi who keeps a critical distance from Bright Future and the Association believes that self-sustaining disability organisations are possible, and groups like his arts and employment centre should seek ways in which 'one activity can nourish another' to directly improve the [material] lives of PWD. As BF members have noted, however, this is less feasible for an advocacy-centred network with no market basis. The question is how long an advocacy focus can be maintained, compared with the desire of members to benefit from network activities through training, job creation and other needs.

In one view, disability groups are most effective when small, up to about ten participants who can really support each other, as was the case with BFG initially. How can this spirit be maintained within the Hanoi Association of 3,000 members, let alone a national association of PWD? To be an effective network or larger organisation, the activist critic suggests, leaders need to be more serious about structure, think about fundraising and sustainability, and find ways to maintain a professional core but participatory methods that meet the needs of members. In this view, it is more important to offer services that people really need than engage in 'movement-building'. This debate between service provision and advocacy is likely to continue for some time.

Cognisant of structural limitations in the Vietnamese context, Bright Future members do not aim to engage in confrontational actions for disability rights. Instead, they have found numerous opportunities to advocate within the system, which they generally view as preferable. Some BF members have become the nucleus of a quasi-governmental association, while others continue to engage in a range of advocacy efforts on behalf of the group. This posture may be viewed both as a weakness and a strength. The Bright Future Group has remained small, retaining many of its original characteristics as a club of educated people with mobility impairments. Although the network is vitally important to the lives of members, its collective voice is often not as strong as the uncoordinated voices of individual members.

BFG has chosen embedded advocacy strategies that are fundamentally elite-based, yet have been effective at influencing policy changes and inspiring other PWD to join in advocacy and self-empowerment. Bright Future's horizontal structure and division of roles and responsibilities among members have kept it away from the bureaucratisation and intra-organisational infighting that have posed an obstacle for many civil society groups (Piven and Cloward 1977: xxii, Lewis 2001: 173). The informal and subsidiary status of BFG has enabled members to focus on advocacy without requiring permission from authorities, on one hand, or incurring the risk of repression on the other. The combination of embedded and community strategies they have pursued has taken shape over more than 20 years and has considerable potential for effective advocacy in cooperation with newer disability activists. As a longstanding network, Bright Future's experience has much to offer other civil society actors, though their strategy is not the only possible one.

4
The China Women's Network against AIDS

In May 2010, a fundraising dinner took place at Shanghai's world-class art museum to commemorate the 27th annual International AIDS Candlelight Memorial Day. Three groups were selected as beneficiaries: the Shanghai Red Cross Society, a Hong Kong-based foundation, and a newly-formed network of HIV-positive women's support groups, the Women's Network against AIDS – China (女性抗艾网络 – 中国, *Nǚxìng kàng'ài wǎnglùo – Zhōngguó*). When the network's secretary-general took the podium, she said, 'Because of this virus in our blood, we sought each other out, talked among ourselves and formed small groups. Finally, we connected into a network... [As] Chinese women affected by AIDS, we are facing the disease while still pursuing life' (WNAC 2010: 4). From its share of donated proceeds of the event, the Women's Network (WNAC) received 40,000 yuan (approximately £4,000), a substantial contribution to the network's budget.[1]

The Women's Network against AIDS formed in July 2009 on the basis of a web-based network of individuals that had existed for several years previously (*China Development Brief* 2009). Most of its 21 organisational members can be better characterised as peer support groups than NGOs. From its organic, virtual roots, the network has transformed into a national body with a significant degree of formal organisation, at least on paper. In a sector already containing multiple and sometimes competing networks of people living with HIV, some observers hoped that WNAC could become a less contentious, more inclusive network than other existing groups. In the network's short history to date, it faces many challenges in its development, and it is too soon to draw conclusions about its success or sustainability.

Less than a month after the successful fundraising dinner in Shanghai, the network closed its Beijing coordination office, citing rising rents and the end of grant funding from its major donor, the Joint United Nations Programme on HIV/AIDS (UNAIDS). Although a new UNAIDS grant was reportedly in process, it had not yet been approved. The network secretariat decided to 'temporarily withdraw the Beijing office until the next phase of the project and then consider whether the application is successful before re-establishing the office' (WNAC 2010: 1). After less than a year of formal operations, the Women's Network's future lay in the balance.

The politics of HIV[2] have been contentious in many settings. People living with HIV (PLWH) are subject to extreme social stigma and discrimination due to both the high morbidity of the virus and its most frequent means of transmission: homosexual and heterosexual contact and blood transmission, including injecting drug use. Since the first Chinese case of AIDS was discovered in 1985, government policy towards HIV has opened considerably, with the attempted cover-ups of the Henan blood scandal and other public health crises such as the SARS epidemic in 2003 forming key turning points (Hu Jia 2007, Kaufman 2010).[3] Government services to PLWH and cooperation with social and community groups began around 2000, leading to policy and attitudinal changes within the state. The 'four frees, one care' (四免一关怀) policy, offering free HIV testing, counselling, and anti-retroviral therapy, was announced at the end of 2003 (Kaufman et al 2006). Comprehensive regulations on HIV and AIDS prevention, treatment, care and support were promulgated in 2006, banning discrimination against PLWH (*Xinhuanet* 2006). The Chinese government has increasingly recognised the role of civil society in HIV prevention and treatment, while still selectively restricting groups' operations (Meng L 2009, Thompson and Jia 2010). International donors speak highly of the Ministry of Health's commitment to accepting civil society roles and find them a relatively open-minded and progressive branch of the government. As a result, while HIV issues are still contentious, the level of political restriction or 'sensitivity' has decreased, with an emerging balance between public health and rights-based approaches.

More than 500 community groups and organisations, including GONGOs, contribute to China's AIDS response (Ministry of Health 2010: 62), including some registered NGOs and many unregistered support groups and networks. Few of these groups, however, represent women affected by HIV.[4] According to official statistics, women make up 30.5 per cent of China's estimated 740,000 PLWH (Ministry of Health 2010: 5). But they have historically been under-represented in HIV policy and programmes (Bu and Liu 2010, UNAIDS 2006). The latest edition of the annual *China*

HIV/AIDS NGO Directory now runs to over 300 pages, but includes only a handful of women's support groups (CHAIN 2010). National surveys show that women have less knowledge about HIV than men, particularly in rural areas (Han et al 2009: 23–4), and less access to HIV treatment (Bu and Liu 2010). The dominant 'scientific' approach to HIV prioritises medical aspects over the social reality of the disease, disempowering women who are affected (He 2006: 8). A major study in 2010 concluded that support to NGOs and groups of HIV-positive women is 'the most important proposal' (Bu and Liu 2010: 10).

Such gendered considerations have not always taken the priority in civil society research that they deserve (Howell 2006). In China, women's organisations and networks began to emerge from the 'monopoly' of the All China Women's Federation (ACWF) following the 1995 United Nations World Conference on Women (Milwertz 2002, Howell 2004b). Two civil society networks on gender and development and domestic violence, respectively, have formed in Beijing among these groups (Keech-Marx 2008).[5] But these networks have not taken an active role in HIV activism and are perceived as a relatively closed group with little success in mainstreaming their issues. As Wainwright describes (2005: 112), 'the encounter of Chinese women with Western feminism gave independent Chinese women's organisations access to a new language and stream of thinking about self-determination, autonomy and self-organised agency'. However, Howell (2004b) critiques some newer women's groups as limited by a service delivery orientation, a perceived lack of legitimacy, and weak networks and alliances with state agencies, together with dependence on international donors. Such mixed influences are also apparent in the experience of WNAC since its establishment as a nationwide HIV network.

Network formation and history

In the early years of China's HIV epidemic, stigma and fear kept most HIV-positive women 'in the closet' about their status, although in many cases they were eventually 'exposed' (暴露, *bàolù*) by neighbours or even health staff (He 2006: 70). Many women (and men) made the unwelcome choice to move away from their homes and families for the anonymity and access to treatment of major cities. For those who were unable or unwilling to do this, their immediate need was to find someone who would understand and offer support. At first, communication took place by long-distance telephone. The spread of the Internet, however, offered new possibilities for connection through instant message boards and chat rooms. In these virtual spaces, people could share their experiences with HIV without telling their real name or identity, even their location. They could also talk to people while revealing nothing at all about their HIV status. Many PLWH went on to develop personal websites and blogs as tools for organising (He 2006: 94). This process led to the formation of the Dandelion Network (蒲公英, *Púgōngyīng*), a virtual predecessor to the Women's Network against AIDS.

> In May 2006, I was losing my mind on receiving a HIV-positive report. Without enough explanation and care from doctors, I had no choice but to search for information and help via the internet. I met many friends who were suffering and struggling against the disease. They helped me solve my initial problems and gave me important advice when I was facing therapy options. Then, when I could finally face my HIV status calmly, my first thought was doing something for the patients with same experience as me who were struggling for care and support and try my best to help them.

> I began to write treatment notes on Sina Blog with the hope that my experience and thoughts could encourage HIV-positive people to fight bravely against the disease. As more accessed, more people made consultations to me. In order to promote the communication between women positives, I created a QQ group[6] in February 2007 named 'Dandelion'. Dandelion is a soft but strong plant that spreads her seeds with love around at her season...

> Based on the QQ group, some active members...decided to set up the Dandelion Network of Women Living with HIV/AIDS in March 2007. We hoped, through the internet, to unite more women to help our friends in difficulties and to raise our unified voice. It's an open organization that has no office space and staff, but with several core members and more than 100 volunteers and members that join or quit at their will. (He 2009)

The use of message boards such as QQ was essential to building links among women in different provinces. Prior to the Internet, such links would have been impossible; as a Hong Kong-based activist says, 'there is no way to overstate the importance' of the Internet.

> Many people think QQ groups childish, but this web-based chatting tool successfully meets the needs of people located in different

geographic areas and provides the requirement of privacy. The members can communicate freely at anytime, from anywhere, as long as the internet is available. In our QQ group, women get along very well, caring and encouraging each other. We discuss reproduction, self-caring, family caring and all topics women are interested in. Communication and discussion help us think about the problems we are facing and enable us to make informed decisions. Visiting the QQ group has become our daily habit. Neighboring members even meet and hang out occasionally. Although the internet is virtual, the friendship between us really exists. (He 2009)

The Dandelion activists and other women's support groups also used existing publications and channels of communication provided by other HIV networks to raise the profile of women's issues. For instance, the November 2008 issue of 'Our Voice' (我们的声音), published by Ark of Love,[7] contains articles entitled 'A person who comes out of the shadows' and 'Infected women: stand up and come out!', the latter by the future WNAC secretary-general, and profiles two women's support groups, Half the Sky and the Guiyang Garden of Health and Care, which later became WNAC founding members (He 2008).

Women's organising took place in the midst of a complex web of overlapping and in some cases competing field of civil society actors. Networks of HIV support groups first emerged after 2001 due to the conditions of government policy openings, international funding, and expanding access to the Internet and other communications technologies. Groups that formed early, were located in major cities, and were led by charismatic, well-connected individuals had built-in advantages.[8] Several previously established groups used their existing connections with government and donors to build national networks of peer groups, particularly those representing gay men (MSM).[9] From others' perspectives, the leaders of these networks could easily appear to be 'gatekeepers' with unfair access to donor funds. Other networks formed expressly for the purpose of accessing international resources, leading to cases in which multiple groups received small grants for overlapping activities in the same cities (Young and Mian 2007). The increased availability of funding fostered competition among HIV support groups and networks, as well as among donors. As one long-term donor describes, 'Everyone wants to be king of the mountain'. Added to great geographic diversity, HIV groups and networks segmented into vertical sub-sectors representing different affected groups: MSM, PLWH, drug users, sex workers, youth/students and women.[10]

In February 2009, 12 delegates from groups of HIV-infected and affected women in eight provinces met in Beijing to hold the first organisational meeting of the Women's Network against AIDS. The group's first media release described their rationale in this way:

> The number of women affected and infected by AIDS is rising rapidly. Although women have always played an important role in the process of the struggle against AIDS, on some occasions women's voices have been weak or even nonexistent. HIV-positive women in many locations have already become aware of the need to form small groups to participate in serving the community and protecting their own rights. At the same time, women have sensed that their own capacity is not sufficient, their access to information is not smooth, and they lack autonomy and the right to speak. Thus, it is necessary to form a working network to develop collaboration. (*China Development Brief* 2009)

According to materials shared by the WNAC secretariat, the goals of this first meeting were to share experiences and explore network strategy. This was followed by group interviews to evaluate needs and existing capacities within the network. A second preparatory meeting followed to discuss a strategic plan and draft network by-laws. After six months of preparation, the official launch of the network occurred on 9 July in Beijing. As the network's secretary-general describes,

> We mobilized the key members of women positive groups and women community workers around the country to establish a nationwide network... We want to expand the existing internet-based network into a substantial one. We hope it could play a strategic role in information sharing, collective actions and establishing an enabling environment for living and treatment, as well as to promote the development of women positive groups... We believe that Chinese women's efforts against HIV/AIDS are on the journey and last forever as the seeds of a dandelion. (He 2009)

Network membership and structure

The Women's Network against AIDS has 21 initial organisational members from 11 Chinese provinces and cities (*Douban* 2009). The membership, strategies and activity plans of the network have been well organised and documented for distribution among members as well as to the

network's external donor, UNAIDS, which began support in the preparatory phase of the network. As a result, WNAC has a more formal structure
than many other civil society networks with a longer history. WNAC's
reported budget in 2009 was 200,000 yuan (£20,000), all of which came
from UNAIDS (CHAIN 2010: 304).

Most WNAC member organisations are local groups of women living
with HIV; several also include women whose family members are affected
by HIV, or carry out other activities. For instance, Bitter Grass in Yunnan
includes HIV-positive women, children and female sex workers among its
members, the only group in China to do so. Silk Road Posthouse, in
Harbin, conducts activities for MSM, youth, migrant workers and other
at-risk groups, and has received three small grants totalling 15,000 yuan
(£1,500) from the Global Fund. Shenyang Firefly, also in the northeast,
has received 35,000 yuan in two GF grants as well as small projects
with the Liaoning provincial Red Cross, the Hong Kong AIDS Foundation, and other donors to conduct a wide variety of activities for
HIV positive women and men. The largest member in terms of project
funding is Ningming Light of the Lotus City, a peer support group in a
Guangxi town near the Vietnamese border, which has an annual budget
of 150,000 yuan and projects with Family Health International and
ActionAid, reflecting the denser presence of INGOs in south-western
China than other regions. One WNAC member is a traditional development NGO, not a HIV support group: the Liangshan Institute, which
implements projects for drug users, sex workers and PLWH with support
from a GONGO and the Global Fund (CHAIN 2010).

In all, at least nine of the 21 organisational members have received
some external funding and are listed in a national directory of HIV/AIDS
groups (see Table 4.1). Regardless of this, 18 of the 21 are unregistered.
The organisational members represent between 50 and 200 participants
each, a total of over 2,000 women nationwide. No membership fees
or dues are charged, as most members would be unable to pay and are
themselves looking for funding. The network supports its members
through training and organising meetings and workshops, but does
not distribute any financial support, in contrast to other HIV networks
that have channelled sub-grants to members.

WNAC began its formal existence in 2009 with three staff: a secretary-
general, administrative officer and an assistant, based in a small apart-
ment in an industrial area of Beijing, near a hospital that provided the
first HIV treatment in the city and still houses several other HIV-related
organisations. The secretary-general, an HIV-positive woman, was the
founder of the Dandelion network; the HIV status of the other two

Table 4.1 **Members of the China Women's Network against AIDS**

Chinese name	English translation[11]	Location (province)
1. 蒲公英女性网络	Dandelion Network for Women Living with HIV/AIDS*	Virtual network (Beijing/Guangxi)
2. 河南金色阳光	Henan Golden Sunshine Children Support/Care Association*	Henan
3. 郑州祥宇	Zhengzhou Auspicious Home	Henan
4. 商丘腊梅花	Shangqiu Winter Plum Flowers	Henan
5. 登封阳光女性家园	Henan Dengfeng Home of Joyful Women*	Henan
6. 新乡爱心协会	Xinxiang Loving Hearts Federation	Henan
7. 巩义康乐家园	Gongyi Happy Home	Henan
8. 凉山社会性别与艾滋病防治研究会	Liangshan Institute for Gender and AIDS Prevention*	Sichuan
9. 临汾绿色港湾手牵手	Linfen Green Harbour 'Hand In Hand'	Shanxi
10. 河北永清半边天	Hebei Yongqing 'Half the Sky'	Hebei
11. 中山阳光公社	Zhongshan Sunshine Commune	Guangdong
12. 柳州雨后阳光	Liuzhou Sunshine After Rain	Guangxi
13. 宁明荷城之光	Ningming Light of the Lotus City*	Guangxi
14. 贵阳健康关爱苑	Guiyang Garden of Health and Care*	Guizhou
15. 南明滋心小组	Nanming Bursting Hearts Small Group	Fujian
16. 浙江互助会-网络支持	Zhejiang Mutual Help Society and Support Network	Zhejiang
17. 上海美丽人生-依依茉莉	Shanghai Beautiful Lives-Supple Jasmine	Shanghai
18. 苦草工作室	Bitter Grass Studio*	Yunnan
19. 七台河爱心家园	Qitaihe Loving Hearts Home	Heilongjiang
20. 丝路驿站	Silk Road Posthouse*	Heilongjiang
21. 沈阳萤火虫	Shenyang Firefly*	Liaoning

Organisations listed in the 2009–10 China HIV/AIDS NGO Directory

staff (one female, one male) is not public. According to materials provided by the secretary-general, the network operates through a hub-and-spokes structure, with the secretariat at the centre and members at the periphery. This may reflect some network communication paths, but in reality some members have closer links to the secretariat than others, particularly Golden Sunshine and Shanghai Beautiful Lives. With nearly one-third of WNAC members coming from Henan, Golden Sunshine plays a regional coordinating role in the province that has intensified in 2010 with the formation of a provincial women's network that it coordinates (Yuan 2010). Outside of Henan, most other provinces are only represented by a single organisation, with a fairly wide national spread, but there is only sparse coverage in the high-prevalence provinces of Yunnan and Guangxi, where a separate HIV network has been organised by the NGO AIDS Care China. There is also no membership group based in Beijing, yet the secretary-general felt it important to have the network coordination office there in order to interact with donors and other HIV organisations. The network has made an effort to reach out to women in other locations, not always successfully.[12] While some existing women's groups joined immediately, others 'don't understand yet what we're about, or are waiting to see what benefits the network might bring them'. Depending on needs and interest, WNAC plans to add five new members per year, although none have joined since July 2009.

Figure 4.1   Structure of the Women's Network against AIDS

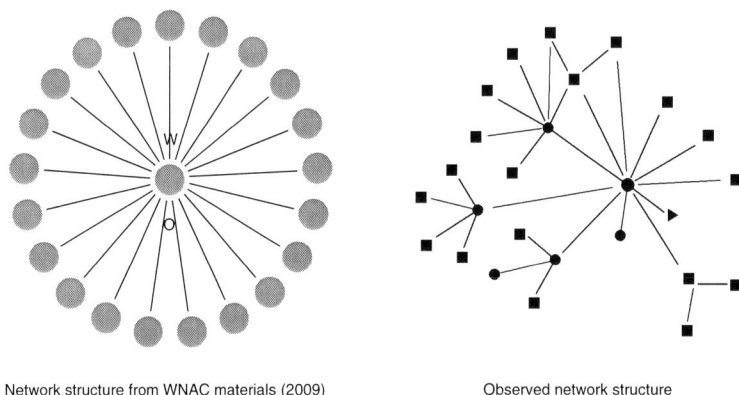

Network structure from WNAC materials (2009)   Observed network structure

Soon after its formal establishment, WNAC developed a strategic plan, objectives and activities covering the period from 2009–12. In 2009, the network aimed to focus on 'establishment and expansion', consisting of participation in local meetings and conferences, development of partnerships, writing for media and internet, and establishing a national office in Beijing. From 2010–12, a three-year strategy includes four objectives:

1. Establish mechanisms for women's leadership and organisational capacity.
2. Develop organisation to implement cooperative projects for HIV-affected women.

3. WNAC extends its organisation and sustains its external development.
4. Advocate for gender-sensitive AIDS policies and measures.

Each of these objectives is then described in chart format with outputs and activities, in a version of the ubiquitous 'logframe' (logical framework) used by many development agencies. For instance, objective 1 consists of a series of capacity building training on service delivery, management and leadership, while objective 2 includes media, internet and publications, as well as income generation for HIV-affected women through handicraft production and exhibitions. The language and tone of these materials could not be more different than the women's online testimonies shared during the formational period of the Dandelion network. The strategy document is clearly intended for a donor audience, not for local women participants in WNAC member organisations.

Advocacy strategies

As a newly-formed network, WNAC does not yet have an extensive record of advocacy activities. However, WNAC members have conducted local advocacy in their respective provinces, in some cases contributing to national-level discussions about HIV-AIDS policies affecting women. WNAC uses primarily community advocacy strategies, aiming to attract more HIV-positive women and support groups to join their activities. Both mainstream media and HIV-specific newsletters and publications are used for awareness raising and mobilisation, with particularly effective use of literature and art as advocacy techniques. Links to policy have been weaker: network leaders have taken part in some policy discussions and expressed their opinions, but since its members are relatively disadvantaged and far from the centres of power, the network has few strong connections with policy-makers.

Table 4.2   Advocacy tactics – Women's Network against AIDS

Advocacy tactics	*Notes*
• Hold public events and exhibits • Write media articles and books • Speak at workshops, conferences • Reach out to HIV-affected women in communities	– Engage women and media through creative use of art and design – Use donor connections to enter higher-level government meetings and discussions – Public opinion is main object of advocacy at present

Network members have engaged in collective advocacy since the formation of the Dandelion network. In 2008, Dandelion members started knitting a 'Red Scarf' to symbolise the lives of HIV-positive women. The scarf was sent by post from province to province, and women in each location displayed it, added to it and sent in on, 'just like the Olympic torch relay' that was occurring at the same time.[13] Knitting the scarf was an 'attempt to check whether we, who were united by internet, could come to a collective action' (He 2009). The scarf campaign received support from Mangrove, a PLWH support group in Beijing, together with ActionAid China. A Chinese-American filmmaker who is active in HIV circles produced a documentary that was shown along with the completed red scarf at Beijing's main avant-garde art centre to commemorate the 2008 World AIDS Day. The exhibit later moved to Shanghai and was shown again in Beijing in 2010 as part of a series entitled 'The Secret Language of Women' (Yuanfen 2010). Not only was the scarf a powerful symbol of women's lives and hopes, it was a key mobilising activity for WNAC.

The Women's Network coordinator is also one of 41 'Positive Talks' speakers nationwide who are open about their HIV-positive status and hold training sessions and talks for government, business, media, NGOs and rural communities. Implemented by Marie Stopes International with funds from UNDP and UNAIDS, this is a form of community advocacy that aims to empower the speakers, communicate to audiences and promote the inclusion of PLWH in 'client-initiated and client-centred' policy development regarding the prevention and treatment of HIV (UNAIDS et al 2010). According to Positive Talks,

> Training sessions in rural areas…are especially important given that rural areas constitute the main sources of migrant workers, who are considered to be key populations at risk of HIV. Training sessions in rural areas generally last half a day, and focus on disseminating key advocacy messages, emphasising that HIV can affect us all, and that the response to AIDS requires participation from all sectors of society, [such as] not discriminating against people living with HIV, or being afraid of becoming infected through casual contact. Training sessions in rural areas are very popular, and generally attract a large number of participants. (UNAIDS et al 2010)

In 2009, after WNAC's launch, members collected personal stories from around China and published these in an illustrated book, *Writing the Life* (写生) written collectively by women living with HIV, their families and community social workers. The book was released in a public event at a Beijing hotel in November, once again timed to coincide with World AIDS Day.

Some, but not all of these activities are included in WNAC's strategic plan, completed in late 2009. As noted previously, the fourth objective of the plan covers advocacy. The Powerpoint slide detailing this objective is copied and translated in Figure 4.2.

This chart reads like a brainstorming of potential new activities, rather than a full advocacy strategy. Although the objective statement mentions 'gender-sensitive AIDS policies', there is no specific policy change described, target audience, nor any details on actors or intended outcomes. This content may be clarified later, or may exist already in an action plan that is not public to outsiders. The strategic plan shows that while the donor and network leaders wish to engage in policy advocacy, most network members do not view this as a high priority and prefer instead to focus on what the network can do for them in terms of access to training and project funding.[14] A more promising alternative would be to build on the network's existing strengths in community and media advocacy, seeking to add members and change local awareness about issues faced by women living with HIV. The uses of art, poetry and story-telling offer powerfully engaging opportunities to reach ordinary Chinese; in that sense, the set of activities in the strategic plan might be fully appropriate, if concrete objectives were clarified that could meet both members' capacities and the donor's expectations.

International linkages

In August 2010, rumours circulated about WNAC in the Beijing HIV activist community. The secretariat's office phone and staff's cell phones were disconnected, and e-mails bounced back. Contacts in other groups said that the secretary-general had gone back to her home in Guangxi province to receive treatment. Others claimed that WNAC's funding from UNAIDS had ended. But the network continued to operate. UNAIDS confirmed that they had received a new proposal from WNAC and were still 'designing' the next phase of funding for the network:

> UNAIDS has supported the women's network for two years now. Our initial support was for development of institutional governance structures, set up in a consultative way. The network's work last year [2009] focussed on advocacy... Advocacy on HIV among civil society is not

Figure 4.2 WNAC advocacy strategy

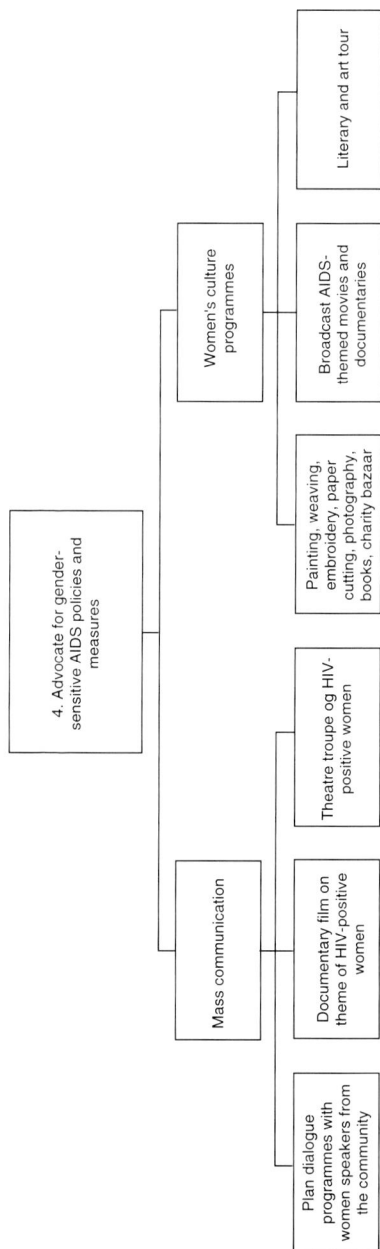

well organised. The field is dominated by MSM and PLWH groups, while the women's voices, sex workers and IDUs [intravenous drug users] are very low. UNAIDS' strategy is to strengthen these groups and help them form networks... Networks are our entry point.

In the early years of the 21st century, large-scale international funding for HIV prevention, treatment, care and support has flowed into China. The largest donor is the Global Fund against AIDS, Tuberculosis and Malaria (GF), which has contributed over US$500 million to HIV programmes since 2001 (Ministry of Health 2010: 58); other major donors have been the Clinton, Ford and Gates Foundations, as well as USAID, DFID and other bilateral government funders. Most of these grants are channelled through the Ministry of Health and other Chinese government agencies; only 1 per cent of GF funding is contributed directly to grassroots organisations. The scale of GF support to China has led to some international criticism, given China's economic resources and greater HIV prevalence in many poorer countries (Chow 2010), although the amount contributed per capita remains relatively low.

HIV support groups, previously under-funded and isolated at the margins of Chinese society, found themselves almost overnight at the centre of international efforts to increase civil society action to reduce the spread of the disease. UNAIDS' funding strategy is to support networks among HIV-affected groups who are not yet included in formal structures. Seeing limited gender responsiveness in existing HIV programming, UNAIDS seeks to 'empower women by providing specific support to CBOs [community-based organisations] and increasing the participation of women's networks, leaders, and women living with HIV' (Aye 2010). Although UNAIDS has its own core funding, it also acts as an intermediary donor; its network funding in this case originates from the Gates Foundation. In addition to WNAC, UNAIDS support in 2009 also went to at least four other networks: CAP+, a separate sex worker forum, a Yunnan drug users' network, and the International Treatment Preparedness Coalition.

UNAIDS funding is provided one year at a time; the initial grant to WNAC during its preparatory phase was for only six months. Although year-on-year funding is not unusual in the HIV sector, the grant duration sends a contradictory message to UNAIDS' stated desire to support the long-term growth of networks. Especially for a new network, short-term core funding may produce high levels of stress and uncertainty and send inadvertent messages that the grantee cannot be trusted, or that the donor is overly controlling. In UNAIDS' view, the short funding cycle encourages grantees to develop strategic plans and carry out 'evidence-based advocacy'.

UNAIDS has encouraged WNAC to link with other Chinese organisations outside the HIV sector. In 2009, UNAIDS introduced WNAC to a Shanghai-based social enterprise group, CSR Pioneers (公益堂, *Gōngyì Táng*). UNAIDS hoped that CSR Pioneers would assist WNAC in organisational development, capacity building and fundraising, while WNAC would introduce principles of gender sensitivity and stigma reduction (*Douban* 2009). A partnership between the two groups was established on paper, but has not resulted in any shared activities to date beyond a short WNAC web page hosted on CSR's site. UNAIDS also has plans to build an 'intimate partnership' between WNAC and the All China Women's Federation, with similar expected mutual benefits (Aye 2010: 19). UNAIDS hopes to increase participation of women in networks, including the ACWF, and 'use them as agents of change in promoting rights of women'. While such a partnership could build on the ACWF's 'dual role' and close links to authorities (Howell 2004b: 62–5, Wainwright 2005), it is difficult to picture how such a partnership might operate given the incongruities between a newly-established civil society network and a GONGO with millions of national members. More disturbing is UNAIDS' unilateral planning: nearly two months after the partnership plan was announced at a regional Global Fund meeting, UNAIDS staff stated that 'we probably should inform the Women's Network about this before we go further with these plans'.

UNAIDS' strategy and support for WNAC are well-intentioned. Yet the donor's focus on 'capacity building' and national-level advocacy may not match the needs of network members. The network secretariat seems to spend the majority of its time preparing reports and documents for the donor, and close contact to donors was the primary reason for setting up the Beijing office in the first place. The network arguably provided more concrete results and support for women living with HIV before it became formalised and received donor support.

Regardless of the positive or negative aspects of a single donor's role, it is generally unwise and undesirable for any organisation or network to depend on only one source of funds (Fowler 1997: 150–1). Yet many newly-formed groups have little choice. WNAC's secretary-general admits the situation is 'not ideal' and is searching for other sources, but finds domestic resources hard to come by. The problem is particularly acute for a network whose members are by definition disadvantaged and relatively poor. Given its wide geographic spread, WNAC is not able to hold informal meetings in coffeehouses or at members' homes. Without external funding, members have few resources of their own to draw on to sustain the network's operations. The Women's Network aims to raise funds through social enterprise, producing and selling handicrafts and books, so that 'we can stand on two feet'. Reflecting the dominance of business management approaches among Chinese NGOs and the increasing role of domestic corporate foundations, income generation from social enterprise is a legitimate strategy for many local organisations. But it is unusual and probably impractical for a national network with organisational members who are themselves seeking operational funds. More realistically, WNAC members might engage in a variety of income-generating activities and contribute a portion of the proceeds to the network. No mechanism for such revenue sharing exists at present.

Network effectiveness: Policy change

WNAC members have faced difficulties in transposing community and media advocacy efforts into effects on policy. Up to now, WNAC has had 'little to no contact with government', including the Ministry of Health. 'China's current HIV policies say little about women', the secretary-general complains. 'In the HIV law, it states that HIV-positive women have a right to have children, for instance, but other laws contradict this. There are no regulations or implementation guidelines to allow this.' In press interviews, WNAC members have spoken about issues such as access to subsidised treatment and second-line anti-viral medication, and called for improved communication and cooperation between authorities and civil society to form 'a united front against HIV/AIDS' (She 2009). In 2010, the WNAC secretary-general was selected as one of 14 people on the steering committee of the China Red Ribbon Forum, a government-civil society dialogue group on human rights (UNAIDS 2010).[15]

In the secretary-general's view, the government has not been too willing to talk directly with civil society networks; instead, HIV groups often advocate through intermediaries. For instance, WNAC has contact with the China Foundation for Prevention of STD and AIDS, a GONGO with no particular focus on women. At the 2009 International Congress on HIV/AIDS in Asia and Pacific in Bali, the GONGO's representative reportedly presented WNAC activities as their own; rather than take offence, the Women's Network secretary used the opportunity to ask for support from the foundation. However, no specific help has been provided.

The most significant civil society effort to improve participation in HIV policy-making has taken place through elections to the Global Fund Country Coordinating Mechanism or CCM (Gnep 2009). Over several years of intense debate, activists succeeded in establishing democratic procedures for election of NGO representatives to the CCM.[16] There were initially 11 NGO committee members, of which one seat was reserved for 'female organizations' and another open to any PLWH (Jia 2009). However, from 2007–09, the CCM committee position reserved for women or children affected by HIV was vacant. The absence of women's participation was 'a great pity', said one WNAC member, but led a consensus about the need for advocacy:

> In the past two years, the number of women groups and women community workers has increased rapidly and their involvement has been strengthened in China... At the end of February 2009, the participants to [WNAC's] first preparatory meeting shared their thoughts on promoting women's participation to the CCM membership election and conducted thorough discussion. They publicized their recommendations on 'Improving Election Options and Promoting Women's Participation', which received wide responses from the community and 39 organizations declared their support. (Yuan 2009)

A WNAC member from Golden Sunshine in Henan province subsequently initiated a campaign and was elected to fill the women's representative position. Women's network members also offered four amendments to the CCM guidelines on gender equity issues, of which two were approved (UNAIDS 2009). Yet despite efforts of WNAC members, no women were elected to the CCM NGO Work Committee, although more women had been nominated than in 2007.

The Women's Network has demonstrated that it is able to carry out collective campaigns and projects for public awareness and mobilise the media. Other HIV networks, however, have formed stronger links to government. The coordinator of the CAP+ network says,

> With government relations, we've always had some difficulties, and also always had some cooperation. There are legal and internal government issues. Every grassroots organisation has to deal with these issues – we're all the same in this way. The difference is in how we deal with it. We don't have particularly close cooperation with government, but also no particular opposition. We stay focussed on issues of concern to PLHIV. We don't get involved in broader political issues around civil society, democracy and so on.

The second major PLWH network, CNNAC states that '[t]he first priority of HIV/AIDS prevention is to influence policies of Chinese government and UN Agencies' (CNNAC 2008). WNAC's secretary-general, for her part, sees UNAIDS as the main object of the network's advocacy; UNAIDS will then channel women's concerns to the government. Without stronger government links, it is difficult to see how the network will have any major impact on HIV policy, as advocacy through an international donor offers only indirect access to 'invited spaces' of policy discussion (Gaventa 2007).

Network effectiveness: Sustainability and political space

As more voices, stories and experiences of PLWH have appeared in public, Chinese society has become more tolerant towards people affected by HIV. These stories not only change images and social assumptions, but have also led to effective and powerful social organising (He 2006). In this case, women being open about their HIV status and reaching out to others through Internet and social networks formed the preconditions for establishment of WNAC. According to Howell (2004b), women's organising on social issues may be seen as a barometer of civil society development and state-society relations in China. The formation of a national network of women affected by HIV and more open public discussion of social impacts of HIV point the barometer firmly in a positive direction. The needle is wavering, however, due to the effects of competition among HIV networks, intensive donor pressure, and limited response to date from government authorities. A Chinese academic survey concludes that HIV networks are 'still in the early stages of development': their advocacy work mainly aims to improve awareness among PLWH, but is under-resourced and lacks technical capacity for larger-scale interventions (Han et al 2009: 40).

As UNAIDS describes,

> The women's network is at the beginning of their development – to develop a resource mobilisation plan will take more time. They are used to working at a local level. But for advocacy, you need to work at a higher level and have a national perspective. This is their weak point at the moment. Networks do want to deliver something to their members: why are we here if not to help ourselves? This becomes harder as networks have more members; then they need a more focussed agenda. If the network is providing services to members, then secretariat capacity and clear leadership is key. When [another network] wanted to do this, they were overwhelmed and had no time for advocacy.

UNAIDS' ultimate stated goal is to create a single nationwide HIV network co-functioning as the Global Fund CCM. Such a national association could have numerous benefits: enabling strategic alliances with the state, strengthening member networks and adding legitimacy (Howell 2004b: 13–14). This objective managed to unite the entire spectrum of Chinese HIV networks as never before, but in opposition to UNAIDS' proposal. One activist terms the concept 'naïve'. Another states that a single network is 'a very bad idea', even if it were achievable. A single voice towards the government would be desirable, but any unified network would make authorities nervous, so they would attempt to control, manipulate or damage it. If donors and government get together to control a sector, the space for networks to advocate independently could be greatly reduced. In this view, multiple networks are beneficial as they amplify voices of civil society and allow for more people to occupy hub positions. Competition among networks, within limits, is a natural and healthy phenomenon.

A centrifugal tendency is also present in the formation of provincial and local networks. The provincial women's network begun by WNAC members in Henan appears to have occurred spontaneously based on local needs, but could be viewed as duplicating or competing with the national network. The Henan network has received funding from the US International Republican Institute, after UNAIDS reportedly intervened unsuccessfully to argue that the funds should be given to WNAC instead. The fact that a network has developed in Henan can be considered a major accomplishment, given that several years ago the province was noted for its division and lack of coordination among NGOs, PLWH and the local government (Young and Mian 2008). The Henan network is also integrated into the WNAC structure, which is not yet the case with the AIDS Care-initiated women's network in the southwest.

As a new network of women activists mostly in their 30s, WNAC holds the potential of developing a more collaborative structure than certain other HIV networks, which remain male-dominated. WNAC has had 'some contacts, but not much cooperation' with the two main PLWH networks, limited to attending each others' events (WNAC 2010).

From a donor or international NGO standpoint, the experience of the Women's Network raises questions of how much support is desirable to help networks form. In a 2007 interview, the *Red Scarf* filmmaker criticised donor ambitions: 'People at the moment feel a lot of the grassroots NGOs are too small, so people get them together in networks or *pingtai* [平台, "platforms"]. But this creates the opposite effect of what is intended: frictions, tensions, criticisms.' A better approach would be 'a wildflower effect: let them grow in their own way and in the end they cover the mountain' (cited in Young and Mian 2007). Yet the leadership qualities necessary to 'cover the mountain' may not be the same as those needed to form a small group. At present, many WNAC members are strong leaders of local support groups, but this does not automatically translate into an effective national network. The mountain is also very spread out geographically and politically, so that a *laissez-faire* approach to organising may not result in full coverage.

Greater cooperation among women's civil society networks also remains elusive. When the WNAC secretary-general met with Beijing-based gender-and-development and domestic violence networks in 2009, she asked them to pay greater attention to women affected by HIV; their leaders replied that their government sponsors did not want them to have projects in sensitive areas, but that the networks might be able to conduct some joint activities or workshops. The formation of WNAC offers an opportunity for these disparate networks to intersect, but this may not be sufficient on its own. One INGO staff observes that women's networks may encounter fewer initial obstacles to formation than networks in other sectors because gender issues are seen as less 'political', but if networks focus on marginalised women, they face the reality that China is still a 'patriarchal society' and 'even NGOs don't see gender as a priority'.

Organising around HIV in China remains controversial: organisations, networks and support groups representing PLWH face additional legal, political and social challenges compared to other civil society actors. In part to overcome stigma, HIV advocates have adopted relatively contentious strategies to draw public and official awareness to their situation. Chinese activists have been arrested for exposing a major blood transfusion contamination scandal (Gnep 2009), held protests (Young and Mian 2008), and in several cases left the country based on perceived threats to their personal safety (Wong 2010, Thurber 2009). HIV networks' use of the internet, however, does not appear to be a major issue with authorities. The QQ message board used by the Dandelion network is a domestic Chinese service, thus less liable to blockage than services by foreign providers such as Google. In all, restrictions on the Internet are an occasional annoyance to HIV activists, but do not effectively deter them from communication.

Conclusion

The Women's Network against AIDS began as an informal lifeline among HIV-positive women. With donor interest and funding, the network transformed quickly, perhaps too quickly, from a virtual social network into a formal organisational network before strong horizontal ties could be formed among members in different locations around China. From the donor's perspective, the network is now making 'quite slow process...

within a few years they will be some of the key voices, [but] now they are still fairly quiet compared to other leaders [in the HIV field]'. Many of the challenges WNAC faces are common to other 'donor-created networks', and that is indeed how some other actors in the HIV sector perceive it.

The development of HIV networks in China follows a worldwide pattern observed by the United Nations that 'organizations of people living with HIV are initially created to provide mutual support and care, and evolve gradually to play wider and more varied roles in the epidemic response as their capacity and collective voice strengthen' (UNAIDS 2006: 212). A UN meeting in South Africa recommended that there was 'a pressing need to professionalize informal structures to enable them to function effectively and participate independently in high-powered organizations and forums'. But UNAIDS also noted that 'Discussions also revealed a tendency for networks to lose touch with the grass roots as they engage with the wider world' (213). How can Chinese networks maintain this balance?

The common donor response to these dilemmas is to provide 'technical skills' and 'capacity-building training' to network members. Many courses focus on project management, proposal writing, and other functional competencies that are necessary to work with donors but may take activists further from their own roots, and do not develop vision or leadership. The broader question is what members need from their participation in a network. In the case of WNAC, women joined local and online peer groups for counselling and social support. These groups then formed a national network in order to reach a wider audience, engage in policy advocacy and attract donor funding – a mixed set of motivations captured variously in poetry, testimonials and logframes.

In principle, gender considerations should be mainstreamed in all development projects, not separated into a sub-sector for women only. In a situation in which existing male-dominated PLWH networks are not willing to change, however, women's groups have little choice but to form their own network. Once their voices are more equal with others, women's network members could then increase cooperation with other networks at the national level. This will require overcoming divisions and mistrust that exist between sub-groups and at the local level, as well as better coordination among donors. If these conditions are absent, the Women's Network against AIDS will continue to be caught between donor priorities and its members' needs.

5
Preserving Hanoi's Reunification Park

In spring 2007, city authorities approved a plan by two private companies to privatise Hanoi's Reunification Park and transform it into 'a small-scale Disneyland' (Trang 2007, Phung 2007).[1] Details of the proposal, including in-depth interviews with the company directors, were published in at least 15 articles in the local state-controlled press and online. Although the corporations insisted that redevelopment would serve the interests of all residents of Hanoi, this was belied by descriptions of a planned five-level underground car park and shopping area, 3-D theatre and nightclub, and an investment of 1,500 billion dong, approximately £50 million (*Dantri* 2007). Local residents spoke out on the Internet against the plans, which were portrayed as corrupt and anti-poor. Influential citizens, including respected retired officials, editorialised against the agreement.[2]

The initially uncoordinated efforts to oppose privatisation came together in the summer of 2007 to form the beginnings of a civil society network. In early August, a Canadian NGO, HealthBridge joined with the Vietnam Urban Planning Association, a quasi-independent GONGO, to organise a one-day workshop on the 'System of Green Public Space in Hanoi' (*Tien Phong* 2007).[3] The academics and architects who gathered at the conference issued a call to 'save green space in Hanoi' that was posted on the Internet. Faced with an upsurge of public outrage, the city government backed down in August 2007, putting the park redevelopment plan on hold.

Reunification Park (*Công viên Thống Nhất*) is the largest public area in the centre of the crowded Vietnamese capital, which has one of the lowest areas of green space per capita of any major world city. The park was built by volunteer labour from 1958–61 on what had been an uninhabited, swampy dump site outside the city centre. Originally named in hopes of national unification, the park's name was changed to Lenin Park in 1980 and then back in 2003. While not as prominent as the public spaces of Hoan Kiem Lake or Ba Dinh Square (Thomas 2001: 308), the park's commemoration of Reunification has symbolic political overtones of 'the power of solidarity, the unity of the nation and of the people of the capital in the task of defending and developing the country' (Dang 2009). Reunification Park is popular with rich and poor alike who pay the equivalent of a few pence each to enter. The park facilities, managed by a state-owned company, are poorly maintained, with shabby carnival rides and informal hawkers occupying much of the open area at the park's main entrance.

Less than a year after the privatisation episode, Hanoi authorities announced plans to build a four-star hotel, 'Novotel on the Park', on land taken from Reunification Park (Hoang 2008). By early 2009, public opinion had crystallised against the hotel, and the network members were ready to act (Steinglass 2009). As in summer 2007, a flood of media articles, online comments and petitions to government leaders followed. HealthBridge played a secondary role this time, helping to organise a public conference on green space in Hanoi in March 2009. A week later, the city authorities reversed their decision, cancelling the hotel project.

As the network formed through these two episodes of collective action, its advocacy strategy shifted from embedded efforts to privately influence leaders to inside-outside approaches, including public statements, use of media channels, public opinion and external resources. Following the cancellation of hotel construction in the park, supporters gathered at a Chinese restaurant in downtown Hanoi for a quiet celebration and 'networking event'. The approximately 20 people attending talked about further cases of public space encroachment in Hanoi and how they should respond. The idea of establishing a more formal network, with a name and dedicated staff, was also discussed at this event and afterwards. No formal structure has since come into being; the Reunification Park network maintains a virtual existence. It is a reality in the minds of its participants, but has no formal name, legal identity, or membership. Despite, or perhaps because of, its lack of formal organisational trappings, the network has demonstrated potential for effective actions to preserve public space.

Existing literature on parks and public space in Hanoi comes primarily from the urban planning and geography fields (Logan 2000, Drummond 2000, Thomas 2001, Kürten 2008), including one joint master's thesis on Reunification Park (Hellberg and Johansson 2008). The first public parks were designed during French colonial rule, creating what one Hanoi architect calls a 'garden city' of parks and lakes. Since the 1945 revolution, city plans for Hanoi have been redrafted seven times according to changing principles and priorities from the socialist period to a current emphasis on cultural heritage. With the coming of a market economy, the Hanoi city government assigned the management of parks to a convoluted group of state-owned companies, responsible to a variety of government departments at different levels of power. Each major park has its own 'one-member corporation' (*công ty một thành viên*) with management authority, while smaller parks are supervised directly by district or ward governments or by companies reporting to them. According to the retired former director of the Hanoi planning department, significant management problems arose as functional ownership of parks shifted from 'the people' to state companies and then to joint-stock companies run as for-profit enterprises by their former state-appointed directors. Overlapping and disjointed management has resulted in the gradual loss of nearly all of the parks, lakes and open spaces in the city (Tran and Linh 2010).

Network formation and history

Over several decades prior to 2007, individual activists engaged in advocacy on public space issues in Hanoi, with little coordination among them. In 1993, five respected scientists wrote separate letters to the Prime Minister and Hanoi People's Committee opposing the transfer of part of Thu Le Park in western Hanoi to build the five-star Daewoo Hotel. This controversial decision was not discussed in the press, and the scientists' letters were not made public. The city government approved the hotel project, promising the scientists that the loss of parkland would be compensated by the construction of a national zoo in another location, which has never happened. Activists achieved somewhat better results in the case of the Golden Hanoi Hotel (*Khách sạn Hà Nội Vàng*) planned by Hong Kong-based investors to overlook Hoan Kiem Lake in the city centre. The plan for an 11-story building clearly violated the height limit of five stories in the area. In 1996, the Vietnam Architects' Association and Vietnam History Association protested the hotel's construction through official letters in what Logan describes as the first successful public protest over urban changes occurring since Renewal (*Đổi mới*), 'a foretaste of what could be expected [and] an important political change' (Logan 2000: 238–9). The architects' intervention halted construction of the hotel, which stood as a half-built shell for over ten years before a bank and boutique shops were completed on the site in 2007. There was no open expression of public opinion on the issue, but the embedded advocacy of professional associations was sufficient to change the minds of city leaders at the time.

Several years later, a major corruption case concerning the planned Thang Long Water Park was exposed by a landscape architect in the Ministry of Construction's Institute of Rural and Urban Planning, acting at considerable personal risk. In 1999, the Prime Minister reversed previous decisions and cancelled the plans; 'correcting such an error after a big project had already been approved and announced by the authorities was very difficult, and many people had to pay the price' (Tran 2007b). In the past several years, citizen pressure and media articles have halted the replacement of the historic 19th December market and proposals for a museum and a high-rise office building on land surrounding Hoan Kiem Lake (Phung et al 2008). In these and other cases of public space activism, limited success came about through existing, embedded advocacy channels, yet these efforts did not coalesce into a civil society network.[4]

Map 5.1   Major parks and lakes in Hanoi

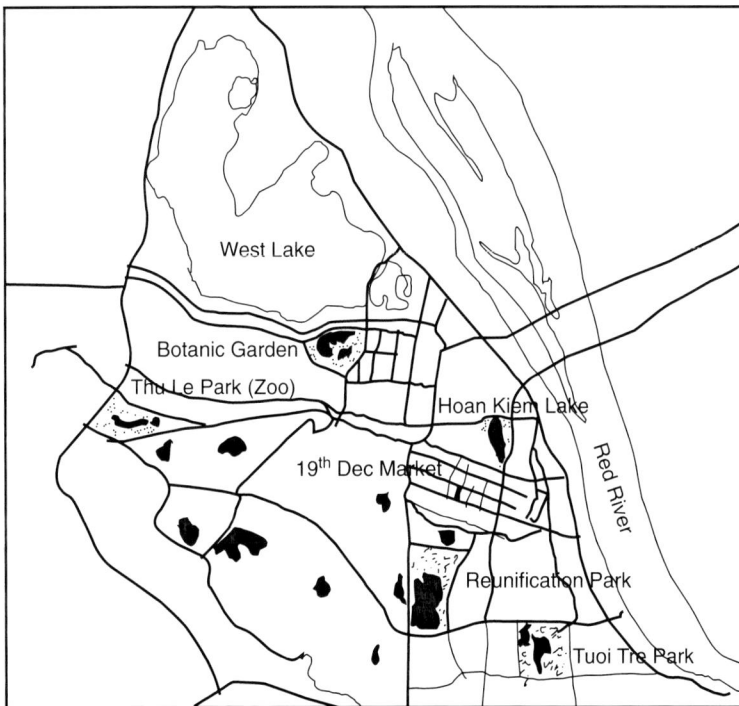

Source: Hanoi Data Ltd. Used by permission.

Saving the park and the city

The 2007 Reunification Park privatisation case attracted the attention of some of the same professional associations and activists as earlier public space campaigning, but differed from these examples due to the facilitation of HealthBridge and the presence of a common cause with well-organised opponents. Initial media reports of the two companies' plans for the park were presented in a neutral to positive light as a business news story, attracting little public comment. Several months then passed without media coverage of the park. According to a journalist, this was not due to any censorship or external intervention, simply that there was nothing new to report. Private discussion behind the scenes, however, was increasing as more Hanoians became aware of the redevelopment plans, and their interest soon turned to dismay and outcry. An architect was the first to put his misgivings on paper in mid-April (Vietnam Studies Group 2007). His polemic, 'Let's save the park! Let's save our city!' was posted on a city issues website, http://dothi.net, then sent by the Hanoi representative of an international NGO to an academic list-serve with over 300 members inside and outside the country.

As an architect who has worked and studied overseas for many years, I always follow every new step and current affairs of my country. When I heard the news that Hanoi will have a new entertainment centre to serve people in the capital...I immediately looked to find out where this centre will be located. When I saw it would be in Reunification Park, I truly couldn't believe my eyes. I can't believe that such a big and strategic project could be approved without any criticism. This is such a big mistake that anyone with just a little professional knowledge would never make...

Historically speaking, this park is very meaningful... The park was built through the efforts of thousands of workers and people in Hanoi. In those days, we lived for the common interest rather than for personal interest. We lived without thinking much about ourselves. We were poor but always smiled. We were much more 'human' than we are now. Our park was born in such a situation like that...

Those people should know that thousands of workers and citizens of the capital, both young and old, will have no green space or clean environment for their morning exercises and no place to play sport in the afternoon... In addition, an entertainment park will make foreign tourists feel uncomfortable. They travel here to find nature, not to go to chaotic entertainment centres that exist only for money and forget human values… We shouldn't trade small and short-term economic gain for serious long-term consequences in the future.

My friends, each of us should contribute our own small efforts to save our park. Please don't destroy history and culture just for money, because no matter how much money we have later, we can never replace their value. SAVE THE PARK, SAVE OUR CITY!

PLEASE SEND THIS ARTICLE TO ALL YOUR FRIENDS. (VSG 2007)

The architect's article prompted 18 responses on the list-serve, all critical of the project; one respondent wrote 'This is one of the saddest things I have read in a long time.' A Ford Foundation programme officer expressed shock that the city had approved the plans without any public hearing and cited rising public anger over the decision (VSG 2007). Other statements soon appeared on Vietnamese-language blogs and websites, including one set up especially for the purpose by a Vietnamese living in Australia.[5] The mainstream media, which had reported news of the redevelopment plans and given a mouthpiece to corporate leaders, did not pick up on the groundswell of public concern until later. By May, *Viet Nam News* referred to 'cries of protest' from Hanoi residents in an article that presented a neutral but confused picture of the debate (Thu 2007).

The debate attracted the notice of HealthBridge, formerly PATH Canada, an international NGO with a range of programming from tobacco control to urban environmental protection. As part of a small project on developing a 'healthy urban living environment', the NGO identified Reunification Park as a priority issue. With assistance from international supporters, HealthBridge developed a plan for a campaign to oppose the construction plan that was revised and approved by the head office in Canada (HealthBridge 2008). HealthBridge had regional experience in Asia, knowledge of advocacy techniques, and a good reputation with Vietnamese authorities, but did not have extensive local connections to draw on or contact with affected people. HealthBridge's in-country staff are all Vietnamese nationals; realising they couldn't do much on their own, they began to look for partners who could join in a local network. 'We found a lot of people – professionals, experts, media – who supported us but didn't speak out. Others didn't know about the park, but when they found out, they wanted to act.' HealthBridge gathered information on the investment plans and city policies, interviewed residents using the park, and posted notices online on students', overseas Vietnamese, architecture, and urban planning websites, with 'many positive responses' (HealthBridge 2008). 'At first, it was hard to identify people – we had to see who could do what', said HealthBridge's organiser. Most meetings and discussions were on an individual basis, since links between people were weak.

On 3 August 2007, HealthBridge and the Vietnam Urban Planning Association organised a workshop on 'Community Green Space in Hanoi', held (ironically) in a meeting room that had been constructed on the grounds of the Botanic Garden, near the Ho Chi Minh Mausoleum. Presenters included architects, lawyers, professors, and central government representatives from the Office of the Government and the Ministry of Construction (HealthBridge 2008). The workshop was scientific and professional in tone, but it was also the first public discussion of Reunification Park since the privatisation project was announced. An international participant recalls high levels of worry and fear, especially from the Urban Planning Association, of the consequences of 'taking on Vincom', known to be a well-connected corporation: 'No one from Vincom showed up at the conference. What a relief. But we were still waiting to see what would come of our comments to the press. We knew that if the story ran, the Party would not be against us.'

An article summarising the workshop appeared in one leading newspaper on the following day, stating that participants found the park project unjustifiable and promising to sue if it went forward (*Tien Phong* 2007). On 7 August, *VietNamNet* (VNN), a leading news website, interviewed one of the presenters at the workshop – the landscape architect who had exposed the Thang Long Water Park scandal in the 1990s (Hoang 2007a). The architect had been a late addition to the workshop: until HealthBridge called to invite her, she had been unaware of the park case. On the same day, VNN also published an angry letter to the State President written by a well-known retired biologist who had previously spoken up in the Hoan Kiem Lake and Thu Le park cases (*VietNamNet* 2007a). These articles became the catalysts for an unexpected groundswell of public opinion, drawing widespread praise (and some criticism) from readers (*VietNamNet* 2007b). The printed comments were only a small fraction of the over 500 responses that VNN received, split roughly four-fifths against the corporations.

Other workshop presenters also gave interviews or wrote articles over the following week. In all, more than 50 articles appeared in print media during August, as well as a series of three television reports on the evening news (HealthBridge 2008). On 10 August, a reporter interviewed the deputy director of the Hanoi Department of Planning, who stated that the final plans for the park had not yet been approved, and promised to 'gather public opinion first' before making a decision (Trong 2007). This brought the city government in compliance with national laws that had been ignored up to that point. According to the Grassroots Democracy Ordinance (SRV 2007a) and other legal documents, the proposal to redevelop Reunification Park should have been posted for public discussion by the Hanoi People's Committee before a decision was made. In practice, the invitation to two well-connected corporations was made behind closed doors, and leaked to the public after the fact (Action for the City 2008: 60).

The director of Tan Hoang Minh Co. responded in print on 13 August with a rambling tirade defending his actions (Do 2007). His response backfired against the investors, leading to more critical readers' comments. In subsequent articles, activists quoted online comments from dozens of readers in support of their arguments, showing that public opinion was overwhelmingly on their side (Tran 2007a). As one activist describes, 'This is the way we won'.

In addition to facts and logic, the often neglected factor of emotion comes forth clearly in both activists' postings and reader responses. History and political meanings led many people to identify viscerally with the park, as in the repeatedly-cited metaphor that privatisation would be like 'removing a lung of the city', a phrase that comes up in seven separate media articles and blogs in August alone (*VietNamNet* 2007b, The Dung 2007a). Some of the strongest statements came from network participants who are sitting central government officials. The director of the Ministry of Construction's Architectural Research Institute emphasised:

> For the welfare of citizens of this city, for the whole community, and as a leader of a professional agency, I forcefully oppose the proposal to reconstruct Reunification Park into an entertainment centre like Disneyland. Not a single modern city or ancient city in developed countries would do anything like this. There is nothing to guarantee that the investors will keep their promises not to take over public space from the people. It's all about profit. (The Dung 2007a)

The director of the Institute for Urban Research and Infrastructure Development, a former vice-chair of the Hanoi People's Committee and Vice-Minister of Construction, continued:

> At a recent workshop on this issue, I already stated my opposition to the proposal to turn Reunification Park into an amusement area.

Let Reunification Park remain as it has been. The 'upgrading' of the park that Hanoi is planning will only benefit the interests of the investors, since anyone can see that this is a gigantic piece of valuable land in the middle of the city. (The Dung 2007a)

These statements by central government officials expanded on their presentations at the conference. Importantly, they had links to the national government, not only to city authorities. When these critics spoke publicly about Reunification Park, they did so as residents of Hanoi with links to a different (and higher) level of government than the one directly responsible for administering the park.

Both officials and ordinary people combined environmental and political appeals to stop the proposed redevelopment of Reunification Park. Access to the park for poor people was a common theme of online postings, even if the bloggers themselves may not have been very poor. Concern about corporate ownership also surfaced repeatedly, but the largest single concern was losing the little remaining public space in central Hanoi. While the physical space of the park was not co-terminus with the political space to discuss its fate – no actual protest activities took place within the park itself – activists made a clear connection between these spaces and quality of life in the city. By claiming Reunification Park as public property, contenders also asserted their right to speak for and as citizens of the Vietnamese polity.

When the city government suspended the redevelopment plans, leaders backtracked on their previous statements:

The city [government] has never agreed for investors to build an amusement centre in Reunification Park. The city only said that this was a project to renovate and upgrade the park... The city will gather public opinion about designing the park. After that, we will see if proposals are compliant with the city plan before allowing any investment. (Doan 2007)

Tan Hoang Minh and Vincom also backed down, stating they had no intention of taking away public space and only wanted to improve the current park (The Dung 2007b).

The 2009 hotel dispute

Less than a year after the 'Disneyland' case was resolved, controversy again erupted around Reunification Park. In June 2008, another group of developers, with no connection to the 2007 investors, announced the groundbreaking of 'Novotel on the Park', a four-star hotel on one hectare of parkland. The hotel would have 400 rooms and cost US $40 million to build (*Dantri* 2009). A brief news article described the investors as the city-owned Hanoi Tourist Co., Singapore-based SIH Investment Ltd., and the international hotel chain Accor. Accor's deputy Asia director told media the hotel would be 'a resort in the heart of the city' (Hoang 2008). As with initial announcements in 2007, this news generated no immediate comment or public reaction, but activists picked up on the statement later to frame the developers as elitist: 'In the plans it says it will be a "resort". People here don't even know what a "resort" is, but they know it's not for them' (Steinglass 2009).

Plans for a hotel in this approximate location had been approved much earlier, in 1991, as Vietnam was just beginning to open its doors to foreign investors. The developers at that time were Swedish, and the structure was to be named the SAS Hotel, located at a major intersection near Reunification Park, but not on park land (a Japanese hotel was later built across the street from this site). However, construction on the original site would have required compensating and resettling several hundred families living there, and the city government did not have the funds or inclination for this. Hence, the hotel site was quietly moved into parkland. Although the investment never materialised, the hotel was listed (in its original site) on the 1992 and 1998 city plans and was mentioned in passing in articles about the park (Do 2007, Hoang 2007b).

Clearance of the hotel site for construction began in late 2008. The speed of these events surprised activists, who were focusing their attention elsewhere. HealthBridge's public space project had ended, and there was no established mechanism for network participants to communicate except by individual phone calls and e-mails. Once activated, however, the network regrouped quickly, instigated this time by the landscape architect who had been a vocal late addition to the 2007 workshop. As in 2007, success initially seemed far-fetched. An international supporter recalls that when he heard construction had begun, 'I thought it was hopeless [as it is] quite tough to close down a project under construction. [HealthBridge staff] said no, we have to try. So we began again with the experience of the first fight.'

The hotel investors attempted to use history to their advantage. They created a shell company, 'SAS Royal Hotel Hanoi Joint Venture Co.' to lead the project. In effect, the partners pretended that they were the successors of the 1991 Swedish investors and attempted to mislead the public. Furthermore, it was later revealed that the Singapore-based partner, SIH Investments, did not stand for 'Scandinavian International Hotels', a company that had not existed for more than a decade. SIH was actually 75 per cent owned by VinaCapital, a large domestic developer comparable to Vincom (Thu and Linh 2009), with the remaining funds from Accor and a third company (*Dantri* 2009). In short, virtually no foreign interests were involved.

Park network participants began uncovering this information in late 2008. The husband of the landscape architect had good contacts with the Swedish Embassy from his previous government job, and he called the ambassador, who confirmed that no Swedish firm was an investor in the hotel and invited the couple to the embassy to discuss the case. Rather than accept this invitation, however, the architect planned a more indirect strategy:

> At first, we just realised that building a hotel in the park was wrong. Then we found grounds for opposing it, based on city planning and the approval process... Instead of going to meet the Swedish ambassador, where we might have been observed, I realised it was better if we got someone from the city government to ask the Swedish embassy themselves. Sometimes we have to take a detour to get the best results.

> I saw from the beginning that we needed an external point of pressure, so I wrote to the foreign investors. If they knew the real situation, they would pull out. I also said that Nguyen The Thao [the chair of the Hanoi People's Committee] was misled and should cancel the project. The problem was that his advisors knew all about it, but they didn't tell him.

The architect's first online article criticising the hotel was published in *Vietnam Week* on 10 February 2009, shortly after the Tet new year holidays: good timing for reaching a wide audience (Tran T 2009). On 12 February, newspapers reported that the city government had approved construction of the hotel (*Thanh Nien* 2009). When the architect's comments came out in the press, 'we all waited. On one website, I counted 27 pages of comments! Unbelievable – we were all afraid, [the Urban Planning Association] would not talk about this on the telephone. We would have to meet face to face.' Over the next week, critical articles appeared by other network participants affiliated with the Urban Planning Association, Architects' Association and HealthBridge. Senior retired officials also spoke out: the former vice-chair of Hanoi and vice-minister of construction quoted in 2007, plus a new participant, a former vice-minister of Environment and Natural Resources. As in 2007, the quantity and tone of public comments overwhelmed advocates' expectations. *VietNamNet* alone published 105 reader comments from 10–12 February, all opposed to the hotel; a small, illustrative sample follows, from the impassioned to the ironic.

Name: Quang Huy
Address: [none given]
Email: bodoicu_ho@yahoo.com[6]

I was truly shocked to read that Reunification Park is being cut up to built a hotel. It's unbelievable that the city could allow a project like this without more awareness of the people's rights. The environment is already so polluted, we need to open more park space in the coming time. Not only are they not expanding, they're planning to take over a park of the city's lung. I can't understand it.

And I'm also concerned that on such an important issue causing so much public criticism, vietnamnet.vn is the only credible source!!! There must be some powerful interest behind this project?

Name: ViệtQuang
Address: Hanoi
Email: vietngoc141@yahoo.com

From a slightly different perspective, there are a lot of benefits to building this hotel. Such as:

1. At present, we're still poor and don't have money to manage and improve the park. We don't even have enough to keep the park clean. If there's a hotel, there will be funds for that. And reducing the park by 1 ha to build the hotel is 1 ha less to clean up.
2. This project will contribute to 'reducing poverty' for a few families. Maybe they're so poor they can't afford to trade in their car for a new model, or are a little money short of building a country estate. Rich people, strong country.[7]

Name: Trần Thọ Quảng
Address: 6 Hẻm 310/90/35, Ng. Văn Cừ, Hà Nội[8]
Email: thoquang@viettel.vn

The Party and the government ought to listen to the opinions of the people in order to serve the long-term interests of the community, if the leaders are really for the people and of the people (*vì dân và do dân*).[9] There are already enough articles from within and outside the country opposing 'cutting up' Reunification Park. I wish the leaders of the Party and government would pay more attention to working people, people who have and continue to selflessly defend the country and the achievements of our revolution.

Name: Chau
Address: Ho Chi Minh city
Email: aidienchau@gmail.com

I'm not from Hanoi, but I love the city, and I love Reunification Park where so many young people used their sweat to enthusiastically build a park on a dump site. I'm really heartbroken that one of the few public spaces in Hanoi is being taken over for private interests of one group of people. Selling a part of Reunification Park is not just selling part of Hanoi's soul, but selling part of all of our souls, because Hanoi is the heart of the country...

(Source for all comments: *Tuan Vietnam* 2009a)

On 13 February, the Hanoi People's Committee held a press conference, announcing that construction of the hotel would continue, as the location had already been set, and 'issues that have been handed down from the past we have to accept for now'. Authorities further claimed that the hotel land did not belong to Reunification Park but was unallocated 'public land' (Le et al 2009). Out of either ignorance or deviousness, a city spokesman also defended the hotel on the basis of 'protecting rights of foreign investors... If anyone causes difficulties for the implementation of the project, this will have a very big influence on the foreign investment environment in Vietnam generally and particularly in Hanoi' (Linh 2009).

Those newspapers most directly controlled by the city government – *Hà nội Mới* (New Hanoi) and *An ninh Thủ Đô* (Capital Security), for instance – reported on the authorities' statements without comment. A columnist in *Kinh tế Đô thị* (Urban Economy) newspaper linked construction of the hotel to Vietnam's historical friendship and debt to Sweden. Other newspapers and websites, however, noted that 'almost all public comments are opposed to the project' and quoted statements by park network members criticising the hotel (Linh 2009). Foreign journalists also reported on the story, quoting one activist with a representative view: 'We protect the genuine wishes of the people. They had no right to use the common land of the community for the interests of their own, and they offer to the foreigners to make money in our country. It's terrible' (Steinglass 2009).

Park advocates drew on powerful visual and emotional frames to mobilise public opinion. In 2007, photos published in the media featured views of the natural environment of Reunification Park and of Hanoians exercising or relaxing in the park. By 2009, network members had collected historical photos and old city maps and began placing these in articles. They also prepared a photo gallery that was published online using lines from a popular, nostalgic song as captions (Nguyen B 2009). The photos recalled the socialist past and volunteer labour that constructed the park, a powerful image with older residents that also outbalanced city authorities' claims of historic debts to Sweden or to other foreign investors. Maps established continuity with the past, and also responded to authorities' claims that the hotel was not actually on park land. City plans from the 1960s until 2001 showed that it was (Tran H 2009). A retired official underlined this argument, stating that 'public land' could not be given away for the purposes of private business, and that city leaders were confusing the meaning of what was 'public'. Although officials claimed to be following the law, in fact a public hearing and auction should have been held if the land was to be sold (Dang 2009).

One particular historical document helped to turn the corner on the hotel case. The retired biologist, who has several rooms full of old documents in his modest house, found a letter that had been signed by then-Prime Minister Vo Van Kiet in 1996 recommending that the SAS hotel project be moved to a location outside the city centre. This document effectively outweighed any subsequent statement or decision by Hanoi city leaders.

With a firm political basis for cancelling the hotel project, the president of the Urban Planning Association then set up a meeting with the Hanoi People's Committee chairman. The association had previously sent an official letter to the city government expressing opposition on 18 February, released to the press on 23 February along with the text of Vo Van Kiet's 1996 decision (*Tuan Vietnam* 2009b). The president and the city chairman knew each other: both of them had studied in Poland at different times, and in the small world of Hanoi intellectuals, they were former schoolmates.[10] The meeting took place on 24 February and included representatives from the Ministry of Construction (*Ashui* 2009). As the landscape architect (who was not present) recounted afterwards,

The chairman said, 'We authorities were put under a great deal of pressure. This is also a foreign relations issue.' Mr. B [the association president] replied, 'I don't know about that. But we are strongly opposed to this project. If there are foreign relations consequences to stopping it, then you have to solve those!' The chairman considered this and agreed that he would ask the Swedes about the case. Everything was going according to our script. If it didn't work, we were prepared to call Stockholm!

As planned in the activists' strategy, the Swedish embassy responded to the Hanoi People's Committee that they had no interest in the case (Kim 2009).

International activists initiated a campaign to boycott Accor Group properties and write to the company in protest of the hotel project. The campaign was designed in coordination with HealthBridge, who calculated that there was a reasonable chance of convincing Accor to withdraw from the project. 'I am outraged by Accor's plan to build a hotel within Thong Nhat [Reunification] Park', a sample letter stated. 'There is simply no legitimate justification – whether it's "job creation" or some rationalized contribution to Hanoi's tourist industry – for Accor to put profit over the public good' (VSG 2009). The boycott and letter-writing campaign resulted in several hundred messages from 'people in professional positions' to Accor's regional vice-president for communications, resulting in complaints from management about the bad exposure they were receiving.

HealthBridge and the Urban Planning Association moved forward with plans for a public workshop, similar to the August 2007 seminar, on the subject of 'Effective Management of Parks and Gardens in Hanoi'. This was held on 17 March in a club overlooking the gate to Reunification Park. The ten presenters, including associations, NGOs, architects and lawyers, described the history of park planning in Hanoi, international comparisons, park design, and legal structures. The sense at the workshop was that the campaign was close to success.

Advocacy came to fruition the following week. Many public comments had suggested that since Reunification Park had become a national concern, the central government should intervene to reverse the decision of city authorities (Linh 2009). On 25 March, the Ministry of Construction recommended that the Prime Minister stop construction of the hotel (*Ashui* 2009). This sounds convoluted, but has force in the Vietnamese unitary political system, where in the absence of an independent judiciary, only a higher level of government can overrule a lower level decision. On April 13, the Prime Minister issued a circular ordering the city to halt the project (AFP 2009).

Network membership and structure

Reunification Park network participants can be categorised into three groups with varying degrees of connections to the Hanoi city government and other authorities. The first, and largest, category consists of leaders and members of professional associations, in this case the Urban Planning Association, Vietnam Architects' Association, and Vietnam Environment Association, among others. These associations' leaders are typically retired officials of medium to high rank (department directors or vice-directors), while rank-and-file members are active practitioners and/or university professors, mostly middle-aged. Association members usually engage in advocacy in an individual capacity, but they may also use the association's offices and stamp when a more official approach is necessary or when it serves their interests. Some associations are seen as more effective than others, depending both on the characteristics of individual leaders and the status and connections of their members. Younger members feel that the older generation is 'too conservative' and state-centred; in contrast, some retired officials are also known for direct and fearless criticism of government policies, as they have nothing to lose from saying what they think.

A second category of network participants (Figure 5.1) consists of journalists employed by print or online media who covered the Reunification Park story and later developed a personal interest. Other semi-professional journalists participate by blogging or submitting articles to online publications; there is some overlap between this group and association-based activists in the first group. Third, and smallest in numbers, are organisational network participants, including HealthBridge and Action for the City. Staff of these organisations are employed to work on issues that relate to public space and engage in advocacy on this basis. Several international NGO-based individuals have also posted comments and taken part in workshops.

Figure 5.1   Reunification Park network structure

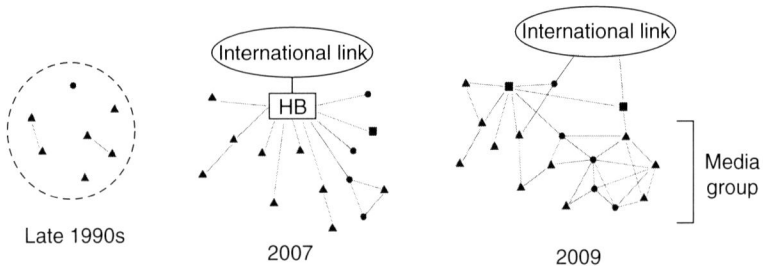

The 2007 campaign resulted in increased ties among members, and by the time of the hotel case in early 2009, the network's structure was more egalitarian, with several well-connected core members and others at the periphery. HealthBridge was still an informal focal point, with one staff person contributing part of her time to the case, but initiatives came from many nodes in the network. Membership has remained loose and undefined, so that while some individuals and organisations do describe themselves as network members, others do not.

The whole network has hardly ever met together in one place, with the exception of the two HealthBridge workshops, which also included outside participants (and in the case of the 2009 workshop, was open to the public), and the networking dinner noted above. Instead, different sub-groups meet as needed to share information and discuss the case, such as a media node made up of online journalists from VNN, *Dantri*, and *VN Express* and a node comprising HealthBridge and several association leaders. For other participants, activism on Reunification Park is only a minor part of a wider set of urban and political issues on which they 'mostly work alone and independently'.

As one network member summarises,

> We all know each other, but we don't meet very often. Mostly I write an article from my point of view, then someone else comments and writes from their expertise (*chuyên môn*). Even if people write using pen names, we still know who it is... We see each other occasionally and talk at conferences and meetings, but we don't write e-mails or meet in public. That might attract attention and they would say 'Aha, they are up to something'. Often we don't even call.

Interviews showed that in fact not all network participants do know everyone else, or at least not very well: several respondents mixed up or could not remember names of other participants who are in other nodes of the network. Even after several years of collaboration, the Reunification Park network remains primarily virtual.

Advocacy strategies

Public space advocacy in Hanoi prior to the Reunification Park case followed an embedded strategy: individuals with connections to government decision-makers attempted to influence them through letters, petitions, workshops and direct personal appeals. In early cases such as Thu Le Park, the contents of the letters were not publicised, and most were never answered. As might be expected, the success rate of this approach is relatively low, although a direct meeting with the Hanoi chairman did play a role in stopping hotel construction in 2009. Recommendations of individual experts can easily be ignored. Network formation was hampered by the lack of a shared identity among potential members, the presence of individual egos, and the fact that most activists were already well established in their careers when they began speaking out about parks and public space. These limitations continue today, as illustrated by the finding that no fewer than five individuals believe that their personal contributions were the deciding factor in either the 2007 Disneyland campaign, 2009 hotel case, or both.

These perceptions notwithstanding, the Reunification Park campaigns were a group effort, and many contributions were essential to their success. Particularly in 2007, HealthBridge was a catalyst in bringing network participants together and offering experience from advocacy for 'livable cities' in other Asian and global contexts. HealthBridge's international status gave them credibility and status with Vietnamese officials, even if they were saying the same thing as local activists. HealthBridge did not attempt to dominate activities or seize the spotlight for itself, nor did it use funding to dominate the network. By 2009, HealthBridge's participation was secondary, helpful but not necessary.

HealthBridge staff view their main contribution to the network as hosting and organising workshops. As an international NGO, HealthBridge feels it has little space for more direct advocacy, preferring 'to be constructive, not criticise the government'. Meetings and conferences with government partners are, of course, embedded advocacy techniques, and this formed the 'inside' part of the new strategy.

The initial efforts of HealthBridge and workshop participants were amplified through the 'outside' component of the strategy, which relied on media and the Internet to leverage public opinion within and outside Vietnam. Originally, HealthBridge also planned to distribute leaflets to people coming to the park, but this idea was dropped since media advocacy seemed more effective (HealthBridge 2008). The response to media stories on the park came as a surprise to everyone involved, including the reporters themselves, who suddenly found themselves working evenings and weekends to respond to public comments. 'We didn't have any plan to cover this issue', says a journalist. 'It just happened. It needed one person to light a match and it started a big fire. We didn't start it, we just reported the news.'

Online postings came not only from Hanoi, but other parts of Vietnam and from the millions of Vietnamese living outside the country, primarily in the USA, Eastern Europe and Australia. In many cases, it was not possible to know where comments originated, as only an e-mail address was given. Through the Internet, the locality-specific park controversies became rapidly transnationalised in a way that previous public space issues were not. For instance, August 2007 workshop papers were posted immediately on the savehanoipark.com website, based in Australia.

Framing of the issue was enabled by the existence of clear opponents. The involvement of private corporate investors, and their arrogant statements to the media, stimulated and targeted public anger in both the 2007 and 2009 cases. For instance, when the Tan Hoang Minh company director criticised several activists by name in August 2007, park network members were able to frame him, probably unfairly, as uninformed and uncultured, while emphasising their own civil behaviour in avoiding personal attacks or arguments in print.

Defenders of Reunification Park did not publicly oppose or criticise government officials, a far riskier tactic. In reality, as network members knew well, some city government officials were aligned with the developers. But other officials – perhaps those who had no way to benefit from the projects – stood aside or were critical. This fragmentation of levels, branches and interests within the state gave the civil society network space to speak out and form alliances (Gupta 2006: 231).

> Advocacy requires divisions among government officials. As long as someone is benefiting and someone else is not – someone gets this cup of tea and someone else doesn't – then the person not benefiting becomes my ally, and I have space to advocate. What's more, *this is always the case.* There are always differences of opinion among the elite, thus spaces to exploit. If all the leaders agreed, then I wouldn't be able to say or do anything. But *all the leaders never agree.*[11]

Advocates did not defeat the corporations or the government head-on, but simply gathered enough allies in other parts of the state, media, associations and international organisations to tip the scales in their favour: that is, engage in 'jujitsu advocacy'. As one activist states, 'we have to have tactics and tricks, because they [opponents] have so many tactics and tricks'. Capital city-based activists may have an advantage over others in terms of greater access to central government, but the principle of engaging multiple levels of the state holds in many situations.

As a stand-alone tactic, Internet postings would not have been sufficient to tip the balance against the park projects: the 'Let's save our city' appeal and the Accor letter-writing campaign both raised public awareness, but did not produce any concrete result. Conversely, embedded actions alone would also not have been sufficient, as shown by previous cases of failure. HealthBridge's role was important but not decisive; the key public statements by network participants occurred after the August workshop was over.

> If a group of intellectuals have a workshop and present papers and talk among themselves, it doesn't change anything in public opinion because no one knows about it. But if articles are published in the media, then it affects what officials say and do, and what people think. Even knowing that there was a conference on quality of life in the city makes them take notice. If I publish an article in the morning, by the afternoon people are reading it, discussing it and commenting on it... Once [officials] see that I write articles that have value, then they come to me and ask about ideas and plans before they are released. They want to know what the public's reaction will be.

A leader of the Urban Planning Association states that in spite of well-written articles and clear presentations at workshops, information is still not strong enough to convince officials at many different levels, some of whom lack awareness and education. A more effective strategy is to stimulate public opinion, which will get better results from authorities who see the media as 'the voice of the people'.

Once inside-outside advocacy efforts began, they produced results in a remarkably short time. At the beginning of August 2007, though many individuals were opposed to privatising the park, there was no organised campaign or public discussion. When this began, it 'went viral' and became, for a short time, the biggest story in Hanoi. The same pattern repeated in 2009 of a long period of preparation and strategising, followed by a one-month burst of online and media attention resulting in government concessions. 'At first, no one took much of an interest in the case, we figured the companies had already won', but once public concern reached a tipping point, there was no turning back. In 2007, this happened almost accidentally, as an unplanned public reaction; by 2009, it was part of a conscious strategy among network members to stop the hotel.

As network participants learned from their previous experiences, their framing of public space issues also became more sophisticated. By 2009, their focus was not just on 'saving the park' but connecting with public expression. Network members made efforts to align themselves with 'the people'. As no political opinion polls or opposition parties exist, public comments on websites were seen as the best way to gauge attitudes (Tran and Linh 2010). This allowed network members to claim they were representing large groups of Hanoians (*Dantri* 2009). By identifying themselves with 'the majority', the activists painted the corporations and their government allies into a corner.

Table 5.1   Advocacy tactics – Reunification Park network

Advocacy tactics	*Notes*
Embedded advocacy • Direct lobbying to officials • Letters, petitions, complaints • Speak at workshops, conferences • Academic and technical research	– Use personal connections to sympathetic officials – Embedded advocacy done by associations and GONGOs as part of a diversified network strategy – International supporters cooperate with embedded actors to organise workshops
Media advocacy • Write articles in print and online media • Blogging	– Journalists participate actively as network members – Use interactive media as a way to demonstrate public opinion on the side of the network

Network members credit much of their success at advocacy to media exposure. As the landscape architect describes,

> The role of the media is extremely important. If the media are afraid of authorities, we wouldn't have any space to advocate. When I took on the Thang Long water park case, the media couldn't intervene or report on this. I had to copy documents and go around from person to person distributing them. Now things are much more advantageous. I can sit at home, write articles and talk to everyone. The media do a much better job now...they give me a forum and are open to balanced views.

> What I do is only one part. The opening of the media is more important. Many people still complain there's no press freedom here. But I think a lot of this depends on us. If we say the right things at the right time, the media will listen.

These varied and nuanced perceptions of media are remarkable in a system in which all media remain state-owned. At different times during the Reunification Park events, media served the purposes of city government and corporate interests, but also interests of activists. The media also followed their own commercial interests. For instance, at one stage in 2007, the editor in chief of *VietNamNet* was reportedly told not to publish any more on the park issue. However, a special VNN feature, the online magazine *Tuan Vietnam* [*Vietnam Week*] had just started publishing several months earlier, and its editor was eager to increase their exposure and market share. The webzine's format is to publish differing views on an issue, then invite readers' responses. The park case was a compelling story for this medium, and no one could criticise the editors as they also presented the companies' views.

On the other hand, the media's role was also limited due both to political restrictions and capacity issues. Journalists did not strategise or plan the campaign, or even engage in investigative reporting. Media responses often happen too late: 'It is better to know about plans in advance, while in the case of Reunification Park, we didn't find out about the [hotel] project until it was already approved', said an activist. 'If we had a more professional media', a journalist complains, 'we wouldn't all have to check in the office at eight every morning. We could go out to research and collect information ourselves, instead of depending on documents someone else gives us.' Debate about Reunification Park could have been shut down at any time by the Ministry of Information and Communications, which supervises the media. The fact that expression was not censored does not mean that the subject is not politically sensitive, but rather that there was no unanimity among leaders to take action. Some leaders at high levels agreed with the park activists, while others supported the corporations; this allowed activists to speak out and the media to report differing views.

The most significant recent change in Vietnamese media has been the emergence of online news and blogs as the industry leaders (Ngoc 2005, Nguyen 2007). Already in the 2007 Disneyland case, print media played a smaller role than the leading news websites such as *VietNamNet* and *dantri.com.vn*. In 2009, the disparity was even more noticeable: all the key interviews and articles involving network participants appeared in *VietNamNet* and *Vietnam Week* first before being re-posted elsewhere (Linh 2009). Online media conducted interviews and published articles, then gathered public comments; the print media then reported on the controversy. Without the political space provided by the Internet, organisation of the Reunification Park network would have been much harder. Physical meetings would have required more logistical preparation and funding, plus the risk of confrontation or restrictions from authorities or corporate representatives. Blogs allowed activists to post their concerns directly without passing through the official media. The Reunification Park campaign was the first public effort in Vietnam to have been conducted in this primarily virtual format.

International linkages

The participation of international NGOs, Hanoi-based expatriates, and overseas Vietnamese was a contributing but not deciding factor in the success of the Reunification Park campaigns. The term 'international' should be qualified in that INGO involvement took place largely via Vietnamese staff of a single, small organisation, not through complex transnational advocacy structures or large external donors. The non-Vietnamese who spoke out about the park all have existing ties to Vietnam, including many who have lived in Hanoi for many years and speak Vietnamese. Overseas Vietnamese participated as individual cyber-citizens posting online comments. While each of these forms of engagement was helpful, HealthBridge's role in initiating a strategy and network in 2007 was the most important. HealthBridge served as the contact point between international supporters and Vietnamese advocates. International participation brought useful comparative perspectives, showing local activists they are not alone, and helped to provide 'cover' that undoubtedly reduced some participants' initial fear of speaking out. HealthBridge's low-budget, supportive but not dominating approach avoided risks of forming a 'donor-initiated network' and demonstrates a model worthy of emulation by other international actors.

No Vietnamese interview respondents felt that international engagement is required for effective advocacy in all cases, pointing to examples where virtual networking and local advocacy succeeded on their own. HealthBridge's role was less significant in 2009 than in 2007, and in earlier cases of activism, no international participants were involved at all. One participant sees the park network as a 'seed' that can inspire and inform other activism, even if the original members no longer participate.

Network effectiveness: Policy change

Participants in the Reunification Park campaigns strategically used available political opportunities to spread their views and reach their objectives. Four inter-related factors combined to bring about success: first, the people speaking out had sufficient and timely access to information; second, they had personal connections to leaders at the appropriate level and branch of government that makes decisions. Third, success requires a base in public opinion that is in favour of the activists. Finally, the media is able to report and reflect activists' and the public's views.

If all of these factors hold, there is no need for a large network. Even a few activists are sufficient: in the Reunification Park cases, fewer than 20 people were active. 'We need to have people who are experts on the issue and who the public will trust. Sometimes even fewer people are involved; even one or two people can lead on an issue but they have to do a lot of work to have their documents and facts straight.' Another activist argues, 'A weak network with strong connections to the state is more effective than a strong network with denser ties'. If the first condition of access to leaders holds, but the media and public opinion conditions do not, an embedded advocacy strategy might be a better choice.

A positive interpretation of this finding is that if conditions can be met, they offer an effective model for advocacy on a range of issues: witness how park activists learned from their unplanned results in 2007 to strategise in 2009. Less optimistically, the conditions also imply that while a few big cases can be won, many smaller cases cannot. Success in a few cases has led advocates to realise how much further they have to go. 'Every day in Hanoi there are hundreds of violations of green space', says one activist. 'We should be working on all of these local issues, not just the big ones like Reunification Park'. An unpublished report on Hanoi wetlands laments that

> we have to accept the truth: rivers and lakes continue to become more polluted and are still taken over for construction. The media is one link in the whole process of discovering violations, raising voices to expose them, protecting and implementing decisions, and monitoring the situation; but clearly not the strongest link. The number of cases that have been resolved is very small compared to the number that have been raised in the media. Especially, the number of cases that have been fully solved are even fewer. This doesn't yet consider the not uncommon situation in which violations continue to occur even after a supervising agency has dealt with the case. Then there are all kinds of cases that have just been identified but not dealt with at all. (Tran and Linh 2010)

In certain cases, the third condition of media interest is present, but the other factors are not. Even then, mass media will only cover national-level or city-wide cases, not community conflicts, and will only have influence over government in big cases. Similarly, blogs can be posted by anyone, but only large, symbolic issues will mobilise public opinion. Experts and well-connected public figures have limited time and social capital, so they will reserve their credibility to speak out on the most important issues. When advocacy conditions are absent, state agencies and private corporations generally act as they wish, including privatising public space for profit, because of economic incentives, weak management and fragmented authority structures. But they can be stopped in some cases if they go too far.

Network effectiveness: Sustainability

Individual activists played key roles, using their contacts in the media and government to advocate for a change in the city's decisions. In the process, they engendered a public debate that involved hundreds if not thousands of Hanoians in reflection about the nature of development in their city and the value of public space. The network's advocacy efforts have been remarkably successful even in the absence of formal structure and dense ties among members.

In 2009, following the conclusion of the hotel campaign, HealthBridge considered taking steps to formalise the network under its own leadership. However, HealthBridge's Vietnamese staff preferred a looser network in which different sub-groups act in different roles. This view is shared by other network participants. 'Advocacy on the web is good – better than an organisation', says one activist. As a variety of people works on different issues, it is often hard to say who is a network member and who is merely an ally. Another participant adds,

> It's better not to have an organisation. If we did, we would have to worry about structure and funding, then if we did something controversial, it would be shut down and then where would we be? It is better this way. We can speak openly without risk of reprisals. The network operates based on events: when there is a need, then people speak out... Depending on what the issue is, different people take the lead.

This mix of reasons combines to form a strong argument for choosing informal network structures rather than more permanent, formalised ones.

The Reunification Park experience also shows that virtual networks have several major disadvantages. Without a coordinating body, collective action depends on volunteer individual leadership, and individuals may be busy, uninterested, or otherwise unavailable. Second, the network stands in basically a reactive pose: 'If another issue comes up', says an association leader, 'we're ready to hold workshops and organise again'. This is doubtless so, as the 2009 case shows, but it leaves much to chance and timing. Ultimately, the reason no formal network has emerged from the park campaigns is that no person or organisation has stepped up to lead it. Funding is also an issue: even a modest annual budget of £5,000–10,000 would be beyond the means of Vietnamese network participants alone, though by international standards this amount is quite small. HealthBridge, the most likely funder, didn't want to impose.

Given that there are important allies within the state and participants from different sectors and types of organisations, there is no reason why a more formal public space network could not succeed, if participants desired it. There are many steps short of full formalisation that the network could take: more frequent meetings, development of a dedicated website, or identification of a staff person as a full- or part-time administrator or coordinator, based in one participating organisation. But no structure can emerge unless participants are ready for it.

Network effectiveness: Political space

From an urban planning perspective, 'the forces of globalization are radically restructuring cities as they intersect with local histories and shifting constellations of power' (Douglass et al 2008: 27), and this process of 'rapid urbanisation...is the backdrop to which the controversies over Thong Nhat Park must be reflected' (Hellberg and Johansson 2008: 29). Globalisation and capitalist development are certainly relevant to the case, as seen in the selection of 'Disneyland' as the corporations' pretext for appropriating public land and links to overseas (and overseas Vietnamese) investment and social capital. Connections to the past are also important, particularly in nostalgia for an imagined purer socialist period in which 'we were more human', and also in the attempt by developers to invoke Vietnam's historical relationship with neutral, social-democratic Sweden as an obligation to build a luxury hotel. It seems too reductionist to describe all these as results of rapid urbanisation. Ultimately, debates over Reunification Park and public space are political, in the sense used in this book of public deliberation over issues of common concern.

Reunification Park network participants have an explicit understanding of their activities as political, and not only because of the role of senior government officials in decision-making. Media websites filed stories on the park under the categories 'politics' and 'society', sometimes both, with 'politics' being used more frequently in the 2009 hotel case. As a journalist states,

> This case is definitely political! In this city, every square meter of land is political – especially something involving a large piece of land in the centre of the city. The state owns all land in Vietnam. It's not private property. So any time land is transferred from one use to another, this has to be approved by the authorities. The companies know this, and there were political interests involved.

Procedurally, the politics of the park can be traced through a series of city government decisions taken and reversed in response to pressure from private investors on one hand and civil society on the other. City officials felt pressure to satisfy investors, as shown in the early worried responses in the hotel case concerning FDI and economic growth; this pressure comes both from the incentives to attract development and policies emanating from the central government and its backers in the World Bank and IMF (Painter 2005: 273–6). The political economy of land rights in a single-party developmental state would predict 'symbiotic clientelism' or 'wicked coalitions' between officials and developers (Lu 2008: 45, Li C 2009: xxvii). Perhaps more surprising, given the Vietnamese political system, is the level of state responsiveness to public opinion as filtered through media and other civil society advocacy. In the absence of formal accountability mechanisms such as elections, what alternative forms of accountability explain government actions?

Interview respondents offer several interpretations. One observation is that current Hanoi leaders are relatively enlightened compared to some of their recent predecessors: they have a background in construction and planning, and 'know how to listen to people'. A second explanation concerns embedded social networks that link current city officials to their former teachers and patrons who are now retired, including some Reunification Park network participants who are able to exert influence on the younger generation, or at least speak their mind freely. Leaders are also city residents, so they would rather not do anything harmful to the city; although they may have received bad advice, they are not foolish or incompetent. Wanting to at least appear to be good, honest officials, leaders have some incentive to respond to citizen demands (Hildebrant 2009). These factors are all potentially valid, but do not fully explain city government actions, which come across as insecure and indecisive. Not too convinced of the rightness of their actions, leaders bend and even reverse policies when expedient or pressed to do so. As noted above, inside-outside advocacy requires a fractured elite.[12]

> The companies weren't afraid of us. They know how to deal with the media. If they couldn't invest in this project, they have a lot of others. But the authorities, they were afraid. What if someone above them calls them up and asks what they were doing? Or what if they are asked about it later in the National Assembly?

Thus, the same fragmentation of authority and flexibility in implementation that allow for regulations to be ignored also gives civil society space to advocate for change. When pressure from below becomes too intense, the state is willing to make concessions to limit the potential for broader social discontent or unrest (Chu 2006: 27). In response to large-scale Catholic vigils in 2008, Hanoi authorities converted two disputed properties, which otherwise might have been sold for commercial use, into public parks (Wells-Dang 2010: 102). Several park network participants view this outcome as a step forward: 'Hanoi needs more parks, we'll take them any way we can get them!' said one. They are strange parks, however, with narrow pathways and signs to keep off the grass, designed like Ba Dinh Square to eliminate the possibility of mass gatherings.

Most park network members say that they feel safe from government crackdowns or reprisals for their actions, since they are not publicly anti-government or oppositional in their stances, though at times harshly critical of corporate and city statements about the park. Activists emphasise that they speak from a position of professional expertise, not like bloggers or dissidents who they view as expressing themselves too generally or unwisely on political subjects. However, definitions of 'unwise' and 'political' vary among the group, as do the limits of what is 'professional'. Several network participants have expressed views on ongoing disputes about Vietnam-China relations, particularly bauxite mining. This may be viewed as a natural outgrowth or complement to concerns about corruption and misuse of power in public space, and could be interpreted as evidence that civil society networks on moderately sensitive topics such as Reunification Park might lead to more oppositional or dissident organising later (Thomas 2002). Alternately, nationalistic controversies such as the bauxite case could be a distracting step backwards from advocacy on topics such as public space where network members have more relevant expertise and better chances of success.

Conclusion

Once the hotel project was cancelled, the city authorities offered to compensate VinaCapital with another piece of land not far from the French Quarter. As the site is too small for a luxury hotel, the company planned to build a shopping complex and high-rise apartments there. In early 2010, however, the Prime Minister put a hold on new high-rise developments in the city centre. The investors then demanded a 2.5 hectare site on the outskirts of the city (DPA 2010). 'They are still making really unfair statements', says the landscape architect. 'They say they lost an opportunity, but really it was just an opportunity to cheat people.'

In 2009, as in the 2007 Disneyland case, advocates succeeded in protecting a small part of Hanoi's limited green space from development. More importantly, as a journalist points out, they demonstrated that citizens have political space to influence policy, and that private investment should be balanced by preserving the positive aspects of Vietnam's socialist legacy (Steinglass 2009). However, the hotel campaign may be interpreted as less than a complete victory, as the investors might end up with more valuable land than they began with, while the hotel land remains fenced off from public use.

While some park network members have moved on to other issues, most have stayed focused on their areas of professional or journalistic interest, expressing more concern about Hanoi than national or international issues and accepting the broader political space for what it is. The ability to write articles and engage in public discussion along with a community of colleagues and the broader public gives them a sense of value and some influence in society. One architect comes every morning to a typical backstreet café in the Old Quarter where he meets friends and discusses both personal and professional topics, part of the 'culture of debate' among intellectuals, media, and some officials. Such a café scene has long been part of Hanoi's artistic and literary environment and is one of the ways that global cities provide 'thick enabling environments' for networks (Sassen 2002: 217). Cafés are also, of course, a specific historical origin of Habermas's 'public sphere' (1962). Thomas notes that '[t]he public are sharing views and gathering together to exchange information and ideas, allowing a "public sphere" to develop in much the same way that it did in Europe in the 18th century' (2002: 1621, also Kürten 2008).

Other analysts of social networks in Leninist settings have reached a contrasting conclusion that by replacing formal organisations and mass media, networks become 'a substitute for a public sphere', rather than the origins of one (Osa 2003: 78, O'Brien and Stern 2008: 17). Neither statement applies exactly to Hanoi networks at the present time. Osa's characterisation of a substitute public sphere in pre-Solidarity Poland fits better with Vietnam in the 1990s, when an intellectual elite engaged in embedded advocacy without engaging the media. The changing role of the press and particularly online media has extended the scope of these debates to include potentially the majority of urban residents. Citizens are now doing more than just 'exchanging information and ideas', but also advocating and networking for policy change, a step beyond Thomas's earlier observation. Whether this is indeed forming a public sphere in the Habermasian sense (let alone repeating the European Enlightenment) is questionable. Public and media discussion on many other political issues in Vietnam, such as religion-state relations or land protests, remains limited. Rather than a single, society-wide public sphere, it may make more sense to envision multiple, overlapping smaller spheres – an 'urban public sphere', a 'green public sphere', an 'artistic sphere' and so on (Yang and Calhoun 2008, Howell 2004a), each composed of one or more networks of organisations and individual activists. One effort among many, the Reunification Park network's experience offers a rich set of lessons and good practices for future advocacy.

6
The China Rivers Network

On 19 August 2003 *China Youth Daily* reported a plan to build 13 dams on the Nu River (怒江) in Tibet and Yunnan.[1] This news shocked environmentalists (Haggart and Mu 2003, Yardley 2004), especially since the area had been declared a UNESCO World Natural Heritage site the previous month. Over a decade earlier, construction of the Three Gorges Dam on the Yangtze had begun without open debate (Dai 1998). The Nu River case was different. In 'an unprecedented public campaign [that] brought together NGOs, scientists, government officials as well as the general public' (Liang and Yang 2007: xii), an emerging, informal network of activists sought to tip the balance of Chinese media and public opinion against the proposed dams. At a SEPA[2] symposium in Beijing in September 2003, 36 Chinese and international experts and NGO participants spoke out against the proposed dams, with extensive media coverage. A subsequent conference in Kunming revealed 'bitter divisions' among state officials and academics (Xue and Wang 2007: 69). Anti-dam advocates found open supporters in central government, particularly SEPA, and attempted to leverage their support against provincial government officials and hydropower corporations (Lu 2005, Sun and Zhao 2008: 158). At the annual conference of the China Environment and Culture Promotion Association (a GONGO) in October, activists collected the signatures of 62 scientists, artists and journalists for a public petition: 'Please preserve the last ecological river – the Nu River' (Yan 2009). In December, a local environmental group in Chongqing collected 10,000 students' signatures opposing the Nu dams (Büsgen 2006: 30). This combination of petitions, direct lobbying and media pressure is widely credited with prompting Premier Wen Jiabao to suspend the project in April 2004, citing the 'high level of social concern' the proposal generated (Yang and Calhoun 2008: 69). The Nu River had been preserved, at least temporarily.

Large dams have a totemic significance in the extractive development model favoured by China's technocratic leadership, symbols of Man's dominance over Nature and by extension, of national sovereignty and economic development (Smil 1993, Economy 2004, Ekins 1992: 88). By the time the Nu River plans were made public in 2003, however, environmental issues had become a higher priority of the central government as well as of Chinese citizens concerned about pollution and other problems. Environmental NGOs (ENGOs) began forming in the mid-1990s; by 2008, over 3,500 were registered, with an estimated 2,000 others unregistered and operating informally, including numerous student groups in both categories (Xie 2009: 3, Xu 2009). The increasingly professional and assertive Chinese media had begun in-depth coverage of environmental issues, including dams (Yang and Calhoun 2008). The controversy around the Nu River project is widely viewed as a key turning point in Chinese environmentalism (Tong 2009), catalysing sustained environmental activism that has continued to the present and explored the boundaries of advocacy in China (Lin 2007).

Opposition to the Nu River dams united a disparate group of scientists, academics, NGO activists and journalists both inside and outside state employment. Initially, this network formed and operated informally. In 2004, core activists formalised their cooperation as the China Rivers Network (中国河网, *Zhōngguó Héwǎng*). When this structure proved unworkable, the network returned to its original informal basis. For the past five years (2006–10), the network has continued to raise awareness about the proposed dams and advocate for alternative forms of development in the Three Rivers area and beyond. In recent years, the focus of advocacy has expanded past the Nu to include the Jinsha-Yangtze, Lancang, and other rivers in Yunnan and Sichuan, as well as other issues of national significance such as the north-south water diversion scheme and the 2008 Sichuan earthquake (Probe 2008, Yang 2009).[3]

In addition to interviews with network members and media articles, this case study draws on an extensive secondary literature on Chinese river activism. Chinese NGOs have probably received more scholarly attention than any other type of social organisation in China, including studies from a development/NGO perspective (Ho 2001, Schwartz 2004, Yang 2005, 2010, Cooper 2006, Lu 2005, Fu 2007, Xie 2009) and a social movement perspective (Dai and Vermeer 1999, Stalley and Yang 2006, Sun and Zhao 2007, Ho and Edmonds 2008, Hildebrant and Turner 2009). Other books and articles focus on rural environmental issues and environment-linked protests (Jun 2003, Ma 2004, Economy

138

Map 6.1 Proposed and completed dams on the Nu, Lancang and Jinsha rivers

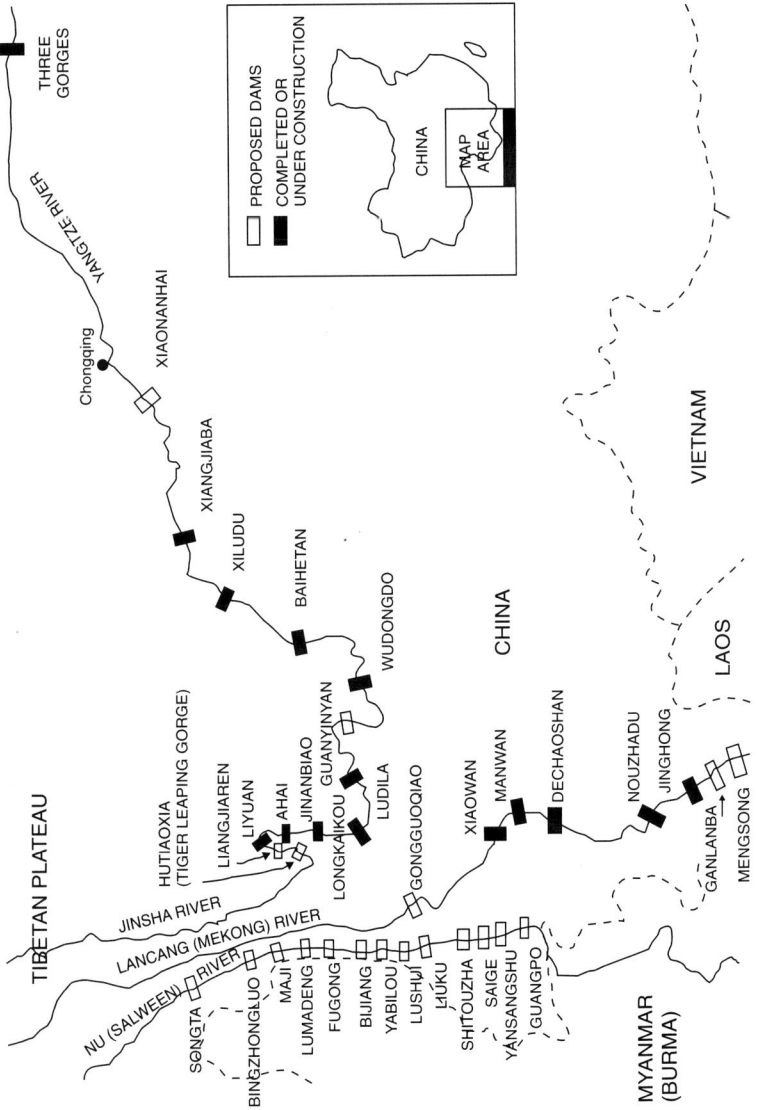

Source: Hanoi Data Ltd. Used by permission.

2004, Brettell 2008). Regarding the Nu River campaign, accounts by participants include Dore and Yu (2003) and Xue and Wang (2007); the most complete secondary sources are Büsgen (2006), Sun and Zhao (2007), and Mertha (2008).

Most studies of the Nu and other rivers are framed in terms of the costs and benefits of dam construction (Xue and Wang 2007, Hensengerth 2010, Brown and Xu 2010). Other texts have examined river activism from a political or sociological angle as a case of environmental movement-building (Sun and Zhao 2008, McDonald 2007, Xie 2007, Tong 2009), NGO involvement in civil society (Büsgen 2006, Garcia 2006, Lin 2007), a 'green public sphere' (Yang and Calhoun 2008, Gu 2008), or changes in public policy and governance led by individual 'policy entrepreneurs' (Magee 2006, Mertha 2008). The above studies are China-specific and emphasise the domestic origins and character of river activism; exceptions are Litzinger (2007) and Chen (2010), who view much of the impetus for activism as coming from transnational advocacy groups.

All of the above approaches are valid frames to approach river activism that has contributed to the growth of Chinese environmentalism and to improved environmental policy. Each provides important insights towards environmental issues, advocacy strategies and political implications. Most analyses, however, have not considered the identity, membership and structure of the network over time. Several sources, looking primarily at NGO activities, mention the China Rivers Network in passing (Fu 2007: 293, Ho 2008b: 36, Mertha 2008), while others do not include it at all (Litzinger 2007, Yang and Calhoun 2008, Hensengerth 2010). Many published accounts end with the suspension of hydropower plans on the Nu River as the culmination of environmental struggle, while concentrating less on recent events and advocacy outcomes. This chapter describes river advocacy organised and led by a civil society network that has changed forms and developed over time, contributing new empirical research based on interviews with network members that serves to update and revise existing accounts.

Network formation and history

The origins of the China Rivers Network lie in personal ties among leaders and staff of environmental non-governmental organisations (ENGOs) in Beijing and Kunming (Xie 2007).[4] Environmental activism in the 1990s was 'relatively quiet', as organisations stayed small and worked separately, but with strong social connections.[5] For instance,

Friends of Nature hosted an annual New Year's party for all the environmental groups in Beijing at the time (Wu 2007). Before there was any programmatic cooperation among organisations, the leaders of these pioneer environmental agencies developed a high level of mutual trust, even though their positions did not always agree. 'At first, we came together out of friendship', recalls one activist. 'We all knew each other for more than ten years. "I trust you, so I support you." This was done through the personal energy of NGO leaders.' Around the same time, international environmental NGOs also established a presence in China (Chen 2010).[6] Many of these organisations hired Chinese directors and senior staff who were also part of local personal networks. The relationship between INGOs and local ENGOs has been 'symbiotic', with significant funding and joint activities (Yang 2005: 57).

Both local and international ENGOs focused initially on environmental education and endangered species protection. The first large-scale campaigns took place in the late 1990s to protect the snub-nosed monkey and the Tibetan antelope (Economy 2004: 149–55, Sun and Zhao 2008: 147–51). 'At that time, we didn't think about a "network"', says an activist; 'it was just an issue, and we thought about how to involve other NGOs and media'. Campaigns brought the Beijing organisations together with emerging NGOs in western provinces, including several Yunnan-based groups.[7] As one NGO staff describes, 'We realised that the space for action was much bigger, and we could get involved in environmental politics'. The perceived benefits of cooperation began to outweigh the potential costs. An activist recalls,

> At this time, environmental groups were still trying to feel each other out. Who was effective? Who was knowledgeable? There were different opinions about this. People realised that there were a lot of issues on which we couldn't work on our own. We needed each other...even though we didn't all like each other too well.

Before long, it appeared that environmental NGOs were always working together, rarely acting on their own, and there was 'an enormous amount of cooperation' (Economy 2005: 18).

The first episode of dam activism took place in June 2003. While travelling in Sichuan province, the founder of Green Earth Volunteers and a media colleague from *China Youth Daily* (中国青年报) heard about plans to build a dam on a tributary of the Yangtze near Dujiangyan (都江堰), an ancient system of water gates that is believed to be the world's oldest operating irrigation scheme.[8] A World Heritage site,

Dujiangyan would have been submerged by the dam. The activists found this a 'truly shameful' violation showing ignorance of China's history and culture (Xue and Wang 2007: 67), and began writing press articles about the case. After returning to Beijing, the two women spoke at a 'journalists' salon' (记者沙龙, *jìzhě shālóng*) organised by Green Earth Volunteers. In the next two months, 180 articles about the plans appeared in the Chinese and international media. For the first time, said the GEV director, the general public 'had a say in a decision on an important project' (Haggart and Mu 2003), as ordinary people posted their opposition on online bulletin boards, creating space for public expression that had not been present before and was not 'given from above'. Activists' framing of the dam as a threat to cultural heritage was a strong argument to attract public attention and influence leaders (Mertha 2008: 20). On 29 August, the Sichuan provincial government reversed their decision and cancelled the dam (Yan 2009).

The spontaneous, informal discussion among ENGO leaders and media in the journalists' salons crystallised into a civil society network. The salons began to be held biweekly, hosting speakers from other organisations and government agencies in what might be considered the beginnings of a 'green public sphere' (Yang and Calhoun 2008). Other NGOs, scientists and academics were affiliated to this core group, but citing their lack of experience, they let the more activist NGOs take the lead, particularly Green Earth Volunteers and Green Watershed (Büsgen 2006: 23). When plans for the Nu River dams were announced, this informal network was ready to take up the challenge.[9]

In August 2004, following the initial successes of Dujiangyan and the Nu River, seven ENGOs joined in formalising the China Rivers Network. Although environmentalists had cooperated on specific issues for some years, the concept of a formal network was new in China. The name China Rivers Network was modelled after the International Rivers Network, a US-based NGO.[10] The idea to start a formal network arose during a trip in early 2004 to the Nu River valley and other proposed dam sites in western China to write articles, document the ecology of the area, and meet with local residents (Yan 2009). The group of 20 included leaders of Green Earth Volunteers, Friends of Nature and Green Watershed, as well as individual activists and journalists.

While we were on the trip, we heard the news that a dam at Tiger Leaping Gorge was going to be built on the Jinsha. I went there myself and came back with a report that it was true, preparatory work had already started and was causing major problems. Back in

Beijing, I spoke about this at the Green Journalists' Salon... It was on the day of that salon that [the founder of GEV] had the idea to form a network, since there was already a group of organisations and individuals who were very interested in the issue.

In an internal report to the China programme of Global Greengrants Fund, which supported the exposure trip with a small grant, the GEV founder wrote, 'After our trip, we created the Chinese Rivers Network, together with other partner NGOs and media persons who are especially concerned with retaining the Chinese natural rivers and streams in recent years' (GEV 2006). The network aimed to work proactively to save rivers, not only respond in emergency cases. In its first year of operation, network members produced a series of further media reports about the Nu, a documentary film, and a website (www.nujiang.ngo.cn) with photo essays and other information.[11] Activists used heated rhetoric: the proposed dams comprised 'government-sponsored anarchy' and 'a messy free-for-all' that would be 'more disastrous than floods, droughts or earthquakes, even more devastating than war' (Xue and Wang 2007: 66–7). While the ecosystem could recover from natural disasters or violent conflict, dams would irredeemably destroy the river, and no compensation could cover these losses. The dam project would thus become 'the hydropower equivalent of the Great Leap Forward' (79).[12] In response, CRN outlined a programme of research and ecological development for riverine communities, with an equal focus on protecting biodiversity and preventing or mitigating costs of resettlement. The network hoped to raise funds for independent studies by scientists that could debunk or balance government studies perceived to be biased, with the results publicised in a 'dam database on the internet' to raise public awareness of the harm caused by dams (GEV 2006).

Despite these ambitious goals, CRN 'never really got off the ground'. In its first year, the network held quarterly meetings of its membership and organised a few public events and lectures, but had 'no big successes'. It had a difficult time establishing an identity, in part as there was no way for a network to register to have legal status, a stamp or a bank account. There were no previous models for a formal network of this type in China; its leaders had no previous experience in forming or managing a network and no clear strategy to carry it out. Management issues, especially staff and leadership structures, took up a great deal of time and effort. CRN began without any external funding: instead, member organisations (some of which did have international funding) put resources into the network. Although network members differ on the precise details, at least six organisations contributed between 5–10,000 RMB each, approximately £500–1,000. On the one hand, this 'self-regulating' behaviour was admirable and formed a new direction in Chinese civil society (Xue and Wang 2007: 87). On the other hand, the amounts members could commit were hardly enough to sustain the network, and fundraising became a major challenge.

No sooner had the network begun to deal with these organisational challenges than it began to face strong pressures from opponents. Beginning in 2005, pro-dam advocates began to speak out forcefully against environmentalists, putting CRN under 'a lot of challenge and pressure'. At a conference in Kunming in April, a group of nine pro-dam scientists attacked CRN members for naively opposing development. The fact that few CRN members have technical backgrounds in water or dam issues made them vulnerable to such criticism. One prominent scholar titled his speech 'A direct attack on fake-environmentalist dam opponents', ridiculing activists for their lack of experience and 'environmental fundamentalism' (Büsgen 2006: 41). Several days later, once most CRN speakers had returned to Beijing, pro-dam advocates held a press conference at Yunnan University and continued personal criticism of CRN members (Shi 2010). Opponents rejected environmentalists' ability to represent people, questioned their grounds of legitimacy, and labelled their advocacy claims 'unscientific', a charge taken quite seriously in China (Bao and Liu 2007).

These arguments dovetailed with a broader tightening of government policy towards NGO activities and accusations of manipulation by foreign interests. The Chinese government was reportedly fearful of 'colour revolutions' such as those that took place in several Eastern European and Central Asian countries in 2005 (Ma 2005, Wexler et al 2006: 56–7). One CRN member organisation, Global Village Beijing, was audited concerning funding they received from the German Green Party's Heinrich Böll Foundation (Büsgen 2006: 41–2, Ho and Edmonds 2008: 219). Other CRN members were threatened with closure, and individual leaders were in danger of arrest. GVB withdrew from CRN as a defensive measure. Conditions in Yunnan were particularly serious, with CRN members unable to travel to dam-affected communities. Mertha speculates that only past revolutionary connections kept the leader of Green Watershed from being detained by police (2008: 144). Instead, his passport was seized for a year and he lost his affiliation with the Yunnan Academy of Social Sciences, but Green Watershed was able to continue operation. The dispute worsened relations between NGOs and the Yunnan provincial government, at the same time that officials took action to address the resettlement problems that Green Watershed had raised (McGray and McDonald 2007: 38, 103). The activist director of FON left the organisation, facing political pressure as well as reported conflict with FON's founder, who was more cautious politically and reportedly felt the director was acting too aggressively.

Authorities did not tell CRN to shut down or take any action against the network itself. Rather, faced with operational challenges and funding difficulties, CRN members decided at a January 2006 meeting to end formal operations and return to an informal structure like the one that had emerged organically in 2003. It appeared that CRN had 'died a natural death'. But the formal network's dissolution was only a tactical retreat. CRN members saw that their public network was becoming a magnet for opponents and took the strategic move of becoming more opaque. The collective decision to disband the formal network structure was informed by actors' perceptions of political opportunities and constraints, together with responses to actions taken by state agencies. Since 2006, network members have continued to meet when needed and coordinate their efforts on a variety of environmental and river-related causes.

Network membership and structure

The seven founding member organisations, according to a former CRN staff, were Friends of Nature, Global Village Beijing, Green Earth Volunteers, Green Watershed, Institute for Environment and Development, Brooks Education Institute (天下溪, *Tiānxià Xī*) and Wild China Films. Up to ten different organisations have participated in CRN at different times.[13] Membership was organisational, but it is not quite accurate to call CRN an NGO network. Of the seven members, 'only two or three were registered at the time', and others, such as GEV and Wild China Films, are volunteer-based or small enterprises, though they also regard themselves as NGOs. The boundaries of the network have always been uncertain: numerous individuals and other environmental organisations joined in river advocacy activities, both before and after the establishment of CRN. Participants met at events and communicated by e-mail and cell phones. Unlike many NGO networks, CRN was formed for the purpose of advocacy, not only for exchanging information or capacity building.

CRN members intended leadership of the network to be shared democratically. The director of Green Watershed served as the first coordinator in 2004–05; after this the network shifted to a secretariat structure and moved to Beijing, where most members were based. The leader of Wild China Films became secretary-general on a voluntary basis and worked out of office space donated by Friends of Nature, which seconded one young staff person as deputy secretary. The FON director at the time was a well-spoken activist who became the main driver for formalisation of CRN's structure. On his own initiative, he drafted an agenda and a strategic plan for the network and presented this at a CRN conference in June 2005. The director's personal involvement and the fact that the secretariat was based at FON, however, posed a risk of the network being too closely identified with a single individual: when he departed, the network was left without effective leadership.

On paper, CRN had a hub-and-spokes structure consisting of a small secretariat and organisational members. In reality, CRN was less a coalition of organisations than a network 'driven by a few committed individuals... Closer networking emerged gradually' (Büsgen 2006: 23). A core group of the most active individuals worked together informally, as they had before the formalisation of CRN; core members included the directors of several environmental organisations plus at least one other individual who had returned from study overseas and was not affiliated to any organisation at the time. The legitimacy of CRN derived from the support and endorsement of these founders, but they had diverging working styles and expectations for the network. The fact that the scientists and academics, as well as some NGO staff, were also government employees with multiple professional backgrounds contributed to a variety of levels of participation within the network. The actual structure was thus concentric circles, with a small core and a large outer circle

Figure 6.1   Formal and informal CRN structures

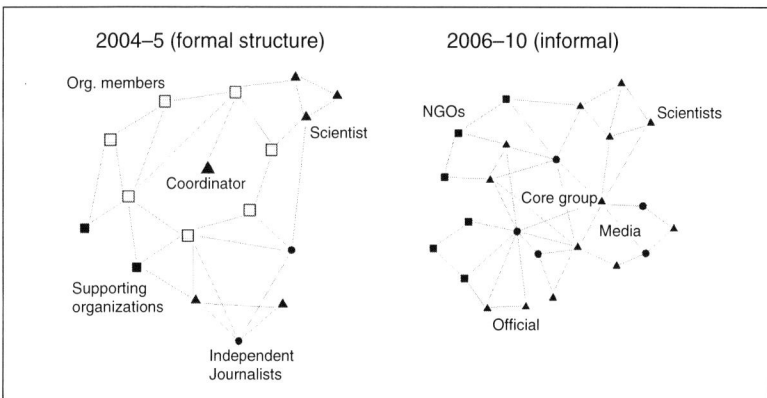

including staff of 'member organisations' as well as journalists, scientists, academics and sympathetic environmental protection officials. The volunteer secretary-general did not stay for long: in summer 2005, she accepted a film contract that she felt unable to refuse. The deputy secretary became coordinator. While enthusiastic, he was unequipped for the challenging task of coordinating among multiple organisations and leaders, many of them with strong personalities. In fairness, no junior employee would be up to this task. Not included in the core group of leaders, he acted more as an administrative assistant, editing films, selling books and organising quarterly meetings. The coordinator position ended after January 2006.

After returning to an informal basis of operations, network participants selected a new structure that was more flexible, allowing for specialisation among members and cooperation on a broader spectrum of issues.[14] As one core activist describes,

> There were seven or eight active groups in CRN at that time [2006]. We tried everything we could to make it work as a formal network, but it didn't happen. Then we said, 'we can function anyway! We have done it before. We don't have to be stuck on this one thing'[15]... Dam issues are politically charged. To give a definite title or name to this issue might defeat the purpose. It could invite adversaries to respond and give them a clear target... [Now] we find it more effective to be informal. We've tested this, and it works.

The current informal network structure is viewed as highly effective by individual participants and continues to show success in advocacy on environmental issues with the Chinese state. 'To this day, a group of people continues to act whenever there is a problem... I still take advantage of the network. Although it's very loose, it's effective.' Since actions are decided by individuals, there is often no need for 'a whole internal organisational process. It is easier just to work on the level of leaders. This model can function very well.' The 'intangible network' is versatile, reduces political risk and sensitivity, and also allows for shared ownership and participation, mobilising people's social capital to the extent that they are comfortable.

The intense period of 2003–06 led to increased trust and cooperation among network members.

> Time tested our relationships. Everyone played a role in this fight. Everybody learned a lot about how to constructively talk about

things – and that being critical also has a value. Being loud continuously can have its benefits, too, to keep an issue on the agenda. In order to be heard, we need a strategy. So although we are different, people now appreciate each other more, and respect each other's limitations too. Everyone has his or her own social network and backdoor influences. Now we are at peace with each other; everyone has won some respect.

Through the informal structure, each organisation or individual member takes the lead on specific actions, and others support them as they are able (Garcia 2006: 65). This reflects a growing specialisation and professional division of labour among ENGOs: as cycles of activism rise and fall over time, members may act as leaders in some areas and followers in others. Some previous individual members are no longer active, such as the former FON director, and several more moderate environmental organisations participate less than they once did. Nodes on the periphery of rivers activism still support network initiatives when needed, such as serving as co-sponsors of an event or signing a petition. In return, network members also contribute to issues initiated by others, as well as participating in other civil society networks. One formerly active member, now on the periphery says,

> I participated in the Nu River efforts before I became director of [my current organisation]. I've known [the GEV founder] for over ten years, since we were in a women's leadership training together. At this point we're still good friends, and I participate in events and the journalists' salon when I am able. I support the network's policy advocacy efforts, and sometimes contribute [donations] to trips to the Nu River area. I still participate as an individual, and sometimes my organisation goes along too.

This individual's participation is through a single personal link to a CRN core member, and as such is not a densely-structured connection. The organisation she directs is a moderate, collaborative NGO that operates very differently from CRN. Compare this statement with that of a core member, who also directs a mainstream ENGO but is much more connected to CRN:

> Organising a network like this is quite difficult. We all have our own work and identity as NGOs. It works because we have a high level of trust with each other that we are all working for the good of the

environment, not for any other reason. That has allowed us to keep going and cooperate for a period of nearly ten years now.

This member is clear that he has two different roles: one in his organisation, and another as a river issues activist. It may be difficult to say which comes first. In his sparsely furnished office, a lone display case contains pictures and memorabilia of trips to the Three Rivers in Yunnan, even though the organisation he leads has no projects in the area.

The rest of CRN's original core group has remained stable, and has not added any new members since 2005. Instead, there is a wider extended membership of 20–30 sympathetic scientists, academics and journalists who serve as expanded network members on a case-by-case basis. Not everyone participates all the time due to time limitations or sensitivity. The small core group is able to reach many other organisations and individuals, some of which have participated actively in recent advocacy efforts. Other members describe a shifting group of participants, with no clear definition who is in or out of the network.

Of the original members, the director of Green Earth Volunteers is perceived by many as the *de facto* network coordinator. GEV was one of the leading groups on the Nu River campaign and has continued to emphasise river activism in an ambitious 'Decade Rivers Project' to document changes in rivers across western China, and through a comprehensive bilingual website of news postings (www.greensos.cn). It is not easy to determine where GEV activities end and the rivers network begins, or what are the individual efforts of GEV's founder.[16] GEV is the only group that contributes full-time effort to rivers issues; all other network members participate on a part-time, limited basis. No Chinese organisation is working exclusively on dams, both because of the sensitivity of the topic and because of funding constraints. This is partly a capacity issue, as the number of dam projects in China is immense, and no single organisation has the ability to monitor all of them. After river issues became politicised, it was hard for anyone to be seen as the public leader and also keep the trust and respect of all participating NGOs.

Advocacy strategies

Through changing structures and political fortunes, CRN has maintained a consistent repertoire of advocacy, combining embedded, media, and community-based tactics into a distinctive inside-outside strategy. Ho and Edmonds (2008: 220) describe CRN as '[a]n excellent illustration of the political leverage of embedded activism', but the network's activities actually extend far beyond an embedded-only model. Different network members emphasise various tactics: journalists and those with close media ties describe their advocacy primarily in these terms, while those with connections to government officials prioritise direct, personal lobbying, and several more activist NGOs have engaged in community organising in dam-affected areas. This could appear to be a scattershot, unfocused approach to advocacy, but is actually a coordinated strategy of alliance-building, based on members' multiple identities.

Their various 'hats' enable rivers network members to present themselves in differing ways to distinct audiences in order to establish their credentials or reduce political risk. When reporting, these journalists draw on their identities as environmentalists; when speaking about environmental issues, they identify as reporters. This gives environmental journalists multiple channels to influence government decision-making (Yan 2009). Other network members use academic identities: when travelling to Manwan in 2004, for instance, the director of Green Watershed identified himself to villagers as 'from the Yunnan Academy of Social Sciences' (Shi 2004), which was his state-linked affiliation at the time, giving him official cover for potentially sensitive activities.

In other words, network members are best described as shape-shifting individual activists, not solely as NGO leaders. The organisations they form are not separate, autonomous entities, but reflections of these multiple identities. In concepts of 'boundary-spanning contention' (O'Brien and Li 2006) and 'organisational amphibiousness' (Ding 1994), people and institutions are seen to move back and forth across the ambiguous line separating the state and non-state sectors. This type of identity shifting also occurs within the rivers network, while at other times individuals use multiple non-state identities. The critical distinction is not state versus society, but which of several identities each network member adopts when engaging in advocacy.[17]

Embedded advocacy

The 'inside' elements of rivers network advocacy include direct connections to government officials, petitions and letters. A journalist describes the first approach as 'making contact with official resources through private networks' (Xu 2009). The most significant personal network in the environmental movement belonged to FON founder Liang Congjie, who was also a member of the Chinese People's Political Consultative Conference (CPPCC), combining 'unique social capital' and 'cultural privilege' (Tong 2009).[18] In cases including the Nu River, he could make proposals and write letters directly to Premier Wen Jiabao and other senior leaders, guaranteeing their attention and at times, action. Environmental activists may at times 'have the ear of very senior people within the government' (Economy 2005: 5), but this influence can also be overstated. In any case, leverage from the central government is key to achieving the network's advocacy goals; without it, there are few other avenues to affect decisions of provincial and local governments (Jiang 2005: 25).

Central government priorities facilitated the expansion of environmental activism in the early years of the 21st century. President Hu Jintao and Premier Wen promoted a 'harmonious society', including environmental protection, over economic growth at all costs (Lo 2007, Lam 2007a). Provincial and local governments, nevertheless, still had pressure and incentives to develop rapidly and place profits over the environment. Yunnan's provincial government, with central support, has followed an infrastructure-led approach to rapid economic growth since the 1990s (Donaldson 2009). Leading electricity and dam-building companies were assigned to exploit different 'powersheds' (Magee 2006) in southwest China: China Electric Company (Huadian) is responsible for the Lancang, the Three Gorges Project Corporation for the Jinsha, and Beijing State Power for the Nu (Xue and Wang 2007: 63). All have connections to top leaders, particularly former premier Li Peng. Advocates find that 'these power conglomerates are very big and powerful, and it makes the situation difficult for us, as the government and corporations are working together'. Like CRN, pro-dam interests draw on sympathetic journalists and allies in various government agencies. In this sense, dam proponents have adopted CRN's tactics and formed a counter-network, though one without any civil society characteristics.[19]

CRN's main government allies are located in MEP, the Ministry of Agriculture, and the CPPCC, among other agencies. MEP is generally regarded as well-meaning but weak: as one journalist writes, 'Environmental protection in China...is a power struggle between different interest groups...when it comes to a battle of strength, [MEP] rarely has the upper hand.' Despite being 'virtually powerless', MEP has 'acquired a great number of enemies' (Liu 2007b). In addition to hydroelectric companies and the Ministry of Water Resources, these include economic growth-focused agencies such as the National Development and Reform Commission (NDRC), previously known as the State Planning Commission (Mertha 2008: 41–5). The rivers network is not well connected at NDRC, although this is the agency that controls energy planning and generation (Liu 2007b). The crackdown in 2005–06 also affected CRN allies in the government: a SEPA official who was a close contact of the network had to step down, while other supportive officials were told to keep quiet (Büsgen 2006: 29–30, Mertha 2008: 122). This has had a significant long-term impact on river advocacy, as key inside sources were no longer available to provide information.

CRN members have used multiple embedded advocacy tactics, but have also gone beyond them. 'The first part of our strategy to affect leaders is to use individual connections to pass memos to key people. Second, we also try to affect public opinion, and through the public also reach the leaders.' The combination of lobbying through personal and indirect channels may actually lead to faster responses from leaders than in democratic systems. 'We can push in only a few places, but if we keep pushing we can get results.' Well-connected journalists are also able to write internal-circulation (内参, *nèicān*) documents, which are viewed as particularly effective (Lu 2005: 2).

> On positive days, I feel that society has created space where leaders have to act...or is it just that leaders don't want to look bad, so then they will act? We can't force leaders to act. Leaders need to show that they are actually answering to issues; this gives them some meaning of legitimacy. But leaders' main interest is where they sit. They want their ministry to be important and effective. MEP also wants the water to be cleaner, and may have genuine care for the environment. So to do responsible policy advocacy, we need to assure leaders that we will act professionally, not embarrass them. The network has ensured the handling of sympathetic officials, not jeopardising individuals' interests.

This statement captures the ambiguity in the rivers network's relations with various parts of the Chinese government. 'NGOs have some friends in the government, but our friends aren't the most powerful ones. These officials see it as in their interest to work with NGOs, but others don't.' The network must join with government allies in order to tip the balance against opposition in other parts of the state.

The primary tactic the rivers network has used in jujitsu advocacy is the open letter: a petition that is concurrently sent to leaders and released (or leaked) to the media and/or posted on the Internet. Since this technique was first used in the Nu campaign in 2003, open sign-on letters have been employed in almost every CRN advocacy episode since. Sent both to allies and opponents, open letters have frequently led to desired results. For instance, in August 2005, 61 organisations and 99 individual activists signed a petition to call for public disclosure of the Nu River Environmental Impact Assessment (EIA) and other major hydropower development plans (Yang 2007: xxviii). That October, the Communist Party Central Committee changed the wording of the Eleventh Five Year Plan from 'proactively develop hydropower projects' to 'develop hydropower projects in an orderly manner while protecting the environment' (Yang 2007: xxix). By the end of 2007, dam companies began to disclose EIA information on the Yunnan provincial environmental protection bureau's website. These events are not proof of causality, although activists believe that their actions influenced the policy process.

In recent years, the number of signatories on open letters has declined compared to the height of the Nu controversy. Network members are willing to act with only two or three members signing their names but believe that larger lists of signatories, including peripheral network participants and supporters, send a stronger message.

> The core group exchanges information and raises issues. When we need something, we all support each other. Others are not so active, but when there's an issue then people participate. They understand the issues and we can mobilise them when needed. We can get 60 organisations and 200 individuals to sign a petition letter, including famous intellectuals and professors who participate. Each member organisation has some links with these people.

Letters are an effective tactic to attract support from moderate environmental NGOs, academics and international organisations who might not support activist methods. Rivers network members do not hesitate to criticise certain INGOs for being too close to the Chinese government, yet the same members draw on connections with these INGOs' senior Chinese staff to gather information from their government contacts. In some cases, INGO staff also participate in CRN advocacy efforts as individuals. Letters are crafted to make the network's appeal representative of all environmental organisations, regardless of political stance, minimising risk to each individual signatory.

Open letters are also sent to hydropower companies. Advocacy towards corporations has somewhat more space than that directly seeking to affect government behaviour, since activists can claim to be supporting government policy to build a 'harmonious society', while criticising lawbreaking activities of companies, even state-owned enterprises, that are causing social disorder. In many cases, dams are now built by companies that are private at least in name and listed on stock markets; this ambiguity enables public criticism since the companies are not directly state-owned. Larger companies connected to the central government may be more susceptible to advocacy, since they have to follow policy guidelines, while smaller provincial companies seem impervious to criticism and have 'so far ignored all inquiries from civil society' (Bosshard 2010).

Media advocacy

The second main component of the rivers network's advocacy links to domestic print and online media. As a network member states, 'the key element of NGO advocacy in China is how we work with the media' – or *are* the media: the core members responsible for developing the network's pioneering media strategy see themselves as journalists first and NGOs second (Lu 2005: 2, Yang and Calhoun 2008: 77–8, Mertha 2008: 11–12). One Chinese sociologist convincingly describes the anti-dam movement as a 'NGO-media network'. Unlike pollution campaigns in which the media is simply used to mobilise resources for activists, in the Nu River campaign media were co-initiators and participants (Tong 2009).

Activists' connections to official media put them in a 'unique position' with regards to authorities. Chinese media remains state-owned and subject to restrictions, but in practice journalists have significant leeway to write on issues of social concern (Zhao and Sun 2007). The power of the media, says one ENGO leader, 'can't be underestimated'.

> If the network were made up of only NGOs, it would be very difficult to quickly tell everyone what is happening. If we depended only on media without an organiser, it would not be so strong, since the media has a short attention span... NGOs are better at motivating the public, while media can get information out quickly and reach the government.

Activists primarily engage Chinese media, but foreign media can also play a role, providing cover for controversial activities. Media also provides access to government leaders, particularly if an article is published prominently in the right newspaper at the right time. For instance, in 2004 Green Earth Volunteers and other CRN members invited the retired vice-director of China Central Broadcasting on a trip to dam-affected areas. On returning to Beijing, he published an article in the CPPCC's newspaper that was reprinted on the same day in major Beijing and Shanghai dailies, calling on officials to pay greater attention to dam policies. According to GEV (2006), this article had great influence on Chinese leaders' awareness, more than if the article had been written by an ordinary journalist.

Table 6.1   Advocacy tactics – China Rivers Network

Advocacy tactics	Notes
Embedded advocacy • Direct lobbying to officials • Letters, petitions, complaints • Speak at workshops, conferences • Exposure trips for opinion leaders	– Use social capital of leaders to reach decision makers – Each network member keeps connections with one or more experts or leaders – Use of open letters as both advocacy and mobilising techniques
Media advocacy • Journalists' salons • Place articles in print and online media • Use of internet and online media	– Include journalists as network members – Bring key journalists on fact-finding tours to dam-affected areas – Circulate information via NGO websites and publications
Community advocacy • Traditional development projects • Video and audio • Community organising (by Green Watershed in particular)	– Frequent visits to dam-affected communities – Document community situation and views, share with other dam-affected people – Bring villagers to public conferences in Kunming, Beijing

Network members use the Internet both for internal communication and for advocacy. E-forums and newsletters are well developed among environmental NGOs (Yang 2005); organisations use their own websites, bulletin boards, e-mail groups and internal publications as mobilisation techniques (Tong 2009). The Internet connects and amplifies voices, increases influence on policy-making, and enables joint advocacy with intensive interaction among organisations (Fu 2007). 'We communicate with each other by e-mail first. If we need to consult experts or other outsiders, we call and they will respond.'

Online media and blogs are also integral parts of advocacy. Although most articles appear in print first, they are then posted and re-posted on multiple websites, giving them a permanent presence in cyberspace and much wider coverage than in a single daily newspaper. Zhou Yongming (2002) describes Chinese intellectual websites as 'an intermediary domain between private intellectual discourse, which is quite free, and a still-controlled official intellectual discourse', resulting in 'expanded space under refined control'. While some topics are still off-limits, print and online media reporting of environmental issues has continued to expand in the past decade, in part due to the media advocacy activities of the rivers network itself.

As coverage of the environment has increased, some observers feel that the media is biased in *favour* of NGOs. While not true of all media, this description may apply to several key papers that give frequent, prominent coverage to river issues, such as *China Youth Daily* and *Southern Weekend* (南方周末, *Nánfāng Zhōumò*), which contains a weekly environment section.[20] These newspapers not only cover activities of the rivers network, but serve as its mouthpiece and even as part of the network, to the extent of publishing laudatory personal profiles of network leaders, which are then posted and sometimes translated into English on GEV's environmental media site and other comparable sites (He and Meng 2010, Zhao 2010). One article summarises the argument with its headline that 'Media has turned into NGOs' (Meng 2010).

The rivers network makes effective use of domestic media in framing its own messages and informal identity (Sun and Zhao 2008: 161). At the same time, media framing also distorts the rivers network's messages in certain ways. Media tends to focus on stories of exemplary individuals, rather than efficient networks or well-managed organisations. At times, these portrayals cross over to the sycophantic, such as likening network members to Superman 'saving the world' (He and Meng 2010). In addition to setting up false expectations, this coverage reinforces the distorting practice of referring to an organisation as belonging to a single leader, and under-represents the coordination that takes place among organisations and network members.

Some of the limitations of media framing can be overcome through the more direct medium of video. During the height of the Nu campaign in 2003–04, activists appeared on prominent national television programmes (Büsgen 2006: 31). One environmental filmmaker produced a 30-minute documentary, 'Voices of the Nu River' (怒江之声, *Nùjiāng zhī shēng*). A second film, 'Rivers, Our Home' (江河-我们的家, *Héjiāng – wǒmende jiā*) was released in 2010. As an advocacy tactic, video is more powerful than a report or article, as viewers see events as they happened, including village meetings along the Jinsha and arguments between pro-dam scientists and environmental advocates. According to the filmmaker, the main intended audience for 'Rivers, Our Home' is local residents in dam-affected areas, so they can see themselves and their neighbours in other river communities and learn about the threat of dams and forced migration. The use of video thus contributes to a community organising strategy in a way that reports never can. For this reason, it is also sensitive, since it could be seen as encouraging local protests (McGray and McDonald 2007: 103). In 2006, 'Voices of the Nu River' was scheduled to be shown at a film festival in Kunming but was cancelled at the last minute due to organisers' fear of repercussions. The screening was moved to a local bar. 'Rivers, Our Home' has not been shown publicly, but only in private screenings in Kunming and Beijing. The filmmaker believes that the 2004 film's circulation might have been partially responsible for authorities' crackdown in 2005–06.

Community advocacy

Network members affirm that increased links with dam-affected communities are desirable, both in principle and as a defence against attacks from dam proponents. The principled argument is that the network's ultimate objective 'isn't [resolving] the environmental problems...the main thing is to raise public awareness'. In a printed article, one activist argues,

> We have also been calling for public engagement on this issue, as we believe that building a dam in an area like this one requires considering the views of all the people who will be affected. But while we have been making these appeals, the surveying of the Nu River has continued apace, and people living along the Nu know little about our appeal or these preparations for dam construction. (Wang 2008)

In 2006, one CRN member stated that over time, the network's goals have 'shifted from biodiversity to people' (Büsgen 2006: 24). 'We focus not just on the destiny of rivers, but also the destiny of people living along the rivers', said a core member in 2009. 'Who is responsible for the migrants? How can we bring this under control, to provide electricity and also provide a livelihood to villagers?' In fact, connections to local communities have always been central to the network's identity (Economy 2005: 30), starting from trips by network members to the Nu area in 2003–04. The group most associated with local river communities has been Green Watershed, both due to its Kunming base and its leadership's willingness to take risks. In addition to taking Nu River villagers to see and meet dam migrants from Manwan, Green Watershed brought a Jinsha community leader and other residents to Beijing for a United Nations consultation on sustainable hydropower in October 2004 (Ge 2004, Büsgen 2006: 33). This was a dramatic statement, but it also led to repercussions from authorities.

The instrumental argument for involving communities, despite the risks, is that it is necessary for success in mobilising public opinion and affecting government policies. One CRN member states, 'We have looked for all sorts of solutions from the market, a legal system, and so on. But we concluded that we need the public to participate, or else there will be no solution.' Such community participation is limited, but it does exist and has been growing in significance. The fact that some local people stand up and speak out serves as an inspiration to others. At a public event in Beijing in August 2010, one CRN member noted, 'If we are just making intellectual arguments in books and reports, it's hard to win'. Another core member agrees: 'Ordinary people (老百姓 *lǎobǎixìng*) are closely connected to our end goal. They understand that this land is world cultural heritage. If they can speak up and participate, that dialogue is the key to success.'

Links to communities also refute opponents' claims that environmentalists are idealists who care only about preserving beautiful landscapes, not about people's desire for development.[21] 'People say we don't care about migrants. But I have been there eight times and done interviews with over 100 migrants!' Efforts to bring literacy and development projects to the Nu and Jinsha areas may be interpreted as symbolic statements of solidarity, in addition to the tangible benefits they bring. In the Jinsha–Tiger Leaping Gorge area, strong community leadership has resulted in well-informed villagers who are able to keep government officials at a distance (Ge 2004), while Nu villagers, according to one network member, are 'easily manipulated, they want to escape poverty and will believe what experts say'. Given these differing opportunities, network members link with communities on a case-by-case basis.

International linkages

CRN has received little international funding (Büsgen 2006: 23). Its independence from foreign donors may be interpreted as evidence of its organic, domestically-focused character, based on pooled social capital. A few donors, notably Conservation International, Global Greengrants and Oxfam, offered limited funds for advocacy activities channelled through GEV and Green Watershed. IRN did not have a direct role, in part due to reluctance on the part of CRN members to be seen as a 'branch office of IRN', which they viewed as too oppositional. In retrospect this might have been a missed opportunity from both sides. Major foundations and environmental organisations also did not speak out, even though they arguably faced less risk than local network members. 'Local NGOs need to lead', says one network member. 'International organisations play it too safe – they can't be leaders.' Other INGOs felt dam advocacy was too sensitive to support directly; instead, they provided 'technical support' by bringing Chinese activists outside the country for training, mainly to Thailand and the USA. This exposed the Chinese to regional and international civil society networks and empowered them to go back to China and increase their activism. In this way, 'the funding was less important than the contacts'. However, CRN members state that they attempted to raise funds from a number of other sources without success. Although information sharing and coordination could continue on a shoe-string budget, the lack of consistent core funding reduced CRN's effectiveness.

Most recently, CRN members have begun to look at the impact of Chinese dams in Southeast Asia and beyond. This is a natural development in the case of the Mekong and Salween rivers that originate in China and flow into neighbouring countries (Manahan 2010). Chinese companies are among those proposing new downstream dams on these rivers (Cronin 2009). Contact between Chinese and regional networks has existed since the Nu campaign, and has increased in recent years. Rivers network members are engaging in regional civil society efforts, such as the Save the Mekong campaign (Hirsch 2010). Green Watershed, with its Yunnan base, is particularly well connected with Thailand. International Rivers has quietly supported some activities and international conferences and adopted a collaborative approach to working in China (Bosshard 2010). Another INGO, Probe International, does not work within China but has translated and posted numerous documents on dam projects. Most coordination, however, takes place not with developed-country NGOs but via regional organisations and networks headquartered in Thailand.

Chinese activists have not historically linked to global anti-dam campaigns (Kaldor et al 2007: 130–3). Conversely, most international campaigns have also not considered Chinese examples or built ties to Chinese civil society. However, transnational links exist and are growing. Advocacy frames are changing to include more international messages, particularly concerning dams on the Lancang/Mekong that have significant downstream impacts. Regional links will likely increase in the future as Chinese networks become more experienced and confident to contribute to, as well as benefit from transnational organising.

Network effectiveness: Policy change

The rivers network's engagement in recent dam controversies shows how its advocacy has developed since the Nu campaign. One recent high-profile case concerns the Xiaonanhai dam, proposed to be built outside the rapidly growing city of Chongqing in a national protected area established as a compromise for lost habitat from the Three Gorges dam. In May 2009, after an internal meeting in Beijing, eight rivers network members sent a petition to the MEP expert committee with responsibility for national protected areas, appealing for them to over-rule the Chongqing authorities in the name of protecting endangered fish species: 'The negative impacts of overdevelopment of hydropower would destroy the river's diverse aquatic life.' As per usual practice, the letter made no mention of a network and was signed in the names of individual environmentalists and scientists. The petition was released to the domestic and international press and enjoyed wide coverage (Chan 2009, Hance 2009, Reuters 2009).

The Xiaonanhai advocacy campaign appeared to be achieving its objective. After the petition's release, MEP suspended the project, but Chongqing authorities persisted with plans to rezone the protected area. In November 2010, 18 months after the start of the campaign, MEP informed Friends of Nature that the rezoning had been approved (Han 2011). Seven network members wrote a joint letter to MEP asking for a public hearing on the issue, and FON followed with an open letter to the National People's Congress (Meng 2011). Some of the most strongly-worded opposition came from the Chinese project manager at the Nature Conservancy, upset that 'a terrible precedent' is being set for protected areas (Watts 2011). In spite of these efforts, construction of the Xiaonanhai dam is poised to proceed.

Controversy has also widened over eight proposed dams on the upper and middle Jinsha (see Map 6.1). At Ludila and Longkaikou, proposed by state-owned conglomerates Huadian (China Electric) and Huaneng (China Energy) respectively, preparatory construction work including dikes and water diversion tunnels, began in 2007 without a completed EIA (Yauch 2010). In June 2009, MEP rejected EIAs for the two dams (MEP 2009, Bezlova 2009) in what one journalist termed 'the severest punishment in the country's environmental appraisal history', yet corporations stated the ruling would have little impact (Li J 2009). MEP ordered additional studies on environmental impacts for other sections of the Jinsha, including Tiger Leaping Gorge (MEP 2009). Several days later, rivers network members issued a joint letter signed by 16 organisations and 20 individuals that called on MEP to suspend construction of all dams on the Jinsha (Probe 2009).

In August 2010, a network member told a sympathetic Beijing audience,

> From 2006 up to now, projects have been postponed, but that doesn't mean the problem is over. Local residents in the affected areas are still very concerned. There is a lot of pressure to start the dam projects. Hydropower is still a national priority, and demand is high. It's possible that one or more new projects will start next year. But I'm also hopeful that they will be restrained... We shouldn't assume that GDP growth will inevitably result in dam building. We need to consider the negative economic effects of pollution, and challenge the whole idea of GDP as the end goal.

In spite of years of effort, CRN has little advance notice or inside information of government plans, which are only publicised when an EIA is completed or resettlement plans are announced (Jiang 2009, Hensengerth 2010: 7). It is sometimes harder now for the network to get unofficial data than in the past, as one key MEP ally who worked on EIAs is no longer in office. Network members search the Internet for public announcements of government projects, sometimes finding information by chance, as when one member happened to see an announcement about the Ahai dam on the Jinsha, just 15 days before construction was scheduled to begin. Rivers network members commented publicly on the EIA but were unable to stop construction of the dam (Wang and Zhou 2010). The 2003 EIA law allows for expert consultation meetings and public hearings, but protocols for observing these are not yet established. Activists try to use the tools they have access to in the law, but it is not followed in all cases. In some cases, activists are able to access information in time to take action. In other cases, they learn of environmentally harmful dam projects only after the public comment period on the EIA has passed (Meng D 2009), or companies begin construction before an EIA is released, making the process 'a mere formality...nonsensical' (Wang and Zhou 2010). Though not successful in every case, network members are convinced that they collectively have played a role in improving the public participation and information around EIAs and large dams.

Network effectiveness: Sustainability

Since CRN ceased its formal structure, its name is no longer used publicly, and most written accounts hardly mention its existence. The network's anonymity does not bother members, some of whom view a low profile as strategically necessary, while others see it as positively desirable. Most would still, in theory, prefer a formal network, but view this as risky.

> We had two choices: we could register CRN legally, then we could have an office, raise funds and so on – but this wasn't possible at that time. The second choice was to keep a loose network, since a close network would have been considered illegal. Everyone agreed to cooperate on activities, write petition letters, and have informal meetings. When there is something to discuss, we all get together.

At a meeting in Hangzhou in July 2010, one member reportedly proposed re-establishing a more formal network structure. Others resisted the idea, feeling it is still too risky and would invite opposition. Their caution is understandable given the network's past experiences and an uncertain future: a formal structure might be politically possible now, but this could change next year. The political context has arguably relaxed since 2005, and CRN has more space to operate than it once did. But most network members still perceive that opportunities are limited.

Fundraising also remains an issue. One member agrees that network members have the capacity to raise funds if needed, but if not done strategically, this could 'defeat the purpose'. The network's lack of registration and formal structure limits funding possibilities. 'If we were to write a proposal, we would have to put someone's name on it who is accountable to donors. Donors won't fund an intangible group.' Another member prefers corporate donations to foundation grants, since the corporations let her do what she wants, while international donors put conditions on their funds and demand formal structures, so that members have to spend time raising money and managing staff.

CRN members have differing ideas about the benefits of an informal network. Some argue that informal networks are a necessary second-best solution because of political limitations, while others favour informality for other reasons. The first argument runs as follows:

> The concept of a looser network prevailed because we had no way to register. If we did sensitive work without registering, it could

bring all the organisations involved into serious trouble... Most organisations and individuals would prefer a formal network if the registration issue could be solved.

The second argument is that 'we prefer to work together closely, but not set up a formal network. We could do this if we wanted, it wouldn't be difficult.' There are, of course, other options: a more formalised, but still unregistered, network; or a strong coordinating organisation that manages the network as a 'project'. So far, however, these possibilities have not attracted strong support. The issue of coordination is one obstacle, as no one is stepping forward as a formal coordinator, and members differ on who would be most effective. Location also plays a role: most members are based in Beijing, where organisations have more opportunities for funding and connections with the government. Beijing members feel coordination should take place there, even though the rivers themselves and several capable organisations are in southwest China. Broadly speaking, CRN has worked with central government allies against provincial government opponents, so it makes more sense to locate near allies where there is more political space.

Political and regulatory restrictions thus remain the major obstacles to an expanded or more formalised network structure (Yang and Calhoun 2008: 84, McGray and McDonald 2007: 46). Capacity and funding are secondary barriers that could be overcome. If network members did re-establish a formal mechanism, however, the political limits would still be there, and might become more intense. If, conversely, the political environment were to relax, it would then be easier to deal with resource issues. Such shifts have occurred before; the space that may be there now could also contract in the future. To be sure, no one knows the exact limits of what might provoke a response from the 'anaconda in the chandelier', as Link (2002) evocatively describes the Chinese security apparatus. Given that some rivers network members are well connected with Chinese authorities, their readings of the tea leaves may be assumed to be accurate, or at least closer than the speculations of foreign researchers.

A mature network, CRN has been able to frame itself as a successful example of advocacy, a perception to which outside researchers have also contributed. As newer networks emerge in China, however, the future and ongoing relevance of CRN is seen by some to be unclear. With its informal structure, the network has no public, coherent strategy, regular meetings, or clearly defined membership. Many of the potential projects outlined years ago have yet to be realised; CRN appears to be reactive, initiating advocacy on dam disputes only when there is an urgent need.

A younger activist who does not participate in the rivers network says,

> Earlier this year [2010] I attended a dinner for environmental activists organised by *Nanfang Zhoumo* [newspaper]…older [rivers network] members were there. As soon as the dinner started, they said, 'Let's go over here and talk about our project', and then they completely ignored the rest of us. They're an exclusive group. If the older generation doesn't want to include me, I'll do my own work. There are lots of things to do, it's not necessary to join their projects!

This anecdote reflects generational differences in the environmental sector, and illustrates limitations of a small, close network based on personal ties. The story also demonstrates something that the younger activist did not realise: the network members must not have met face-to-face for some time, and they needed to use the newspaper's dinner as an opportunity to talk.

Rivers network members are clear that they never intended to become a large, public group; they had an elite structure from the beginning.

> It's easier if we have fewer people involved. With many members, including a lot of new younger NGOs, there would be a lot of different agendas in the network, and this would be ineffective for making consensual decisions. Besides, some information is sensitive and we need to be careful with it. It's better for us to reach out to different groups depending on the issue.

This member expresses concern that with more public exposure, river activism could get 'out of control', with competing NGOs, copycat groups, and too much political attention. In short, the issue could become the basis for a broader social movement. Activists in many countries might be delighted with this prospect, but the older generation remembers that Chinese experiences with such movements have not turned out well.

As environmental protection and transparency have become priorities of the Chinese state, activists can frame advocacy to align with central government policies (Lo 2007, Mertha 2008: 18–23). The more moderate the frame, the more people the network can bring in as co-signatories or supporters. Conversely, if network leaders get too far ahead of their constituencies, this could lead to dissension within their ranks: as one core member describes, 'we involve influential [supporters] on a case-by-case basis, but do not want to demand their involvement on issues that are sensitive'. Friends of Nature is the only network member with a large membership base of its own, but it does not yet have any members' groups in Chongqing, Sichuan or Yunnan. Even if they had, FON is hesitant to ask them to take action on dam issues due to possible local repercussions.

Thus, the hypothesised shift towards community advocacy has not yet taken place in the case of the China rivers network; if anything, community connections were stronger in the early years of the network before strong opposition arose from local governments. The relative role of media and online advocacy has increased somewhat in recent years, as these sectors continue to develop, while embedded advocacy has taken a slightly less prominent position, in part because several key government allies have stepped down.

Network effectiveness: Political space

CRN's initial accomplishments in blocking Nu River dams expanded political space for environmental activism, but due in part to opponents' reactions, did not become the breakthrough for civil society that some hoped. The political opportunity structure surrounding river activism is 'restrictive and conducive at the same time' (Ho 2008a: 3), with elements of openness as well as state control. Pressure from authorities was not the only reason for CRN's formal dissolution in 2006; registration, funding and capacity questions also played a role. Yet if political opportunities had been different, these other issues could have been solved: 'maybe if [CRN] had existed longer and developed, it would have opened up later'.

The backlash of 2005–06, as unwelcome as it was for CRN, is significant in a number of ways. It serves as a reminder that civil society development is not a linear progression or a game theory matrix with clear winners and losers. Whether a victory or a crackdown, a single event is rarely the end of the story, as political contention extends across episodes and cycles (Tarrow 1998: 141, McAdam et al 2001). Not only can activists not win every time, there are also costs to winning, one of which is retribution from opponents who may have lost a policy decision but remain strongly connected to sources of power. Reprisals illustrate the pendulum of the Chinese (and Vietnamese) political system, alternating between repression and opening (Shieh 2010). While certain aspects of network formation and strategising are potentially significant in all political contexts, there also remain particular features of the Chinese political opportunity structure that cannot be generalised.

The China rivers network has consciously chosen network structures, advocacy strategies, and message frames to express their criticism of certain hydropower projects without opposing the Chinese government as such. At times, some network members have used provocative language to express what they see as the potentially catastrophic damage of dam projects. At no point have they aimed to change the overall political system. There is little evidence of 'self-imposed censorship' (Ho 2008a: 8) in the network's activities. Nor do activists limit their concerns to 'politically safe and innocuous issues' (Yang 2010: 101). Instead, they see conservation and participation as linked. The network aims to protect rivers and ecosystems, stop or limit effects of dams, and support sustainable development for people in affected areas. Network members speak openly and passionately about these goals, which are broadly consistent with the government's own stated policy for environmental protection. The network seeks 'fundamental, not radical' political change (Büsgen 2006: 27) within the existing Chinese regime.

For these reasons, it is misleading and possibly damaging to characterise rivers network members as 'water warriors', in the unfortunate title of Mertha's otherwise valuable 2008 book.[22] Mertha uses particularly strong language to describe Green Watershed, which he situates '[o]n the extreme end of the spectrum of viable Chinese NGOs' (62), using 'unprecedented' methods and 'guerrilla tactics' (144, 113). At times, this seems an appropriate characterisation, as Green Watershed's community advocacy activities in 2004–05 were indeed groundbreaking and viewed as sensitive by government officials (Lu 2005: 3). In another respect, however, Green Watershed is a 'typical advocacy group' (Fu 2007: 294) whose strategy and activities lie fully within the mainstream.[23]

CRN members have applied learning from rivers advocacy in the formation and operation of new networks on earthquake relief and climate change, primarily for information sharing but with some engagement in advocacy. Compared to the rivers network, the Climate Change Action Network has greater political opportunity and access to resources. International NGOs emphasise responses to climate change more than dam issues, in part because they favour constructive approaches to the Chinese government, but also because even activist INGOs have set international strategies that local staff cannot easily affect.

Political barriers to community advocacy persist in rural areas affected by dams. The deputy director of public relations in one Sichuan district along the Jinsha River told reporters in July 2010, 'Resettlement work has strong political nature, is extremely policy-guided and very sensitive. Since the Hanyuan incident in October 2004, the provincial government has strict regulations on the coverage of resettlement for hydropower projects' (Xu 2010). In Hanyuan county, Sichuan, 20,000 villagers protested the low resettlement compensation they were offered for the construction of the Pubugou dam in western Sichuan. The protests led to delay of construction for a year and the dismissal of key local government officials (Cai 2008: 170–1; Mertha 2008: 65–93). While Chinese writers view the protests as successful, Mertha notes that 'there was next to no impact on policy' (66), and that by shifting the frame from dam construction to political protest, the villagers lost the chance to attract support of environmental and media allies, including members of the rivers network.

> In general, NGOs played a very limited role. Individual NGO officers acted as intermediaries communicating what was unfolding on the ground to Chinese media outlets. Several of these individuals made visits to Hanyuan wearing their journalist hats in the summer of 2004. However, like the rest of the media, once events in Hanyuan became overtly political, these NGO representatives recognised their limited ability to influence them. The political 'spaces' disappeared, replaced by the overwhelming imperative to maintain social stability. (Mertha 2008: 89)

Mertha concludes that political considerations keep 'policy entrepreneurs' such as rivers network members from community mobilisation, since this could be interpreted as a threat to authorities (93), and feels that local protests are insufficient to achieve policy change (115). Yet disputes over dam construction continue to occur, and will likely escalate as more dams are built (Buckley 2009). On 2 June 2010, people displaced by construction of the Xiangjiaba dam on the Jinsha River protested at the dam builders' project office; dozens were injured in a resulting clash with police (Xu 2010). The rivers network is not able or willing to take part in such protests. The network's existing 'elite hierarchy' (Ho 2008b: 34) of environmentalists and journalists has enabled effective advocacy in many ways, but it may be less of an advantage using these newer methods; in particular, it is difficult to represent community interests through an informal network structure. Chongqing Green Volunteers Union has pioneered the use of lawsuits to block or delay dam construction, and other rivers network members are currently considering similar strategies in different cases.

Realising that community-level work is often most effective when linked to service delivery, Green Watershed and Green Earth Volunteers have begun charitable and poverty alleviation projects in Jinsha and Nu River communities; some of these ideas were envisioned by CRN from the beginning. While the content of the projects is traditional, such as livelihood support and construction of local libraries, the purpose is linked to community advocacy, building connections with villagers and encouraging them to speak and act about environmental issues. Network members have also distributed printed materials, copies of videos, and information about relevant Chinese laws.

Some analysts claim that the rivers network's advocacy has promoted 'democracy' (Xu 2009) or 'pluralism' (Mertha 2008: xv). At first glance, this seems exaggerated. However, if democracy is interpreted not as a regime type, but as increased popular participation within the current political system, then the claims make more sense. The rivers network members have certainly asserted their own right to participate in the policy-making process. Even so, the question should be raised of how much broader societal participation this has promoted. As a result of media exposure, sections of the general public are more aware of environmental issues, and dams in particular, than they were before the rivers network formed. Communities in dam-affected areas are also better informed, and in some cases more actively involved, although there are still limits on their participation.

Conclusion

Nearly a decade after the formation of the China Rivers Network, both the network's future and the Chinese government's dam construction plans remain in limbo. On the Nu River, SEPA approved an EIA for a reduced plan for four dams, which are listed in the 2010–14 Five Year Plan. Dam companies are able to start 'preparatory work' on this basis, including construction of access roads, buildings and electric lines (Jiang 2009). 1,000 people were relocated from proposed dam areas during 2006–08; their housing and health have worsened, and the compensation they received is not enough to build new houses. The national government continues to put a hold on construction, most recently restated by Wen Jiabao in May 2009 (Shi 2009, Bezlova 2009). Network members continue to campaign for protection of the Nu, as well as conduct research and study trips, but community organising is not possible due to opposition from the local government. The situation on the Jinsha and other rivers is broadly similar.

In a 2006 article, Stalley and Yang argue that Chinese environmentalism 'lacks sustained contention' since 'there is no network of organisations or individuals who are a persistent source of external pressure on environmental policy', and 'scattered protests and campaigns' fail to add up to a broader movement (336–7). Yet the experience of the China rivers network suggests otherwise. In spite of political obstacles and limitations on capacity and funding, the network has sustained its advocacy over an extended period and contributed to incremental political change towards more open decision-making processes on dam construction, a core concern of China's environmental movement and civil society.

7
Conclusion: Civil Society Networks and Political Change

The four health and environmental networks presented in this book share numerous common features. Despite their differences in issue focus, history and geographic locations, the case studies may be assembled into a composite story of how civil society networks form and operate, using a method called analytic induction (Becker 1998: 194–212). This narrative demonstrates the possibilities of a network-based approach to civil society that is distinct from the standard three-sector division as well as from theories of partial or state-led civil society. If networks can comprise civil society in the perhaps unexpected settings of China and Vietnam, then a focus on networks might also be productive in other contexts.[1]

The story of civil society networks begins with personal connections among a group of individual activists. These 'pre-existing social networks nurture critical thinking and incubate resistance' (O'Brien and Stern 2008: 17). Personal or virtual ties transform into civil society networks in response to the combination of perceived need and political opportunities. For instance, both the Bright Future Group and Chinese activists against the Three Gorges Dam mobilised around common grievances, but their initial attempts at advocacy were blocked by authorities. When the political field later shifted, networks emerged and began to participate in politics. Other mobilising resources, such as funding, organisational structures, and identified leaders, can be helpful but are not necessary or sufficient for network formation: of the four case studies, only the Women's Network against AIDS had access to these resources at the time it began. External funding can support an existing network to operate and grow, but cannot create a new network as a development project (Desmond et al 2007: 17).

Contrary to Keck and Sikkink's findings (1998: 9), networks do not depend primarily on international or domestic NGOs but are largely comprised of dynamic, often inspiring individual members who are consciously at the forefront of organising around their issues. Civil society networks stress human values of trust, solidarity, creativity and emotion in counterpoint to dominant discourses of economic growth and scientific progress. However, the processes of network formation, structuring and advocacy are not smooth or easy, and should not be romanticised. Every aspect of these networks is contested through multiple, overlapping relationships with central and local authorities over registration, legitimacy and policy directions; with state and private corporations who are objects of advocacy, but also counter-actors with their own strategies; with donors and international organisations who are often supportive allies, but sometimes with strings attached; and finally within networks themselves, in debates over identity, goals and tactics. Many individual activists are connected to both organisations and networks, often multiple networks, and wear multiple hats linked to state agencies and media. Thus, there is no clear separation between state and non-state actors. Of the profiled networks, only WNAC could be described as autonomous from the state, yet due to its close ties to a single donor, it is in other respects the least autonomous of the four. Autonomy is not a crucial or even relevant indicator of a network's effectiveness. Instead, networks negotiate complex relationships and structural challenges to create opportunities for pathbreaking social change.

Within this overall narrative, each of the four network case studies follows a distinct trajectory, summarised in Table 7.1. The evidence does not show any fundamental differences between Chinese and Vietnamese contexts. With their focus on group identity and equal participation, the disability and HIV networks presented in Chapters 3–4 are more similar to each other than either resembles the other case study from the same country. The same is true for the public space and environment networks in Chapters 5–6, which share a common mission of increasing public participation in planning and decision-making.

Chapter 2 presented six hypotheses concerning network structure, advocacy and effectiveness. Some, but not all of these postulates are confirmed by case study findings.

The **denser ties hypothesis,** that networks with closer cooperative ties will be more effective, is supported by the observation that the networks that have existed for a longer period (Bright Future and CRN) have had greater impact overall in the senses of effectiveness as network sustainability and political space. Networks with a capital city base, some level of independent resources, and links to authorities and elites

Table 7.1 Comparison of network case studies

Network	History	Structure	Advocacy strategies	International links	Effectiveness
Bright Future Group	Long-standing club of individual activists took on more public role as opportunities emerged	Concentric circles with elected exec committee. Decisions through discussion and consensus.	Primarily embedded advocacy with govt allies, though some members reaching out to community	None at first; important for legitimacy and advocacy in 1990s; multiple small project funding since	High level of policy impact, though gaps between law and practice. A model for other disability groups.
Women's Network against AIDS	Newest of the networks. Began virtually, then developed formal structure with peer support groups as members	Hub-and-spokes structure with paid staff in secretariat. Provincial clusters emerging	Creative use of media and arts aiming at changing public perceptions of HIV-affected women. Few links to govt	Few initially; reliance on single donor in formalisation of network	Little policy impact yet. Potentially a strong model for other networks, but sustainability is uncertain.
Reunification Park public space network	Coalesced from personal ties in response to an external threat	Informal structure with de facto core group. Strong media involvement	Inside-outside strategy combining embedded and media approaches	One INGO and several indiv. play effective facilitating roles	Effective at stopping large park privatisation projects. Unclear sustainability or broader impact
China Rivers Network	Personal network became formal network in 2004–05, then reverted to informal status	Concentric circles. Informal alliance of NGO leaders and journalists.	Inside-outside, some use of all 3 strategies	Some members are internationally funded and connected to regional networks	Postponed numerous dam projects. Strong demonstration value, diffusion to other networks

have had greater impact on policy. In China, there has been noticeably greater cooperation to date among environmental groups than in the HIV sector, perhaps because environmentalists are united by a common external mission rather than identity-based politics. The Women's Network against AIDS is too new a network to reach definitive conclusions on effectiveness, but given further time to develop, its social capital may also increase. Further exploration of this hypothesis should also consider examples of rural networks with fewer links to elites but potentially other forms of social capital.

However, the **size and structure hypothesis** that larger networks with more formal structures will be more effective, is not supported by the evidence.[2] Size does not appear to be a relevant factor for effectiveness in any of the three senses. Contrary to expectations, formal networks (WNAC and CRN prior to 2006) do not demonstrate greater effectiveness than informal structures; in fact, many members prefer informality, as the experiences of CRN and Reunification Park reveal. The structure networks adopt is determined by the political and resource contexts they face, together with members' capacities for leadership. Where political obstacles exist, respondents argued that it is better to form multiple small networks focused on practical goals, rather than a single large structure. This confirms Melucci's counter-intuitive finding that new social movements 'seem to mutate towards informality' (1996: 331).

The **change over time hypothesis** posits that the advocacy strategies of embeddedness, media and community participation comprise a cumulative, chronological process. This hypothesis is partly supported in that the three longer-existing networks have gradually moved away from a reliance on embedded tactics alone to combined inside-outside strategies. However, the hypothesised shift towards community advocacy has not yet occurred, largely because of political constraints on NGO-community links from both Chinese and Vietnamese authorities. Informal network structures offer one possible way around this restriction, and community-based strategies may increase in the future if opportunity structures shift.

The **elite allies hypothesis** states that networks select strategies based on the presence of allies at different locations within the elite. All four networks have identified and sought out elite allies, including government officials, academic experts, and prominent journalists. The CRN and Reunification Park strategies are the most similar in that both networks seek to leverage allies to prevent their opponents, private or state-owned corporations, from implementing development projects that network members view as harmful. BFG has mainly aimed to influence the attitudes and actions of central government allies. For the Chinese women's network, donor relations have so far been more important than domestic alliances, suggesting that this hypothesis might vary among different types of networks.

The **multiple advocacy strategies hypothesis** is well supported by the case studies. **Diverse membership** also applies to all cases but comes through especially strongly in the two Vietnamese cases. By comparison, CRN could probably benefit from more diverse membership, but has chosen instead to remain small and informal, while WNAC's membership is diverse geographically while emphasising solidarity around a common positive identity.

These findings are significant for the internal operations of networks, for donors and other supporters, and more broadly for theory on civil society, social movements and networks. This concluding chapter considers implications of these findings relating to network formation and leadership, selection of network structures, resources, and multiple aspects of effectiveness, and finally on the potential significance of network activism on political change in China and Vietnam.

Network formation and leadership

Civil society networks form for a combination of external reasons, such as advocacy opportunities or grievances, and internal identities. The motivations for individuals to join existing networks are similarly mixed. In the view of one Chinese activist, these include psychological reasons to belong to a group, perceived access to funding or power, and protection from opponents through strength in numbers. An Asia Foundation study in Vietnam (2008: 37) concludes that networking increases public perceptions of organisational cohesiveness, facilitates fundraising and access to resources, creates alliances for advocacy, and builds capacity through training and information sharing. A member of a Vietnamese child rights network emphasises external opportunities: 'In order to have a voice with government, we needed to form a network... If we do this, we can unify our voices and speak out on questions of orphans, domestic violence and education.' The coordinator of an HIV network in China, by contrast, stresses benefits to members. 'We aren't creating a network just for the purpose of creating a network, but in order to do things to help people. It's not just about getting money...it needs to be based on real needs and conditions of its members.' Successful networks must do both: without support to members, networks may disintegrate, while too much internal focus could weaken the civil society focus of the network, reverting to a personal network for members' private benefit only.

Some individuals and groups do not join networks, preferring to work alone or limit cooperation to loose structures for exchange and information sharing. In an uncertain political environment, some fear that joining a network will lead to reprisals. Not knowing which other people or organisations can be trusted not to get in political trouble, they keep their distance to avoid being labelled by association. These attitudes seem particularly strong in locations with less perceived political space and among religious groups. Other NGOs see networks as a waste of effort compared to service delivery: 'it seems that networks make people crazy and use up resources and energy', says one Chinese activist. Another NGO staff asserts, 'What is the result of all this advocacy? Leaders of these NGOs are very famous, but the people don't get services they need. We do more and talk less.'

Setting a balance between advocacy and capacity building depends on effective leadership. Case study findings confirm that a single individual leader is rarely sufficient to develop a network; this is a weakness of a paid coordinator structure. Networks develop more strongly if they have at least two or three key drivers with ideas and commitment. This reduces the risk of a cult of personality forming around a leader who uses the network as a basis for individual ambition; such leaders eventually retire or move on, taking the network with them. Reliance on a single charismatic, authoritarian individual is seen by some respondents as a cultural characteristic (see also Ma 2006: 129), but network experiences show this need not be the case. 'For people to cooperate, we need to be clear on sharing benefits and success. If one group stands up and takes credit, it's hard to work with them.' Duplication of roles within a network may appear inefficient, but actually serve as a resource to counteract defections and repression, keeping a network intact through troughs in waves of collective action.

The case studies presented also demonstrate the emergence of subgroup agendas, often linked to generational change and conflict. Both Chinese and Vietnamese activists note differences between the older generation who lived through the American War and Cultural Revolution, and those who grew up since. An activist in her 20s explicitly draws this connection:

The main factor for network success is leadership. Are the leaders really open? Are they representing members' interests, or on their own agenda or power trip? Leaders need to be capable to lead and represent their members, while staying open and flexible... In China, this is a generational issue. Older adults tend to be inflexible and want to hold on to power. If we want change, we need to get younger people involved.

The counter-argument to shared leadership is that strong leaders may be necessary, especially at the early stages of a network, to motivate and bring people together. Networks that operate on an all-volunteer basis, without full-time staff, never become professional. Paid network staff or a secretariat is seen as desirable for financial management and accountability. Yet networks with paid staff risk dependency on donor support. Most donors lack the capacity to evaluate or fund a whole network; instead, they want a 'one-stop shop', working through an individual leader who can reach the membership.[3] 'A good donor will choose the right person to fund', says a Chinese activist. 'If the wrong group gets the funding, it will all fall apart.' In sum, there are risks to both too much leadership and too little. The most effective networks are led by a small, committed and diverse core group of individuals who may be employed with member organisations, or have multiple affiliations, but are not paid directly as network staff. A second prevalent model, seen in the cases of WNAC and many of the networks profiled in Table 2.3, consists of a single coordinating agency or secretariat with paid staff. The experience of the China rivers network is revealing in this regard, as it experimented with the coordinating agency model, then chose to return to a more informal core group. Leadership choices also have implications for network structures.

Formal and informal structures

Respondents' preference for informal over formal network structures is an unexpected finding of this research. This was affected, to be sure, by the choice of issue-based, advocacy and membership networks as case studies rather than NGO coalitions and forums, but arguments for informality emerged from many sources. Networks with formal organisational structures have not been noticeably more successful at advocacy. Nor do states prefer to deal with more formal networks. Both the Bright Future Group and China Rivers Network experimented with formal structures earlier in their existence; CRN gave up for both political and organisational reasons, while BFG successfully spun off a formal association. For the Women's Network against AIDS, it is too early to tell whether a formal structure can be sustained, or whether it might return to its original virtual network form. In all these cases, personal ties among network members and long-term commitment to issues have mattered more than organisational structures or funding.

One variant of this argument is that formal networks may be desirable in some circumstances, but in settings with limited political opportunity structures, informal or virtual organising is the only viable option.[4] In this view, political context determines network structure. Formal networks are limited directly by the lack of a legal framework for networks to register and indirectly by restrictions on potential network members in terms of fundraising, geographical operations, and issue sensitivity. Establishment of a formal network requires funding and staff or volunteer capacity, which potential individual or organisational members may not be able to provide. These conditions apply in China and Vietnam, as well as other settings where states, conflict, or economic deprivation hinder development of formal organisational structures. As one Hong Kong-based activist describes,

> We try to stay low profile and network informally. There are more formal networks based in Beijing, but these are more likely to be donor-driven or co-opted by the government. Formal networks aren't worth the effort, and they tend to get dominated by the same people.

A stronger, universal argument for informal networks is that they are more effective vehicles for advocacy (while formal structures may still be better for information sharing or other purposes). In this view, networks are not second-best arrangements in restrictive environments, but virtual communities or 'soft organisations', compared to less flexible 'hard organisations' such as NGOs.[5] Both Chinese and Vietnamese activists argue that the most successful networks are informal, independent and set up on their own. For instance, several respondents suggested creating a new website and internet forum for social networking around public space issues in Vietnam, as this is not costly, can be managed by just a few people, and can reach many people with little political risk. The availability of the Internet and communication technologies create different structural incentives for advocacy than in previous generations. In a cultural version of this argument, the importance of personal connections and *guanxi* in China and Vietnam also favour informal networks, but this does not explain why civil society networks have formed at some times rather than others. At most, perhaps, cultural preferences compensate for the real, though not particularly effective attempts by governments to restrict online organising.

One Vietnamese activist combines both arguments in a practice of 'organisational non-ego', both a philosophy of activism and a response to political uncertainty:

> The issue needs to come first. Everything we do, we do in service of the issue. The organisation follows: it is a vehicle for the issue. If the organisation is shut down, the movement continues. If the growth of the organisation is your main goal, then you won't get where you want to go; you will get somewhere else instead… Big organisations or organisations that take controversial stands may attract notice from powerful people who will try to shut it down. Whereas [with] a network or a web, if one member closes, the network is still strong.[6] Also, smaller organisations are more sustainable and easier for fund-raising. Instead of one big organisation with a lot of pressure to raise funds to stay big, this is spread out among many organisations who can sustain themselves in different ways. I don't want a united civil society that replaces government. I want diversity, not hier-archy. But we can still take advantage of economies of scale by joining together and acting as a network.

A Chinese respondent states, similarly, that the emergence of civil society networks is 'more than a strategic response to difficult political con-ditions'. There is also a cultural component of building trust and sharing resources that has traditional roots in both China and Vietnam, yet runs counter to much of the aggressive materialism in present-day societies.

In the informal structure of the China rivers network since 2006, several organisations specialise on each issue; when needed, they organise campaigns with the support of other network members. Core individual participants are 'sleepers' between campaigns and can act as leaders in some areas, followers in others. This structure allows for waves of col-lective action without having to maintain formal network structures. Complete internal democracy, with rotating leadership, may not always be possible, but a network with multiple centres is more balanced and is not dominated by a single leader. The four case studies also suggest poss-ible steps that networks could take towards greater levels of activity while remaining informally structured: more regular meetings (even social events), clearer communication pathways, proactive rather than reactive plan-ning, and development of concrete advocacy strategies with position papers, clear objectives and indicators of success. These changes do not require large amounts of funding or time commitments and are within the present capacities of members. Indeed, several networks are currently making efforts or discussing such moves towards increased substantive cooperation, not just information sharing. As networks become larger, bureaucratic structures and a more focused agenda become necessary. 'The more members we have, the more complicated it becomes', says one Vietnamese network coordinator. 'But since we want to raise awareness of the whole society, if we only worked with NGOs that would be too narrow.'

The majority of CRN members favour the context-specific argument for informality, stating that a formal network could not succeed because it could not be legally registered and would become a target for criticism and retaliation by opponents. This seemed to be the case in 2005, but may no longer hold. In the past several years, formal networks have emerged in China and Vietnam that have found ways around legal and political restrictions, for instance by operating the network as a project of a coordinating organisation.[7] The selection of structure may vary depending on the perceived sensitivity of a network's activities, as well as on the preferences and desires of its members.

In informal networks, the question of membership is often unclear even to others in the network. According to Knoke and Kuklinski's 'realist criterion' (1982: 22), a network member is someone who self-identifies as such. This criterion fits with an actor-centred approach, but may be too narrow for networks such as CRN, which comprises not only a small group of NGOs but also journalists, scientists, and even certain central government officials who have joined in advocacy, whether these individuals identify themselves as CRN members or not. Just as there is no firm boundary between state and non-state actors in civil society networks, it is best to assume no strong distinction between a core group of committed individual or organisational members and a wider associated group of supporters who are linked to core members and join certain, but not all, network activities. In such cases, it may make more sense to speak of network participants rather than members.

Resources and donor roles

Resources in the forms of funding and time are needed to grow and sustain any network, increasing with size and level of formality. Case study findings show that networks with greater internal resources (members or individual donors) have more options for strategic and structural choices, as shown in the social capital of CRN compared to the Women's Network against AIDS. International presence and support, with or without funding, can help open political opportunities, as with the Bright Future Group in the 1990s, and allow for a high level of autonomy, if networks do not have to worry about core funding. External donors can also bring risks of political blowback, as some CRN members experienced in 2005, as well as donor interference in the network's operations. Large-scale funding opportunities, as in the HIV sector, can lead to conflict over resources, while ironically networks in under-funded sectors may have more incentive to cooperate.[8] Whether donor support is helpful or harmful depends on the case and the donor's willingness 'to share respectfully, not to lead'. A Chinese activist adds, 'So many networks are kept alive artificially by carrots. People only participate in order to get funds, or they do "capacity building" to satisfy donors' needs for reports and proposals'. If all funds are provided externally, then members do not see a need to contribute by bringing their own resources: networks need to be demand-driven, not external resource-driven.

Availability of external funds may also lead to bureaucratisation, as leaders seek to build formal organisations rather than escalate advocacy (Piven and Cloward 1977: xxii). This recalls Eccleston's (1996: 67) findings that north-south collaboration can increase advocacy effectiveness of southern partners, but can also lead to internal management problems and adverse government reactions. As one Vietnamese network coordinator states,

> There are groups of people living with HIV in different districts of Hanoi. They may be operating well on their own, but there is no broader movement. Then a donor comes in and gives grants to one or more groups. This may lead to conflict. Even if not, if there is a policy issue, each group will be busy with their own project and they won't be able to work together.

The main advocacy focus of the civil society networks considered in this book is domestic government authorities at the national or local level. Some network members have international connections, and a few networks include foreign participants resident in their countries, but the level of transnational campaigning remains low. This is in part a result of language barriers; few Chinese and Vietnamese activists can speak a common language. It also reflects political reality in several ways. First, and probably most importantly, networks are focused on the immensity of social and political issues in their own countries and communities, not on international issues or on their country's behaviour overseas (although there is some sign this is starting to change in China around issues of climate change and corporate responsibility).

Second, there is potential political risk in being closely identified with foreign networks and civil society. Most NGOs and networks wish to cooperate with government where possible and seek to protect their existing connections. In a reversal of Keck and Sikkink's (1998) 'boomerang model', in which civil society activists leverage external allies against their national governments, international connections can easily boomerang back on the activists themselves if the state uses perceived external interference as an excuse to crack down on domestic civil society, as occurred to some CRN members in 2005 as well as members of HIV and dissident networks referenced in Chapter 2.

Civil society networks that are able to draw on internal resources and diverse sources of external funding both avoid dependence on a single donor and reduce risk from state-imposed restrictions on access to international funds, which tightened in 2010 in both China and Vietnam. In China, the growth of domestic corporate foundations offers a potential opportunity for local network fundraising, although most foundations prefer social enterprise and direct service projects and are new to the idea of advocacy. Such foundations are not yet common in Vietnam, but may be expected to become more important in the coming years.

Donor support of networks appears more effective when funds are channelled to existing networks rather than creating new ones.[9] Evidence shows that donor-initiated networks restrict members' independence and may cause more problems than they solve. In the words of a foundation officer, 'A network is about individuals. It's not a project or funding. A donor can't solve it…the problems of consolidation and maturity have to be solved internally.' A Chinese HIV activist says, 'most infighting takes place because of the intervention of outsiders, not from the community themselves. But the community always gets blamed for it'. If no network exists on a particular issue, a supportive donor could encourage informal and personal networking among existing actors from all sectors (including NGOs, informal groups, academic researchers, and media, among others), focusing first on trust-building and learning (Nooteboom 2006). Donors should not expect network members to engage in advocacy immediately, but rather give small grants to meet immediate needs and allow networks time to develop strategies. Rather than one-off advocacy training workshops, networks benefit more from small-scale, ongoing coaching, for instance on developing communications and media strategies, the 'least normative and interfering option' (Wexler et al 2006: 39) for donor support. In the longer term, no amount of funding will be sufficient to maintain network members' motivation to continue in uncertain and risky advocacy activities. Many effective networks, says the HIV activist, 'never have [external] funding, but still do impactful work. These are the groups that keep the movement going.'

Effectiveness

Networks may demonstrate effectiveness in three aspects: policy change, network sustainability, and/or changes in political space. The first and most direct measure of success is influencing policy and achieving the advocacy objectives of the network ('winning').[10] Evaluating advocacy results is notoriously difficult, since it can be nearly impossible to measure exactly what the network has contributed compared to state responses or other actors (Wilson-Grau and Nuñez 2006: 2).[11] In most cases, if the objective is achieved the network can claim to have influenced it in some way even if they are not solely responsible. Piven and Cloward (1977: xix, 32) define success as concessions from the state or other opponent, but note that such victories are rarely total and often come at a price.

A second type of effectiveness is longer-term and internal: does the network persist and develop organisationally, and is it useful to its members? This may be measured in terms of membership growth, geographic coverage, longevity, steps towards formalisation, or more stable funding.[12] Although both winning and network sustainability are considered as measures of effectiveness, they are to some degree inversely related (Covey 1995: 175). Quick success may sometimes lead a network to disband, as might complete failure. Rapid growth of membership could lead to a lack of focus and the eventual loss of civil society functions; however, too little focus on organisational sustainability could lead to disintegration.

A third way to conceptualise effectiveness assesses the impact of advocacy on the operating environment and political opportunity structures. A network could conceivably fail to achieve many of its policy objectives and leave no ongoing structure behind, yet have a positive demonstration effect for succeeding waves of collective action (Swarts 2003: 79). Action can have unpredictable results, sometimes expanding political opportunities for civil society, but also potentially increasing the influence of opponents (Tarrow 1996: 58–60). A successful network in either of the first two senses could provoke state responses that reduce opportunities for subsequent advocacy. More often, effects are mixed: state responses may contract opportunities for certain groups in the short term, while examples of successful policy advocacy and organising nevertheless create possibilities for future movements (Piven and Cloward

1977: xiii). In these cases, the greatest legacy of networks lies not in specific achievements but in the 'growing repertoire of tactics and strategies from which future campaigners may select' (Mattausch 2000: 195). Especially in authoritarian contexts, activists often need to 'look beyond quick policy and procedural victories and eschew simple notions of success and failure' (O'Brien and Li 2006: 96). Systemic outcomes on political space are the hardest to predict, as they depend most heavily on external factors; however, all three types of effectiveness come about through the interplay of internal network capacities and external opportunities and constraints.[13] When networks succeed, they can 'break the cycles of history' (Keck and Sikkink 1998: x), but there is no certain measure of success in complex, contingent environments.

Each of the network case studies has demonstrated its effectiveness in one or more of these aspects and shown changes over time: the Bright Future Group did not have many policy results to show in its first decade, but much more since, while the Women's Network against AIDS is too new to be assessed fully (Table 7.1). The longer-existing networks (BFG and CRN) have contributed more in terms of changes in policy formation and implementation, with the Vietnamese Disability Law and the Chinese Environmental Impact Assessment Law as prime examples. The Hanoi public space network has affected implementation (or prevented mis-implementation) of laws and regulations, but not yet affected policy formulation. WNAC, similarly, has been able to improve implementation of HIV policies in a few instances to be more inclusive of women's concerns.

Considering sustainability, BFG has maintained itself as a core of activists for over 20 years; though it has not grown significantly in size as a network, BFG set up the Association of People with Disabilities, a legal association under which BFG has formally registered. Though this required compromises with the state that some BFG members question, the Association is definitely a sustainable structure. The China rivers network may appear less sustainable by comparison, moving away from a formal structure and continuing as an almost submerged group of individual activists. Yet it has continued strong advocacy over a period of seven years.

Impact on social and political space is harder to measure. BFG has had a significant impact on the disability sector in Vietnam, opening opportunities and models for other self-help groups to start, and indeed providing advice and material support to many of these groups. The efforts of the Women's Network against AIDS, along with other HIV and women's groups, have contributed to heightened awareness of HIV in Chinese society, lower costs to becoming 'exposed' as HIV-positive, and more public discussion of sexuality and gender issues, making it easier for new groups of women affected by HIV to form around the country. The impact of this advocacy has mostly been on the media and public opinion, but state agencies' awareness has also been affected. Bright Future and WNAC are identity networks representing the interests of particular constituencies, with some internal democratic and participatory mechanisms. Through the BFG and DPO Hanoi executive committee elections, and to some extent the CCM elections in China, both BFG and WNAC can claim to be accountable and representative of their constituencies.

The Hanoi public space network, on the other hand, began without a constituency but demonstrated through its media advocacy that it speaks for the majority of Hanoians. In this sense, the network may be the most representative of public opinion, even though it is the least organised of the four case studies and has no internal mechanisms. As for CRN, its members speak for a large number of Chinese who care about protecting water resources and the environment, including dam-affected villagers, but some segments of public opinion are also against them. Both CRN and the Reunification Park network have demonstrated new repertoires of collective action based on media outreach and public opinion that may be used by other networks to affect state planning or oppose damaging development projects. Not all networks share the same degree of connections and sophistication as these, but their advocacy has increased political space by showing the potential of an inside-outside strategy.

Interview respondents and secondary sources cite a number of factors as key to success of network advocacy, in one or more of the senses considered here. A Vietnamese activist suggests that the three main factors leading to effectiveness are use of e-mail and Internet; links to international knowledge and resources; and inclusion of prominent individuals in the network. Two Chinese analysts of community campaigns see capable leadership as the most important factor; successful leaders are persistent in using personal channels as well as media to influence high-level leadership (Shi and Cai 2006: 321–9). Desmond and colleagues (2007: 17) hypothesise two criteria for network success: organic formation and membership of sub-national organisations. All of these explanations fit well with the experience of network case studies. These networks' effectiveness may be summarised as based on the presence of influential allies, a balance between inside and outside ties, support from public opinion, and leadership from either a committed core group or a leading organisation. However, a sole focus on internal capacities risks committing the 'fundamental attribution error' of interpreting a situation as based on individual strengths and weaknesses, rather than systematic and structural issues (McAdam et al 1996: 9).

Civil society networks have been able to raise public awareness on their issues of concern and, in the case of environmental and public space networks, stop or postpone some of the most egregious examples of what they view as destructive projects. These are significant achievements given the strength of the opposition these networks face. Yet dam-building, land grabs, and corruption continue, as does stigma against people with disabilities and HIV. Networks alone cannot resolve all of these issues or produce regime-level political change (Marsh and Rhodes 1992: 260). And following Gamson's (1990: 41) theory of movement success, effective networks focus on single issues and seek limited goals that do not displace elites.

Collective action has a demonstration value for both allies and opponents (Tarrow 1996: 58). The informal networking and advocacy strategies developed by civil society networks can also be used by counter-movements and opponents for private gain. Advocacy outside institutional politics might develop into a pattern of embedded insider contacts and deal-making that is opaque and undemocratic. When networks that represent private or corrupt interests use the same strategies, they will likely be at least as effective as civil society actors, since they may be expected to be better resourced and connected to elites. If this pessimistic assessment is correct, civil society networks will lose more often than they win, and informal networks may in the long run be a poor alternative to more transparent and accountable institutional practices linking society to the state.

Civil society networks, social movements and political change

The social and political changes sought by Chinese and Vietnamese civil society networks are limited ones. Their advocacy seeks to engage and cooperate with state agencies, not confront or press for regime change. Instead, the networks profiled in case studies seek to work within and around existing structures to stop dams, support disadvantaged constituencies, and protect public space. The political boundaries are generally clear enough: if activists avoid explicitly anti-government statements or positions, it is possible to accomplish many things, while open dissidence will lead to the network being shut down and even members' imprisonment.

Although chances of regime change in China and Vietnam appear slim in the foreseeable future, authorities continue to show concern about possible 'peaceful evolution', such as evidenced in the 'colour revolutions' in Eastern Europe and Central Asia, or the 2011 'Arab Spring'. In the pre-1989 Eastern European experience, civil society networks that began without an explicit agenda for regime change came together with others and became politicised, for instance via Solidarity and certain Catholic youth groups in Poland (Osa 2003). Reform outcomes are more likely when multiple movements converge and issues are 'coupled' (Kingdon 2003: 181, Tarrow 1996). There is little to suggest such meta-network organising capacity among Chinese or Vietnamese networks at present. Networks' impact on democratisation is remote: a functioning civil society is only one of many prerequisites for a democratic transition (Schmitter 1997: 240, Linz and Stepan 1997: 17). Networks that operate with internal democracy, such as the Bright Future Group or the China Global Fund CCM, may claim with justification that they are modelling a more democratic society (Jia 2009). But the influence of this demonstration effect on the regime remains small. In contrast, dissident networks such as Vietnam's Bloc 8406 or China's Charter 08 and China Democracy Party (Wright 2004) have few allies and are repressed before they can transform from personal into civil society networks (Béja 2009).

The Chinese and Vietnamese states have demonstrated their ability to crack down on unwelcome political action at any time, sometimes using external events as a timely excuse. The nature of the state system and structural opportunities change slowly, yet civil society networks have found ways to organise even in the midst of apparently more restrictive periods. A core question asked by activists is how to promote change without provoking a negative response from the state. 'You have to be strategic in highlighting sensitive issues without irritating government officials', says a Chinese environmentalist (quoted in Ford 2009). 'If you are seen as a troublemaker...they will shut your mouth and shut you down.'

Whether networks may come together to form a broader social movement thus depends on many external factors, including state attitudes or repression, external events like natural disasters, economic shocks or epidemics, and actions of other networks. In Sidney Tarrow's view of movement formation, 'ordinary people' face political opportunities, constraints, and resources; this leads to episodes of contentious politics, which sometimes develop into full-fledged social movements. One of the conditions for forming social movements is 'dense social networks' (1998: 19, 71). The picture presented in this book is similar in many respects, but begins instead with the view that society is formed of personal networks. Facing political opportunities, constraints and resources, some personal ties develop into civil society networks, which engage in collective action and advocacy using a strategic repertoire that can include institutionalised and/or contentious politics. If networks have adequate resources, leadership, and political space, they might come together to form longer-term coalitions and social movements.

It is a matter of debate whether present-day disability, environmental, or HIV solidarity groups in Vietnam or China meet these conditions. The sector that has received the most scholarly attention is Chinese environmentalism, which some identify as a social movement (Sun and Zhao 2007) while others hesitate (Stalley and Yang 2006). One informant, an expatriate with long experience in China, thinks 'movement' is a western linear model, not rooted in Chinese culture; many groups say they prefer to be part of a 'circle' instead. A Chinese environmental activist says that while perhaps not meeting all the characteristics of a 'western-style movement', it could still be one 'in a Chinese sense', and that there is a Chinese tradition of social movements historically.[14] Such a movement would employ a different repertoire of collective action than the historical western European repertoire, though both are related via transnational brokering and diffusion. The roles of state and business interests in Chinese environmentalism are quite strong and also adopt progressive and environmental causes for their own benefit (Hildebrant 2009). As these interests cannot easily be separated, it is difficult to identify a single 'green public sphere' (Yang and Calhoun 2008) out of what continues to be a mix of competing interests.

The same argument applies for the Vietnamese disability movement or for HIV activist movements, which each comprise multiple networks with varying degrees of effectiveness, but have not yet demonstrated a capacity for sustained, large-scale collective action. Informal networks may be effective at mobilising people to join collective action but not enough to sustain a movement (Kyaw 2004: 390, Tarrow 1998: 124–31). The cases in this book demonstrate that informal networks may indeed have substantial staying power and show increased networking and organisation over time. Yet they have so far not coalesced into any challenge to the Chinese or Vietnamese regimes (Bernstein and Lu 2003, Thayer 2009). When larger movements do arise, as with the 1989 Chinese student movement or Falun Gong, they will likely result in 'dogged protest-containment efforts' by authorities (Béja 2009: 8), whether or not the movements claim to have radical or regime-changing goals.

In Tilly's formulation, social movements are characterised by public displays of 'WUNC': worthiness, unity, numbers and commitment (2004: 4). Some, but not all of these elements apply in the cases of civil society networks. Network members demonstrate worthiness by speaking the language of state authorities, keeping important links and relationships with officials, and refraining from anti-government activities or statements. They also show obvious commitment through their years of activism and contributions of time and resources to the network. However, there is a much lower premium placed on unity and numbers. The multiplicity of views and roles within networks is one of their greatest assets, and most networks agree on the value of remaining small. In place of unity and numbers, an element of flexibility forms a core network competency.

The revision of 'WUNC' to 'WCF' may be viewed as a contextual adaptation. Tilly emphasises the specificity of his conception of social movements to western Europe since the 18th century (2004: x), while Chinese and Vietnamese actors draw on different historical legacies and political institutions. A more structural approach would posit that the difference is primarily not cultural or historical, but rather one of scale: large social movements do in fact require unity and numbers, whatever their national context, while networks are smaller and more flexible (Khagram et al 2002: 6–9, Bandy and Smith 2005: 3). Varieties of social movement have existed in China and Vietnam in the past, and may well emerge again; the current rarity of such movements is a temporary political condition, not a cultural constraint.

In the contemporary contexts of China and Vietnam, civil society networks will continue as a modular form of citizen advocacy as long as the issues and grievances that prompted their formation continue or recur, resources are available, and the current opportunity structure persists. With their features of worthiness, commitment and flexibility, these networks will likely remain small, largely informal and unregistered, and maintain a focus on social and political issues, not organisational growth or regime-level political change. They will include a diverse membership of activists, some with links to authorities, others independent, and use multiple strategies of embedded, media, and community advocacy. By expanding their web of ties, linking previously unconnected nodes, and leveraging other actors and resources, civil society networks have the potential to create new political spaces for advocacy.

Notes

Chapter 1   The Dynamic Societies of China and Vietnam

1   These options correspond to William Connolly's analysis of situations in which an existing concept does not apply well: preserve the concept but lose its relevance, change the meaning of the concept to preserve the original criteria, or (the option taken here) revise the concept to preserve its original meaning (1974: 31, see also Chamberlain 1998).

2   China-focused scholarship has been in advance both theoretically and empirically. Vietnam specialists have adopted concepts from the China civil society literature, such as Frolic's 'state-led civil society' (Lux and Straussman 2004) and Ding Xueliang's 'amphibious organisations' (Hannah 2007), but have not engaged with the literature in depth. On the other hand, some Vietnam scholarship, such as Kerkvliet's (2001a/b, 2003) on state-society relations, has no parallel in China studies.

3   Broader comparative studies of civil society in Asia have been conducted or coordinated by Yamamoto (1996), Shigetomi (2002), Schak and Hudson (2003), Lee (2004), and Alagappa (2004). Of these, only the two Japanese volumes include chapters on both China and Vietnam; Schak-Hudson and Alagappa include China but not Vietnam, while Lee limits his discussion to Southeast Asia and covers only Vietnam. On environmental issues, Hirsch and Warren (1998), Kalland and Persoon (1998), and Lee and So (1999) offer regional perspectives, but none of these includes China or Vietnam. Gu Chengyong (2002) compares NGOs in China and Southeast Asia; a university dissertation by Pěrinová (2005) compares civil society in China, Vietnam and Myanmar, stressing the mutual interaction of associations and the state.

4   Other bi-country comparisons have been conducted of China and Mexico (Lindau and Cheek 1998) and China and India (Friedman and Gilley 2005). On Southeast Asia, Anderson (1998) and Mulder (2003) compare Indonesia, Philippines and Thailand, while Hedman (2001) compares the 'dyads' of Philippines/Thailand and Indonesia/Malaysia. Kerkvliet writes on both Vietnam and Philippines, though usually not together (Scott and Kerkvliet 1986); Scott (2009) has also taken an original look at 'anarchist' history of non-state areas. Read and Pekkanen (2009) group neighbourhood associations and quasi-NGOs from East and Southeast Asia (including China and Vietnam) together in a category of 'straddlers' that does not fit all cases equally well.

5   In two exceptional cases, interview respondents have subsequently been subject to harassment or arrest by security forces, but this had nothing whatsoever to do with their speaking to a foreign researcher.

6   In a study of NGO advocacy in China, a team of Chinese and Chinese-speaking Americans carried out interviews with 40 organisations and reported no clear differences in responses among researchers (Wexler et al 2006: 44).

Chapter 2   Redefining Civil Society: Networks and Advocacy

1 An initial step is to broaden civil society to include both a metaphorical 'realm', as well as the actors who operate in this space (Walzer 1995: 7, Hughes 2003: 138). Other approaches to civil society as a wider 'social process that generates trust and mutual understanding' across various degrees or 'thresholds' are proposed by Deakin (2001: 7), Jorgensen (1996: 44–7), and Hedman (2006: 184). Schak and Hudson (2003: 1) argue that civil society in Asia should be understood as a dynamic project in process, while Hannah focuses on 'social and political processes involving civil society and the state' along a continuum of possible roles (2007: 58, 92).

2 www.civicus.org/csn. The only identified use of the term 'civil society network' in a sense close to this book is in a short article on Malawi (James and Malunga 2006). Even writers who take an actor-centred view of civil society (Hannah 2007, Wischermann 2010) or personal ties (Büsgen 2006, Xie 2007) still use NGOs as their unit of analysis.

3 The nesting paradigm, adapted from conflict resolution literature, considers both the narrower and broader aspects of a social structure, ranging from issues to more systemic concerns (Dugan 1996, Lederach 1997).

4 Men are represented in network diagrams by triangles, women by circles and organisations by squares. Thus, the pyramid in this example is an individual membership network, the clique an organisational network, and the others have mixed individual and organisational members. Organisation A in the web diagram has the greatest density and prominence, while individual B is at the margin. In the segmented-decentralised network, the shaded individual acts as a broker between two organisations.

5 This description evokes Eyerman and Jamison's alternative cognitive definition of social movements as 'temporary public spaces [and] moments of collective creation' (1991: 4).

6 The author has previously been an active member of both the Jubilee and landmine ban networks. Keck and Sikkink describe transnational advocacy networks, including these, but many of their core examples are single country-focused. One historical example given is the campaign against foot-binding in China, led by both western missionaries and Chinese reformers.

7 Xie Lei (2007: 51–3) contrasts individual membership networks (which she terms 'personal networks') with organisational networks. She notes that 'individuals can't be reduced to the organisations they belong to', since in individual membership networks, members cannot be readily replaced by other individuals within the same organisation. The aggregation of individual networks does not automatically result in institutional linkages among organisations.

8 Fisher (1998: 4–9) divides NGOs into two types (grassroots membership organisations and 'grassroots support organisations' or intermediary NGOs) and examines networks of both types. Membership organisations form either 'formal umbrella networks' such as associations and cooperatives; informal economic networks (such as of the 'collaborative groups' mentioned above); or 'amorphous grassroots social movements'. Intermediary organisations also form formal and informal networks among themselves and with grassroots

organisations. This typology covers much of the variety in network forms, but is restricted to NGOs.

9 A Philippine study identifies NGO networks, issue-based coalitions and task forces, the latter described as 'issue-oriented [but] typically more narrowly focused and less permanent than issue-based coalitions' (Silliman and Noble 1998: 12).

10 The eight are the Microfinance Working Group, Vietnam NGO Alliance, GenComNet, Vietnam Rivers Network, CIFPEN, Vietnam Water Partnership, Cooperative Development Group, and People's Participation Working Group. Members of six of these eight were interviewed for this book (excepting the microfinance and water groups); three are included in Table 2.3.

11 Some interview respondents take a narrower view of advocacy as 'one subset of engagement', namely direct lobbying of government officials. Advocacy is used here in a more specific way than Kerkvliet's (2008) 'forms of engagement with the state', which also includes service delivery. Vietnamese and Chinese studies emphasise that 'mere' service delivery can also be an important way for organisations to involve in public issues (Kerkvliet et al 2008: 7, Wexler et al 2006: 10, Schwartz and Shieh 2009).

12 Keck and Sikkink (1998: 25) describe four basic network tactics: generating and disseminating information, using symbols to make sense of events, leveraging help from powerful allies, and holding actors accountable to stated claims and principles. Mass mobilisation techniques are rarer.

13 Businesses and other social groups, including humanitarian organisations, may also be involved in corruption, defined as 'the abuse of entrusted power for private gain' (Transparency International 2010: x). Corruption, such as bribery of government officials, is outside the scope of advocacy, although the line between engagement and abuse may be difficult to draw at times. Cultivating a relationship through shared meals and study tours is a legitimate advocacy activity if it is done for a public purpose and not for private gain; this distinction is consistent with Transparency International's definition.

14 In Hannah's definitions, 'advocacy' is restricted to mean action on behalf of constituents for policy implementation, differentiated from lobbying for policy change, watchdog actions that expose corrupt officials or practices, and public criticism of policies or the regime (2007: 93). I consider all of these as forms or tactics of advocacy.

15 The regulations were widely interpreted as being aimed at a single independent think tank, the Institute of Development Studies, which announced its closure the day before the new decree took effect.

16 These categories correspond roughly to what Wexler, Xu and Young describe as different types of advocacy by international NGOs in China: constructive engagement, media campaigns, and raising visibility and voice of marginalised groups (2006: 61–5).

17 As with corruption, it can be difficult to tell where embedded advocacy ends and back-room deals or interest group politics begin. This system of influence is not unique to China or Vietnam, as the western public policy literature shows (Marsh and Rhodes 1992, Sabatier and Jenkins-Smith 1993). The difference is that the objects of advocacy in China and Vietnam may also have the power to register or shut down the advocates themselves, an inherently unequal and hazardous situation.

18 This list is similar to Lin Teh-Chang's (2007) repertoire of seven methods used by Chinese environmental NGOs: petitions, signature campaigns, media debates, public forums, investigative field trips, photo exhibits and websites. Most of these are embedded tactics, but some extend to media and community advocacy.

19 In 2003, the same activist also stated that 'Chinese environmentalism cannot always rely on non-confrontational tactics to achieve its aims' (cited in Ho and Edmonds 2008: 221). In 2010, a Chinese newspaper profiled her as an 'extreme environmental activist' – and meant this as a compliment (He 2010).

20 'Boundary-spanning contention', according to O'Brien, 'goes on partly within the state and hinges on the participation of state actors.' Such a campaign 'is not prescribed or forbidden, but tolerated (even encouraged) by some officials, and not tolerated by others' (2004: 107).

21 O'Brien's 'rightful resisters' 'use the vocabulary of the regime to advance their claims… They launch attacks that are legitimate by definition in a rhetoric that even unresponsive authorities must recognize, lest they risk being charged with hypocrisy and disloyalty to the system of power they represent' (1996: 35).

22 For details on press freedom and the above cases, see Human Rights Watch (2010a, 2010b), US Department of State (2009), OpenNet (2007), Cullum (2010), and Hayton (2010: 136–40).

23 In China, 87,000 cases of rural protest were documented in 2005 (Cai 2008: 163). In Vietnam, an official estimated 15,000 land disputes took place in 2007, 70 per cent concerning compensation (Hayton 2010: 41).

24 This hypothesis echoes Keck and Sikkink's finding that 'networks are more effective when they are strong and dense' (1998: 206).

25 In other respects, however, 'resistance' is not an appropriate way to describe network advocacy; for a critique of the 'rightful resistance' approach, see Mertha (2008: 153).

26 This strategy has relevance beyond the cases considered here: a similar combination of confrontational and consensual strategies has been used to describe Hong Kong environmentalism (Chiu et al 1999: 59, 75–6), Chinese peasant protests (Bernstein and Lu 2003: 13), and contemporary Russian civil society (Nikitin 2010). Filipino activists describe a *bibingka* or sandwich strategy, consisting of allies at the top and the bottom (central government and communities) against local elites in the middle (Franco 2004) – in terms of this book, a combination of embedded and community advocacy.

27 The martial arts metaphor also echoes Gramsci's (1971) 'war of position' among competing social forces.

28 In her book on Chinese environmentalism, Economy (2004: 131) also refers to a 'tightrope act', but only between NGOs and the state. Of course, no metaphor should be stretched too far: advocacy is not a linear process that only moves forward.

Chapter 3   The Bright Future Group of People with Disabilities

1 The National Coordinating Council on Disability (NCCD) includes representatives of 15 ministries and other government-linked agencies. It holds monthly

meetings in Hanoi with participation from people with disabilities, including Bright Future members (IDRM 2005).

2 The INGOs are Catholic Relief Services, Handicap International France, and Medical Committee Netherlands-Vietnam; the company's name is August Technology and Application. Of these, CRS and MCNV have been among the ongoing supporters of BFG since the mid-1990s.

3 There is also a self-help group of HIV-positive people with a similar name, Bright Futures, which is part of the Vietnam Civil Society Partnership on AIDS. There is no connection between the two groups.

4 2.4 million veterans, including many people with disabilities, who fought on the revolutionary side in the American War are members of the Veterans Association of Vietnam (*Hội Cựu Chiến Binh*), a mass organisation set up in the early 1990s as a state response to independent veterans' organising in Ho Chi Minh City (Abuza 2001: 162–73). MOLISA (2005) estimates that 23 per cent of disabilities come from war-related causes, but the source of this data is not clear.

5 The Disability Forum *(Diễn đàn Người Khuyết tật Việt Nam)* is an 'information-sharing network' of self-help groups and individual participants (IDEA, undated) that meets on a bimonthly basis and maintains an e-mail list-serve. The forum evolved from an international NGO-led Disability Working Group that formed in the late 1990s, coordinated by Health Volunteers Overseas (HVO), who sought to transform the group into a Vietnamese-led network. HVO eventually localised their own operations, forming a local NGO, Inclusive Development Action (IDEA) in 2006. While the Forum and IDEA could be viewed as competing networks to the Bright Future Group in some respects, in fact the groups are closely connected. The Disability Forum coordinator during the HVO-led years was a BF member and is now serving as Bright Future's chair. Several IDEA staff, including the recently-appointed executive director, are also BF members.

6 Bright Future Group has a stub Wikipedia page in English, http://en.wikipedia.org/wiki/Bright_Future_Group_for_People_with_Disabilities, with information gathered from secondary sources.

7 According to Vietnamese regulations, legal registration via a government-affiliated organisation is required in order to open a bank account and receive foreign funds (SRV 2003, Decree 88, Articles 22–3). In the mid-1990s, there were few options to do this; now there are more. In Vietnamese terms, BFG didn't have its own 'red stamp', and had to ask to borrow someone else's.

8 The network maps in each case study are approximate for purposes of illustration. Connections among members are based on general impressions from interviews, not actual observation or quantifiable demonstration of network ties. As in Figure 2.2, men are represented by triangles and women by circles. The chair of the network at each stage is shaded. Each diagram was discussed and developed with several network members during interviews.

9 The Independent Living Centre opened in 2009 and is jointly sponsored by the Nippon Foundation and the Disabled People's Organisation in Asia Pacific (DPIAP) through 2011 (Tharp 2009).

10 *Nâng cao nhận thức*, literally 'increasing knowledge', sometimes also referred to, especially by older members, as *tuyên truyền* ('propaganda'), a term used by the Party-state in its original (positive) meaning.

11 The Association of Support for Vietnamese Handicapped and Orphans (*Hội Bảo trợ người tàn tật và trẻ mồ côi Việt Nam*) was set up as a GONGO in 1992. In the view of one BF member, this was in part intended to compensate for the government's initial refusal to register Bright Future.

12 Similar events took place in China following the release of the Law of the People's Republic of China on the Protection of Disabled Persons in 2008 (CANGO 2008: 4). Both the Chinese and Vietnamese laws contain rights-based provisions in accordance with the 2007 UN Convention on the Rights of the Disabled, which both China and Vietnam have signed.

13 This has also been the case in China, where most cities have banned motor-ised tricycles for passenger transport, putting many people with disabilities out of work. In a case in Hunan province, disabled and non-disabled tricycle drivers organised protests at a district government in November 2000. When there was no reply from the authorities, 44 PWD occupied a government office overnight (Chen 2007: 258–9).

14 On Ba Dinh Square, the political centre of power in Vietnam (Thomas 2001). These demonstrations occurred in December 2007, shortly before the ban was to take effect, with the largest on 31 December.

15 In the Chinese case referenced by Chen (2007: 259), the local government also agreed to compensate drivers at a roughly similar level, though without rescinding the ban on three-wheeled vehicles. While the facts of the two cases appear remarkably similar overall, the Chinese writer concludes that 'disruptive behaviour' was the main cause leading to government conces-sions, while 'obedient tactics' helped to sustain the movement (277), a somewhat different conclusion than here.

16 For instance, the China Disabled Persons Federation (残联), a GONGO led by Deng Xiaoping's son Deng Pufang, held its fifth national congress at the Great Hall of the People in Beijing in November 2008, several days before the much more modest BFG anniversary celebration in Hanoi (Ding 2008: 75).

17 Danish funding was also used to organise training courses for Association members and to publish the Association's newsletter, *Nắng Xuân* (Spring Sunshine). A new phase of PTU support began in 2009 to expand the Association into additional new districts in Hanoi (Embassy of Denmark 2010).

18 The Vietnam Blind Association (*Hội Người Mù*) was established in 1969 with initial support from fraternal socialist countries. Unlike other disability groups, it has long-term sources of funding from European donors and from the Viet-namese government, which has paid salaries of association leaders. In NCCD meetings in 2007–08, Blind Association representatives pointed out that the Blind Association already had local chapters in over 40 provinces, while few PWD Associations existed at that time. The Blind Association members appeared to be concerned that the formation of a national DPO would cause their association to lose its separate status.

19 The *mít-tinh*, which constitutes part of the Vietnamese repertoire of collec-tive action, originates from a 19th century French borrowing of the English 'meeting'. In contrast to political demonstrations (*biểu tình*), these rallies are typically highly staged events, lacking spontaneity or participatory char-acter, as in traditional Communist Party propaganda events (Woodside 1976: 266). Holding a (legal) *mít-tinh* in contemporary Vietnam requires a

permit from local authorities, which can be issued or denied arbitrarily (US Department of State 2009: 12–13).

20 In addition to being the Vietnamese term for '(social) movement', *phong trào* is also the phrase used for Party-led propaganda campaigns, and can thus have a positive or negative connotation depending on the situation and speaker.

Chapter 4   The China Women's Network against AIDS

1 An abridged version of this chapter has been published online in Chinese and English by *China Development Brief* (Wells-Dang 2011b).

2 In keeping with current international practice, this chapter refers to the Human Immunodeficiency Virus (HIV) and people living with HIV (PLWH). This usage is preferred by most advocates over referring to AIDS (Acquired Immunodeficiency Syndrome), a disease that affects people in late stages of HIV infection. In Chinese, the word AIDS (艾滋病 , *aìzībìng*) is commonly used, and some international programmes continue to use AIDS or 'HIV/AIDS' in their titles.

3 A similar transformation took place during the same time period in Vietnam, where HIV had previously been labelled as a 'social evil' (Government of Vietnam 2004).

4 'Affected' by HIV is a broad term that can include people living with HIV (PLWH) as well as those with a HIV-positive family member. In China, different from most international usage, PLWH commonly refer to themselves as 'infected' (感染者 , *gǎnrǎnzhě* 'the infected ones'). This chapter refers to PLWH in recognition of the limits of designating people by an acronym for an 'illness identity' (He 2006: 19).

5 The Gender and Development in China Network has over 40 organisational members, with large bi-annual conferences and a research focus. The gender-based violence network has developed an integrated intervention model including NGOs, the ACWF, hospitals and police. A third network on gender and public policy is newer and more advocacy-focused, with support from an international NGO.

6 QQ is a popular Chinese message board, similar to Yahoo or Windows Messenger.

7 Ark of Love (爱之方舟 , *Aì zhī fāngzhōu*) is a Beijing-based NGO that coordinates one of two national PLWH networks, the China Alliance of People Living with HIV/AIDS (CAP+), with support from the Ford Foundation. From an initial 24 members at its launch in 2006, the network has now expanded to 109, although these do not all participate at the same level. The second network, the China National Network of AIDS CBOs (CNNAC) has 133 members, largely comprised of MSM support groups. It is coordinated by the Aizhixing Institute (爱知行 , 'Love-Knowledge-Action'), a long-standing activist NGO in Beijing. In addition to workshops, training, and some work on legal aid, CNNAC has set up a community fund that provides small-scale financial support to between 30–40 members. The departure of Aizhixing's director to the US in May 2010 has weakened CNNAC's standing, but also given it an opportunity to restructure its operations. A third

cluster of HIV networks, with closer links to CAP+ than CNNAC, has formed in south-western China through the coordination of AIDS Care China, and focuses mainly on service delivery and community support to PLWH, rather than policy advocacy (International HIV/AIDS Alliance 2010, Robertson 2007).

8 International experience was also helpful, but not essential. Many network leaders, including WNAC, do not speak foreign languages.

9 The neutral term 'men who have sex with men' (MSM) is commonly used in international health and also in China, where many MSM do not self-identify as gay. The prevailing Chinese slang used by MSM to describe themselves is 同志 (*tóngzhì*, 'comrade'), with the full political irony of the term intended (Young and Mian 2007).

10 The *China HIV/AIDS NGO Directory* lists 80 PLWH support groups and an additional 116 MSM groups (CHAIN 2010). The directory is produced by the China HIV/AIDS Information Network together with the China Centre for Disease Control's HIV programme. In its brochure, CHAIN describes itself as a 'platform for information exchange and open discussion' that was co-founded by three GONGOs in 2002. It operates a website and circulates printed information about HIV, but is not a membership network.

11 Translations of members' names are by the author except for organisations listed in the HIV NGO Directory, in which case the English name listed there is given, even if it is not a complete translation of the Chinese name.

12 The secretary-general cites the story of one sex workers' group in Guangzhou who was invited to participate, but insisted on being provided air tickets to Beijing rather than the train tickets that were budgeted.

13 Although WNAC members do not mention the connection, this is similar to the original AIDS Quilt in the USA, which was a highly effective awareness-raising and advocacy tool in the 1980s. Red is a universal colour used by HIV movements and has no political meaning within China.

14 A similar dynamic was observed in several Vietnamese networks (Desmond et al 2007, Hoang and Bui 2008).

15 The Red Ribbon Forum has no connection to the Red Scarf campaign described earlier.

16 This process has significance beyond the HIV field: these were the first independent national elections of any kind in China organised by non-members of the Communist Party. As a result, 'the CCM represents a rare instance in which government officials sit as equals with civil society on a decision-making body' (Thompson and Jia 2010).

Chapter 5   Preserving Hanoi's Reunification Park

1 The two companies were Vincom, a real estate corporation whose directors made money in Ukraine and invest in Vietnam, and Tan Hoang Minh, a taxi and trading company whose aging yellow vehicles were known for a poor safety record before disappearing from Hanoi streets since 2007. Vincom owns a shopping and office complex that towers over the eastern edge of Reunification Park. The developers intended a private theme park modelled after Disneyland; the

Walt Disney Corporation was never involved in these plans, but as in other cases of brand piracy, was probably not harmed by the publicity.

2 Portions of this chapter concerning the 2007 park preservation campaign are adapted from an article published in *Pacific Review* (Wells-Dang 2010).

3 Douglass et al (2008: 5) differentiate between 'civil society space' (metaphorical), 'public space' (which can also include government in the sense of public services), and 'civic space' (free community spaces that are open to all, but can be public or private, as in the case of cafes and pubs). As David Koh describes in a chapter on Hanoi, civil society can also use market spaces to double up as civic spaces (Douglass et al 2008: 168). I use public space as a general term including both public and civic spaces in these senses.

4 Similar advocacy, led by scholar-activists, has taken place in Beijing, Tianjin and other Chinese cities to preserve *hutong* neighbourhoods and remaining historic structures, with more failures than successes (Meyer 2008, Johnson 2004). An excellent case study of Shanghai citizens resisting development of a park can be found in Zhu and Ho (2008) and Shi and Cai (2006).

5 The website, www.savehanoipark.com, was not maintained and has been unavailable since 2009.

6 The e-mail address translates as 'Old soldier of Ho [Chi Minh]'.

7 Cynically evoking the beginning of the pre-eminent Party slogan, 'a rich people, a strong nation and a just, democratic and civilised society'.

8 An address deep down an alley in a poor area of the city across the Red River, home to many migrant workers.

9 This phrase, originating from Abraham Lincoln, is used frequently in Vietnamese political discourse.

10 This may seem like a weak link to influence policy, but research on *guanxi* in China also suggests that classmate (同学) relations are an important facet of social networks (Gold et al 2002: 6). As proof of the 'strength of weak ties' (Granovetter 1973), this was enough to get the association president in the mayor's door, and the case unfolded from there.

11 This insight recalls Shi Tianjian's (1997) description of 'political participation' in Beijing.

12 As one Hanoi architect jokes, 'there are three models of administration. The first is that the government fears its people, as in the US. The second is that the people fear their government, as in China. Then there's Hanoi: the government and people fear one another and go about their business' (cited in Meyer 2008: 121).

Chapter 6   The China Rivers Network

1 The Nu ('Angry') river, known downstream as the Salween in Myanmar (Burma), is the westernmost and most remote of the Three Parallel Rivers in southwest China. It is the last undammed major river in China. The other rivers are the Lancang (澜沧江), which flows south into Laos and Thailand where it is know as the Mekong, and the Jinsha (金沙江) which passes through 'Tiger Leaping Gorge' (虎跳峡), then turns east and is the major source for the Yangtze (长江). Dams are proposed or underway on all three rivers, beginning with the Manwan dam on the Lancang, completed in 1994. Three other Lancang dams have been built

since, and four more are proposed, raising concern from downstream Mekong countries due to potential effects on water levels and fisheries (Osborne 2007). Eighteen dams are planned for the Jinsha and upper Yangtze, plus 200 on its tributaries (Biello 2009), including a dam at Tiger Leaping Gorge. Two dams on the Jinsha, Xiluodu and Xiangjiaba, will be the second and third-largest dams in China when completed in 2015 and 2012 respectively, requiring the resettlement of over 100,000 people (Xu 2010).

2 The State Environmental Protection Agency (SEPA) was elevated in status to become the Ministry of Environmental Protection (MEP) in 2008.

3 One scientist, a member of the rivers network's extended membership, aroused controversy in 2008 by pointing out possible links between the Sichuan earthquake and the Zipingpu Dam just miles from the epicentre (Xu 2010).

4 This follows Diani's finding on Italian 'green networks' that informal ties among members of different environmental organisations helped to develop a common identity (Tarrow 1998: 135).

5 China's first ENGO was formed in Liaoning province in 1991 (Xu 2009), but the most prominent groups developed in Beijing later in the 1990s, including Friends of Nature (自然之友, *Zìrán zhī yǒu*), Global Village Beijing (北京地球村环境教育中心, *Běijīng Dìqiúcūn Huánjìng Jiāoyù Zhōngxīn*), and Green Earth Volunteers (绿家园, *Lǜjiāyuán*). For more on these groups, see Economy (2004, 2005), Liang and Yang (2007), Fu (2007), Xu (2009), and Zhao (2010).

6 INGOs operating environmental programmes in China include World Wildlife Fund, Conservation International, Oxfam, The Nature Conservancy, and Greenpeace, among others.

7 The most significant of the Yunnan ENGOs in river activism have been Green Watershed (绿色流域, *Lǜsè Liúyù*) and the Centre for Biodiversity and Indigenous Knowledge (CBIK). See Xu (2009), Büsgen (2006: 28), and Mertha (2008).

8 Dujiangyan is near the epicentre of the 2008 Sichuan earthquake. Following the quake, the city is being reconstructed with a focus on historic preservation (Yan 2009).

9 A chronology of river activism (in Chinese) is online via Friends of Nature (2010).

10 IRN is an NGO, not a network, and has since shortened its name to 'International Rivers'. The search for international models is common in Chinese environmentalism: Friends of Nature's name was adopted from Friends of the Earth (Xu 2009), and another well-known activist began his career by setting up a local environmental group in his high school, which he called 'Greenpeace' after a banner he had seen on TV.

11 This website, originally hosted by the Institute for Environment and Development in Beijing, is still operational. A second, CRN-specific website, www.chinarivers.org.cn, has gone offline since 2008.

12 A minimum of 30 million people died in the Great Leap Forward and resulting famine in 1958–61 (Yang 1996: 38).

13 Büsgen (2006: 24) lists eight 'NGOs', not seven, subtracting Wild China Films and adding Green Island and Green Hanjiang. Ho (2008b: 36) cites Büsgen's list. This information was also provided by a key network member, showing that participation in CRN varied over time and was not always

clear even to members themselves. Mertha's list is identical to mine, but misspells the name of Tianxia Xi (2008: 61). Tong (2009) lists nine organisations as part of a Nu River NGO alliance, including Green Island but not Tianxia Xi/Brooks, plus two other organisations that were to my knowledge not involved in CRN. A chronology of the Chinese environmental movement posted on FON's Chinese-language website also states that nine organisations founded CRN, but does not specify which ones (Friends of Nature 2010).

14 This change is reflected by the use in this chapter of 'China Rivers Network' in upper case during the formalised period in 2004–06, and 'the rivers network' in the informal period thereafter.

15 Compare this statement to the virtually identical description of the Bright Future Group's internal process after their initial application to register was denied by the Vietnamese government.

16 The GEV founder's position in the network is analogous in some ways to that of the landscape architect in the Reunification Park case (Chapter 6), although the architect does not work through any organisation at all. The two networks share other common challenges in coordination and organisation, yet have engaged in advocacy regardless.

17 Some observers attribute these conditions to self-censorship in which 'true NGOs' hide their identity as 'entities they are not' (Ho 2008a: 10, also Jiang 2005), while others suggest they are not 'real' NGOs at all (Liu 2007, Stalley and Yang 2006). Both are misconceptions that result from a normative assumption that NGOs should be autonomous, separate organisations in their own sector of society.

18 Liang passed away in October 2010. As the son of a famous architect who unsuccessfully urged Mao Zedong to preserve Beijing's old city (Meyer 2008: 275–93) and the grandson of an even more famous late Qing dynasty reformer, he possessed impeccable academic and political connections with Beijing's intellectual elite (Ho 2008b: 33–4; Mertha 2008: 20, though he associates Liang with the wrong organisation).

19 In an example of 'astroturfing' (corporations creating fake 'grassroots' support), two Nu villagers were brought to Beijing in 2005 to speak in favour of the dam's potential to improve their lives. When a journalist re-interviewed the two in 2006, he found they were actually local cadres, and one of the two didn't actually support the dam (Liu 2007a).

20 Mertha (2008:10) terms *Southern Weekend* a 'maverick' publication, while *China Youth Daily* is one of the 'traditional bastions of official propaganda'. This does not necessarily result in differences in their coverage.

21 Litzinger (2007: 292) shares the view that elite NGOs favour preservation over the needs of local residents; this may have been true in 1990s endangered species campaigns, but is not the case in the Three Parallel Rivers.

22 The phrase is based on what were known as 'water wars' in Bolivia and other developing countries (Manahan 2010). These struggles are usually over access to clean, affordable drinking water, not about dams, and war analogies are unhelpful for understanding the China Rivers Network.

23 In addition to advocacy on river issues, Green Watershed has engaged since 2005 in a range of development projects along the Jinsha, parti-

cipated in Sichuan earthquake relief, and formed a new network on green finance. Many of these activities are in cooperation with other CRN members.

Chapter 7   Conclusion: Civil Society Networks and Political Change

1 This reasoning follows Casanova's on Ukraine (1998: 203): 'if a civil society can emerge in such an unexpected setting as Ukraine, it could possibly emerge in many other unlikely places'.

2 This is also contrary to Keck and Sikkink's conclusions (1998: 206), perhaps because they only consider formal networks.

3 There is a structural basis for this preference: many private foundations are legally bound to fund only registered organisations, not individuals or networks.

4 Sidney Tarrow argues that in undemocratic conditions, transnational advocacy networks 'provide a second-best but safer alternative to social movements' (1998: 189). However, Tarrow's claim that transnational activism replaces domestic organising does not apply in Chinese and Vietnamese cases, nor does his assumption that domestic actors are 'resource-poor' and depend on cross-border linkages.

5 A comparison with Taiwan may be revealing in this regard: with a similar cultural heritage, Taiwan has a consolidated democracy, while civil society still uses informal forms of engagement (King 2010).

6 This echoes Mayfair Yang's (1994) statement about 'rhizomatic networks'; see also Yang Guobin (2008: 133) and Vala and O'Brien (2008: 116) on networks reducing risks of political repression.

7 This model is used by the 5–12 Sichuan Earthquake network, CIFPEN, and the Vietnam Rivers Network, among others.

8 With these conflicts in mind, Korten argues (1990a:124) that 'the surest way to kill a movement is to smother it with money'.

9 Michael Edwards (2004: 105–7) reaches a similar conclusion that donors look for existing, independent associational life and focus on the ecosystem level.

10 Keck and Sikkink (1998: 201) define effectiveness as influence on politics, but include within this the importance of framing debates and getting issues on the agenda. Advocates may fail to meet their substantive goals, but still have procedural success (160).

11 Wilson-Grau and Nuñez list four 'types of achievements for an international social change network': operational outputs, organic outcomes, political outcomes, and impact on society in the long term (2006: 10). These categories are related to, though conceived differently from, the three forms of effectiveness presented here: for instance, the measure of policy effectiveness might include aspects of both 'operational outputs' and 'political outcomes'.

12 As Tarrow (1998: 162) notes, citing Melucci (1996), success for some movements may consist more in establishing a collective identity than in achieving policy change.

13 Keck and Sikkink consider that domestic opportunity structures are critical in the formation of networks, but are insufficient to explain why some networks are effective while others are not (1998: 202).

14 Milwertz (2002: 4) argues that 'organizing by women in Beijing qualifies as social movement activism, even though it does not fit neatly and precisely' into existing definitions.

Bibliography

Abrami R, Malesky E and Yu Zheng (2008) 'Accountability and inequality in single-party regimes: A comparative analysis of Vietnam and China', Harvard Business School Working Paper.

Abuza Z (2001) *Renovating Politics in Contemporary Vietnam*. Boulder: Lynne Rienner.

Action for the City (2008) 'Citizen participation in planning & management of public spaces – A case study of Thong Nhat Park in Hanoi, Vietnam', research report, October.

Agence France Presse (2009) 'Vietnam PM halts controversial hotel in park', 15 April.

Alagappa M, ed. (2004) *Civil Society and Political Change in Asia: Expanding and Contracting Democratic Space*. Stanford: Stanford University Press.

Anderson B (1998) *The Spectre of Comparisons: Nationalism, Southeast Asia and the World*. New York: Verso.

Anheier H, Glasius M and Kaldor M, eds. (2003) *Global Civil Society 2003*. Oxford: Oxford University Press.

—— (2002) *Global Civil Society 2002*. Oxford: Oxford University Press.

Ashui (2009) 'Bo Xay dung kien nghi dung xay khach san trong cong vien' [Ministry of Construction recommends stopping construction of hotel in the park], 26 March. http://mag.ashui.com/index.php/duan/kinhte-phapluat/60-kinhte-phapluat/847-bo-xay-dung-kien-nghi-dung-xay-khach-san-trong-cong-vien.html Accessed 6 August 2010.

Asia Foundation (2008) *Training Needs Assessment of Civil Society Organizations in Vietnam*. Hanoi, November.

AsiaNews (2008) 'Communist party attacks archbishop of Hanoi', 24 September. http://www.asianews.it/index.php?l=en&art=13303&size=A Accessed 1 October 2008.

Aye, NweNwe (2010) 'China: Rolling the agenda for women, girls, gender equality and HIV', presentation by UNAIDS Country Office China to Global Fund SWA Regional Meeting, 29 June.

Bandy J and Smith J, eds. (2005) *Coalitions Across Borders: Transnational Protest and the Neoliberal Order*. Lanham MD: Rowman and Littlefield.

Bao Hongmei and Liu Bing (2007) 'Different voices in the debate on "revering nature"', in Liang Congjie and Yang Dongping, eds. *The China Environmental Yearbook 2005: Crisis and Breakthrough of China's Environment*. Leiden: Brill, 117–32.

Baum R (2008) 'Political implications of China's information revolution: The media, the minders, and their message', in Li, Cheng, ed. *China's Changing Political Landscape: Prospects for Democracy*. Washington: Brookings Institution.

Becker H (1998) *Tricks of the Trade: How to Think about Your Research While You're Doing It*. Chicago: University of Chicago Press.

Béja J-P (2009) 'China since Tiananmen: the massacre's long shadow', *Journal of Democracy*, 20(3): 5–16.

Bell D (2006) *Beyond Liberal Democracy: Political Theory for an East Asian Context*. Princeton.

Bentley JG (2004) 'Survival strategies for civil society organizations in China', *International Journal of Not-for-Profit Law*, 6 (January). www.icnl.org/knowledge/ijnl/vol6iss2/art_1.htm

Bernstein T and Lu Xiaobo (2003) *Taxation Without Representation in Contemporary Rural China*. Cambridge: Cambridge University Press.

Bezlova A (2009) 'China reins in dam builders', *InterPress Service*, 18 June.

Biello D (2009) 'Damming the Yangtze: Are a few big hydropower projects better than a lot of small ones?' *Scientific American*, 13 October.

Blee K and Taylor V (2002) 'Semi-structured Interviewing', in Klandermans B and Staggenborg S, eds. *Methods of Social Movement Research*. Minneapolis: University of Minnesota Press, 90–117.

Bosshard P (2010) 'China: Not the rogue dam builder we feared it would be?' blog posting, 31 March. http://www.internationalrivers.org/blog/peter-bosshard/china-not-rogue-dam-builder-we-feared-it-would-be Accessed 18 October 2010.

Bratton M (1990) 'Non-governmental organisations in Africa: Can they influence public policy?' *Development and Change*, 21: 87–118.

Brettell A (2008) 'Channeling dissent: The institutionalization of environmental dispute resolution', in Ho P and Edmonds RL, eds. *China's Embedded Activism: Opportunities and Constraints of a Social Movement*. London: Routledge, 111–50.

—— (2007) 'China's pollution challenge: The impact of economic growth and environmental complaints on environmental and social outcomes', in Guo S and Guo B, eds. *Challenges Facing Chinese Political Development*. Lanham, MD: Lexington Books, 155–75.

Bright Future Group (BFG) (2010a) 'Gioi thieu nhom Vi tuong lai tuoi sang' [Introducing the Bright Future Group], http://www.ttsongdoclaphn.vn/modules.php?name=News&op=viewst&sid=73 Accessed 10 July 2010.

—— (2010b) 'Muc tieu va nhung hoat dong chinh cua nhom Vi tuong lai tuoi sang' [Objectives and Main Activities of the Bright Future Group], http:// www.ttsong-doclaphn.vn/modules.php?name=News&op=viewst&sid=74 Accessed 10 July 2010.

—— (2010c) 'Ban dieu hanh moi nhom Vi tuong lai tuoi sang' [New Executive Committee of the Bright Future Group], http://www.ttsongdoclaphn.vn/modules.php?name=News&op=viewst&sid=117 Accessed 10 July 2010.

—— (2008) 'Ky niem 20 nam thanh lap nhom 'Vi tuong lai tuoi sang' cua nguoi khuyet tat' [Commemorating 20 Years of Establishing the Bright Future Group of People with Disabilities], paper distributed at workshop, 16 November.

Brown P and Xu K (2010) 'Hydropower development and resettlement policy on China's Nu River', *Journal of Contemporary China*, 19(66): 777–97.

Bu Wei and Liu Xiaohong (2010) *Study of Gender and HIV/AIDS Policy*. Beijing: Research Center for Communication and Youth/Children, Institute of Journalism and Communication, Chinese Academy of Social Sciences, commissioned by UNIFEM and UNAIDS.

Buckley C (2009) 'China's giant water scheme opens torrent of discontent', Reuters, 27 February.

Bui Quang Dung (2007) 'Xa hoi dan su: khai niem va cac van de' [Civil Society: Concept and Issues]', *Tap chi Triet hoc* [Journal of Philosophy], 15 April. http://www.chungta.com/Desktop.aspx/ChungTa-SuyNgam/Van-Hoa/Xa_hoi_dan_su_khai_niem_va_cac_van_de/ Accessed 30 July 2010.

Büsgen M (2006) *NGOs and the Search for Chinese Civil Society: Environmental NGOs in the Nujiang Campaign.* The Hague: Institute of Social Studies Working Paper No. 422.

Cai Yongshun (2008) 'Disruptive collective action in the reform era', in O'Brien K, ed. *Popular Protest in China.* Cambridge MA: Harvard University Press, 163–78.

Casanova J (1998) 'Between nation and civil society: Ethnolinguistic and religious pluralism in independent Ukraine', in Hefner R, ed. *Democratic Civility: The History and Cross-cultural Possibility of an Ideal.* New Brunswick NJ: Transaction, 203–28.

Castells M (1996) *The Rise of the Network Society*, vol. 1. Oxford: Blackwell.

Chamberlain H (1998) 'Civil society with Chinese characteristics', *China Journal*, 39(1): 69–82.

Chan A and Wang Hongzen (2003) 'Raising Labor standards, corporate social responsibility and missing links – Vietnam and China compared', paper presented at conference on 'The Labor of Reform: Employment, Workers' Rights, and Labor Law in China', University of Michigan, March.

Chan A, Kerkvliet B and Unger J, eds. (1999) *Transforming Asian Socialism: China and Vietnam Compared.* Lanham, MD: Rowman & Littlefield.

Chan J (2009) 'China activists say dam will kill off rare fish', 23 June. http://www.cuyoo.cn/html/zhongguo/2009/0623/10374.html Accessed 26 August 2010.

Chan K (2005) 'NGOs under a post-totalitarian regime: China', in Weller R, ed. *Civil Life, Globalization and Political Change in Asia: Organizing between the Family and the State.* London: Routledge, 20–41.

Chang Pao-min (1997) 'Vietnam and China: New opportunities and new challenges', *Contemporary Southeast Asia*, 19(2): 136–51.

Chapman J and Fisher T (2000) 'The effectiveness of NGO campaiging: Lessons from practice', *Development in Practice*, 10(2), May, 151–65.

Chen Feng (2008) 'Worker leaders and framing factory-based resistance', in O'Brien K, ed. *Popular Protest in China.* Cambridge MA: Harvard University Press, 88–107.

Chen Jie (2010) 'Transnational environmental movement: Impacts on the green civil society in China', *Journal of Contemporary China*, 19(65): 503–23.

Chen Xi (2007) 'Between defiance and obedience: Protest opportunism in China', in Perry E and Goldman M, eds. *Grassroots Political Reform in Contemporary China.* Harvard Contemporary China Series 14. Cambridge MA: Harvard University Press, 253–81.

China Association for Non-governmental Organization Cooperation (CANGO) (2008) 'Studying law of the People's Republic of China on the protection of disabled persons', *NGO Cooperation Forum* newsletter 59(4) (July/August), 4–5.

China Development Brief (2009) 'Zhongguo Nuxing Kang'ai Wangluo diyici choubei huiyi zai Beijing zhaokai' [China Women's Network against AIDS convenes first preparatory meeting in Beijing], 2 March. http://www.chinadevelopmentbrief.org.cn/newsview.php?id=228 Accessed 16 August 2010.

China HIV/AIDS Information Network (CHAIN) (2010) *2009/2010 China HIV/AIDS NGO Directory.* Beijing.

China National Network of AIDS CBOs (2008) 'Working Report of the Third Secretariat', 10 December.

Chiu S, Hung H and Lai O (1999) 'Environmental movements in Hong Kong', in Lee Y and So A, eds. *Asia's Environmental Movements: Comparative Perspectives.* Armonk NY: ME Sharpe, 55–88.

Chow J (2010) 'China's billion-dollar aid appetite', *Foreign Policy*, 19 July. http://www.foreignpolicy.com/articles/2010/07/19/chinas_billion_dollar_aid_ appetite Accessed 29 September 2010.

Chu L (2006) 'Catholicism vs. communism, continued: The Catholic church in Vietnam', paper presented at the Midwest Political Science Association, Chicago (April).

Cohen J and Arato A (1992) *Civil Society and Political Theory*. Cambridge, MA: MIT Press.

Coleman J (1990) *Foundations of Social Theory*. Cambridge, MA: Harvard University Press.

Collier D and Levitsky S (1997) 'Democracy with adjectives: Conceptual innovation in comparative research', *World Politics*, 49(3): 430–51.

Connolly W (1974) *The Terms of Political Discourse*. Lexington MA: D.C. Heath and Company.

Cooper C (2006) '"This is our way in": The civil society of environmental NGOs in southwest China', *Government and Opposition*, 41(1): 109–36.

Covey J (1995) 'Accountability and effectiveness in NGO policy alliances', *Journal of International Development*, 7(6): 857–67.

Cronin R (2009) 'Mekong dams and the perils of peace', *Survival*, 51(6), December 2009–January 2010, 147–60.

Crossley N (2002) *Making Sense of Social Movements*. Buckingham: Open University Press.

Cullum B (2010) 'Spotlighting digital activism in Vietnam', online article, http://www.movements.org/blog/entry/spolighting-digital-activism-in-vietnam/ Accessed 21 December 2010.

Cui Xiaohuo (2010) 'Old mine may house garbage-burning plant', *China Daily*, 5 February. http://www.chinadaily.com.cn/business/2010-02/05/content_9435448. htm Accessed 27 August 2010.

Cunningham G, Goulet L, ND Vinh and DT Vinh (2007) *Asset Based & Community Driven Development*. Materials for course held at An Giang University, Vietnam, December 2007. Coady International Institute, St. Francis Xavier University, Canada.

Dai Qing (1998) *The River Dragon Has Come! The Three Gorges Dam and the Fate of China's Yangtze River and its People*. Armonk, NY: ME Sharpe.

Dai Qing and Vermeer E (1999) 'Do good work, but do not offend the "old communists"', in Ash R and Draguhn W, eds. *China's Economic Security*. New York: St. Martins Press, 142–62.

Dalton RJ and Ong N (2004) 'Civil society and social capital in Vietnam', in Mutz G and Klump R, eds. *Modernization and Social Change in Vietnam*. Munich: Munich Institute for Social Science.

Dang Hung Vo (2009) 'Khong the vin vao boi canh du an ma xay khach san' [Don't seize on the background of the project to build a hotel], *Tuan Vietnam*, 17 February.

Dang Kim Son (2007) 'Ba Ban Tay: Thi truong, nha nuoc va cong dong ung dung cho Viet Nam' [Three hands: The market, state and community applied to Vietnam]. Ho Chi Minh City: Nha Xuat Ban Tre.

Dantri (2009) 'Bien cong vien thanh khach san khong phai no luc cua cong dong' [Changing a park into a hotel is not in the community's interest], 12 February. http://dantri.com.vn/c20/s20-307996/bien-cong-vien-thanh-khach-san-khong-phai-no-luc-cua-cong-dong.htm Accessed 6 August 2010.

—— (2007) 'Cong vien Thong Nhat se sanh tam khu vuc' [Reunification Park will attain regional standards], 11 March. http://www.cauduongcang.com/tintuc/73D449.aspx Accessed 3 August 2008.

Deakin N (2001) *In Search of Civil Society*. Basingstoke: Palgrave Macmillan.

Della Porta D, Andretta M, Mosca L and Reiter H (2006) *Globalization from Below: Transnational Activists and Protest Networks*. Minneapolis: University of Minnesota Press.

Della Porta D and Tarrow S, eds. (2005) *Transnational Protest and Global Activism*. New York: Rowman and Littlefield.

Deng Guosheng (2010) 'The hidden rules governing China's unregistered NGOs', *The China Review* 10(1): 183–206.

Desmond M, Hoang Ha, Pham Quang Nam and Treasure-Evans J (2007) 'Establishment of local NGO network on poverty policy monitoring and evaluation, Phase 2 Review', unpublished paper, Oxfam Great Britain, Hanoi, April.

Deutsche Presse Agentur (2010) 'Hotel investors demand 80 million dollars from Hanoi government', 1 April. http://www.earthtimes.org/articles/show/316731, hotel-investors-demand-80-million-dollars-from-hanoi-government.html#ixzz-0kCPV3WLh Accessed 5 April 2010.

Diamond L (2010) 'Liberation technology', *Journal of Democracy*, 21(3): 69–83.

Diani M (2002) 'Network analysis', in Klandermans and Staggenborg, eds. *Methods of Social Movement Research*. Minneapolis: University of Minnesota Press, 173–200.

Diani M and McAdam D, eds. (2003) *Social Movements and Networks: Relational Approaches to Collective Action*. Oxford: Oxford University Press.

Dickson B (2002) 'Collective identity among business entrepreneurs', in Goldman M and Perry E, eds. *Changing Meanings of Citizenship in Modern China*. Cambridge MA: Harvard University Press, 255–87.

Ding Qiwen (2008) 'Canlian yinggai youde shehui shiye' [Disabled People's Federation should have a social vision], *NPO Magazine* (Beijing), November, 74–5.

Ding Xueliang (1994) 'Institutional amphibiousness and the transition from communism: The case of China', *British Journal of Political Science*, 24(3): 293–317.

Dixon C (2004) 'State, party and political change in Vietnam', in McCargo D, ed. *Rethinking Vietnam*. London: RoutledgeCurzon, 15–26.

Do Anh Dung (2007) 'Tan Hoang Minh giai trinh du an cong vien Thong Nhat' [Tan Hoang Minh explains the Reunification Park project], *Tuan Vietnam*, 13 August http://tuanvietnam.net/vn/thongtindachieu/988/index.aspx Accessed 3 August 2008.

Doan Loan (2007) 'Cong vien Thong Nhat se khong bi bien thanh Disneyland' [Reunification Park Will Not Become Disneyland], *VN Express*, 18 August. http://www.vnexpress.net/GL/Xa-hoi/2007/08/3B9F94E1/ Accessed 7 July 2008.

Dogan M and Pelassy D (1984) *How to Compare Nations*, 2nd edition. Chatham, NJ: Chatham House Publishers.

Donaldson K (2009) 'Why do similar areas adopt different developmental strategies? A study of two puzzling Chinese provinces', *Journal of Contemporary China*, 18(60), June: 421–44.

Dore J and Yu Xiaogang (2003) 'China plans to dam the Nu/Salween River', *Watershed*, 9(2) (November): 4–5.

Douban (2009) 'Women's network against AIDS is established, cooperates with CSR pioneers', 4 August. http://www.douban.com/group/topic/7510656/ Accessed 27 September 2010.

Douglass M, Ho KC and Ooi GL, eds. (2008) *Globalization, the City and Civil Society in Pacific Asia*. New York: Routledge.

Drummond L (2000) 'Street scenes: Practices of public and private space in urban Vietnam', *Urban Studies*, 37(2): 2377–91.

Dugan M (1996) 'A nested theory of conflict', *Women in Leadership*, 1(1).

Eccleston B (1996) 'Does North-South collaboration enhance NGO influence on deforestation policies in Malaysia and Indonesia?' in Potter D and Taylor A, ed. *NGOs and environmental policies in Asia and Africa*. London: Frank Cass, 66–89.

Economy E (2005) Testimony to the U.S. Congressional-Executive Commission on China, roundtable on 'Environmental NGOs in China: Encouraging Action and Addressing Public Grievances', 7 February.

—— (2004) *The River Runs Black: The Environmental Challenge to China's Future*. Ithaca NY: Cornell University Press.

Edwards M (2004) *Civil Society*. Cambridge: Polity Press.

Edwards M and Gaventa J eds. (2001) *Global Citizen Action*. London: Earthscan.

Ekins P (1992) *A New World Order: Grassroots Movements for Global Change*. London: Routledge.

Embassy of Denmark (2010) 'Danish Society of Polio and Accident Victims – PTU: Support to persons with disabilities', http://www.ambhanoi.um.dk/en/menu/ DevelopmentPolicy/DanishNGOsinVietnam/Danish++Society+of+Polio+and+Ac ident+Victims+(PTU)/ Accessed 13 July.

Emirbayer M (1997) 'A manifesto for a relational sociology', *American Journal of Sociology*, 103(2): 281–317.

Emirbayer M and Goodwin J (1994) 'Network analysis, culture and the problem of agency', *American Journal of Sociology*, 99(6): 1411–54.

Encarnación O (2006) 'Civil society reconsidered', *Comparative Politics*, 38(3): 357–76.

Erlandson D, Harris E, Skipper B and Allen S (1993) *Doing Naturalistic Inquiry: A Guide to Methods*. Newbury Park CA: Sage Publications.

Esarey A and Xiao Quang (2008) 'Political expression in the Chinese blogosphere: Below the radar', *Asian Survey*, 48(5): 752–72.

Evans P (1996) 'Government action, social capital and development: Reviewing the evidence on synergy', *World Development*, 24(6): 1119–32.

Eyerman R and Jamison A (1991) *Social Movements: A Cognitive Approach*. Cambridge: Polity Press.

Fay B (1996) *Contemporary Philosophy of Social Science: A Multicultural Approach*. Cambridge, MA: Blackwell.

Fei Xiaotong (1992) *From the Soil: The Foundations of Chinese Society*. Berkeley: University of California Press.

Feng Yongfeng (2008) 'The different roles involved in garbage collection', Friends of Nature newsletter, Spring 2008. http://www.fon.org.cn/content.php?aid=9932 Accessed 27 August 2010.

Fforde A (2009) 'Economics, history, and the origins of Vietnam's post-war economic success', *Asian Survey*, 49(3): 484–504.

Fiedler K and Zhang Liwei, eds. (2005) *Growing in Partnership: The Amity Foundation 1985–2005*. Hong Kong: Amity Foundation.

Fisher J (1998) *Nongovernments*. Bloomfield CT: Kumarian Press.

Florini A, ed. (2000) *The Third Force: The Rise of Transnational Civil Society*. Tokyo/ Washington: Japan Center for International Exchange and Carnegie Endowment for International Peace.

Ford P (2009) 'China quake: From rubble, civil society builds', *Christian Science Monitor*, 10 May.

Fowler A (1997) *Striking a Balance*. London: Earthscan.

Fox J (1996) 'How does civil society thicken? The political construction of social capital in rural Mexico', *World Development*, 24(6): 1089–103.

Franco J (2004) 'The Philippines: Fractious civil society and competing visions of democracy', in Alagappa M, ed. *Civil Society and Political Change in Asia: Expanding and Contracting Democratic Space*. Stanford: Stanford University Press, 97–137.

Friedman E and Gilley, B eds. (2005) *Asia's Giants: Comparing China and India*. New York: Palgrave Macmillan.

Friends of Nature (2010) 'NGO guanzhu jianghe shijianbiao' [Chronology of NGO River Activities], http://www.fon.org.cn/content.php?aid=11750 Accessed 11 October 2010.

Fritzen S (2003) 'Donors, local development groups and institutional reform over Vietnam's development decade', in Kerkvliet B, Heng R and Hock D, eds. *Getting Organized in Vietnam: Moving In and Around the Socialist State*. Singapore: Institute of Southeast Asian Studies, 234–70.

Frolic M (1997) 'State-led civil society', in Brook T and Frolic M, eds. *Civil Society in China*. Armonk, NY: M.E. Sharpe, 46–67.

Fu Gang (2006) 'Zhengzhi goutong zouxiang wangluo, yuenan xianxing yibu' [Vietnam is a step ahead in online political communication], *Nanfang Shiping*, 26 October. http://www.southcn.com/opinion/gjgc/200610260244.htm Accessed 4 October 2010.

Fu Tao (2007) 'Development of environmental NGOs in China', in Liang Congjie and Yang Dongping, eds. *The China Environmental Yearbook 2005: Crisis and Breakthrough of China's Environment*. Leiden: Brill, 291–310.

Futrell WC (2008) 'Evolution of international NGOs in China: Broadening environmental collaboration and shifting priorities', in Yang Dongping, ed. *The China Environment Yearbook, Volume 2: Changes and Struggles*. Leiden: Brill Academic Publishers, 225–57.

Gadsden A (2008) 'Earthquake rocks China's civil society', *Far Eastern Economic Review*, 171(5), June, 25–9.

Gallagher M (2004) 'China: The limits of civil society in a late Leninist state', in Alagappa M (ed.) *Civil Society and Political Change in Asia*. Stanford: Stanford University Press, 419–54.

Gamson W (1990) *The Strategy of Social Protest*, 2nd edition. Homewood IL: Dorsey Press.

Gamson W and Meyer D (1996) 'Framing political opportunity', in McAdam D, McCarthy J and Zald M, eds. *Comparative Perspectives on Social Movements: Political Opportunities, Mobilizing Structures, and Cultural Framings*. Cambridge: Cambridge University Press, 275–90.

Gao Bingzhong (2007) 'Understanding the revival and survival of grass-roots associations in China: The perspective of four categories of legitimacy', *Horizontes Antropológicos* (Brazil) 13(27): 49–68.

Gao Bingzhong and Yuan Ruijun (2008) *Zhongguo Gongmin Shehui Fazhan Lanpi Shu* [Blue Book on Civil Society Development in China]. Beijing: Peking University Press.

Garcia J (2006) *Whose Development Is It Anyway? An Analysis of Civil Society Engagement with Multilateral Development Banks in Mekong/SE Asia*. Washington: Bank Information Center.

Gaventa J (2007) 'Levels, spaces, and forms of power: Analyzing opportunities for change', in Berenskoetter F and Williams J, eds. *Power in World Politics*. London: Routledge, 204–24.

Ge Quanxiao (2004) 'The relationship between dam construction and the rights of original inhabitants to participation', paper prepared for the UN Symposium on Hydropower and Sustainable Development, Beijing, 27–29 October. http://www.internationalrivers.org/files/dampar.pdf Accessed 9 September 2010.

Geertz C (1973) *The Interpretation of Cultures*. New York: Basic Books.

Global Times (2011) 'Trash incinerator plans scrapped after resident outcry', 21 January. http://beijing.globaltimes.cn/society/2011-01/615212.html Accessed 14 March 2011.

Gnep Y (2009) 'Mobilising the community: Modalities and ambiguities of HIV carriers' participation in China's fight against AIDS', *China Perspectives* 2009/1, 8–15.

Gold T (1998) 'Bases for civil society in reform China', in Brødsgaard K and Strand D, eds. *Reconstructing Twentieth Century China: State Control, Civil Society and National Culture*. Oxford: Clarendon Press, 163–86.

Gold T, Guthrie D and Wank D, eds. (2002) *Social Connections in China: Institutions, Culture and the Changing Nature of Guanxi*. Cambridge: Cambridge University Press.

Goodwin J and Jasper J (1999) 'Caught in a winding, snarling vine: The structural bias of political process theory', *Sociological Forum*, 14(1): 27–54.

Government of Vietnam (2004) *National Strategy on HIV/AIDS Prevention and Control*, March.

Gramsci A (1971) *Selections from the Prison Notebooks*, ed. Hoare and Smith. London: Lawrence and Wishart.

Granovetter M (1985) 'Economic action and social structure: The problem of embeddedness', *American Journal of Sociology*, 91(3): 481–510.

—— (1973) 'The strength of weak ties', *American Journal of Sociology*, 78(6): 1360–80.

Gray M (2003) 'NGOs and highland development: A case study in crafting new roles', in Kerkvliet B, Heng R and Koh D, eds. *Getting Organized in Vietnam: Moving In and Around the Socialist State*. Singapore: Institute of Southeast Asian Studies, 110–25.

—— (1999) 'Creating civil society? The emergence of NGOs in Vietnam', *Development and Change*, 30: 693–713.

Green Earth Volunteers (2006) Grant report to China GreenGrants Fund, 26 May.

Gu Chengyong (2002) 'Fei zhengfu zuzhi: Zhongguo yu Dongnanya' [Non-governmental organizations: China and Southeast Asia], in Curley and Liu, eds. *China and Southeast Asia: Changing Socio-Cultural Interactions*. Hong Kong: Centre for Asian Studies, University of Hong Kong, 69–77.

Gu Hongyan (2008) 'Participatory citizenship and sustainable development: Redefining "public" in contemporary China and Japan', paper presented at 17th Biennial Conference of the Asian Studies Association of Australia, Melbourne, 1–3 July.

Gu Xin (1993) 'A civil society and public sphere in post-Mao China? An overview of Western publications', *China Information*, 8(3): 38–52.

Gupta A (2006) 'Blurred boundaries: The discourse of corruption, the culture of politics, and the imagines state', in Sharma A and Gupta A, eds. *The Anthropology of the State: A Reader*. Malden, MA and Oxford: Blackwell Publishing, 211–42.

Habermas J (1962) *Strukturwandel der Öffentlichkeit*. Neuwied am Rhein: Luchterhand.

Haggart K and Mu Lan (2003) 'People power sinks a dam', 16 October. http://www.probeinternational.org/written-probe-international/people-power-sinks-dam Accessed 23 August 2010.

Han Jialing, Tang Mengjun, Liu Hongyan, Liu Zhongyi and Gao Xing (2009) *A Literature Review on Spousal Transmission of HIV in China*. Beijing: Social Development Resource Centre, Beijing Academy of Social Sciences.

Han Ziyu (2011) 'Razing the last refuge', *China Dialogue*, 9 February. http://www.chinadialogue.net/article/show/single/en/4095 Accessed 15 March 2011.

Hance J (2009) 'New Yangtze River dam could doom more endangered species', 22 June. http://news.mongabay.com/2009/0622-hance_dam_yangtze.html Accessed 26 August 2010.

Hannah J (2007) *Approaching Civil Society in Vietnam*. PhD diss., Department of Geography, University of Washington.

—— (2005) 'Civil-society actors and action in Vietnam: Preliminary empirical results and sketches from an evolving debate', *Towards Good Society*. Berlin: Heinrich Böll Foundation, 100–10.

Haynes J (1997) *Democracy and Civil Society in the Third World: Politics and New Political Movements*. Cambridge: Polity Press.

Hayton B (2010) *Vietnam: Rising Dragon*. New Haven: Yale University Press.

He Baogang (2003) 'The making of a nascent civil society in China', in Schak D and Hudson M, eds. *Civil Society in Asia*. Aldershot: Ashgate, 114–39.

—— (1997) *The Democratic Implications of Civil Society in China*. Basingstoke: Macmillan.

He Haining (2010) 'Sheri Liao: Extreme environmental activist', *Nanfang Zhoumo*, 6 January. http://eng.greensos.cn/showArticle.aspx?articleId=338 Accessed 27 August 2010.

He Haining and Meng Dengke (2010) 'The superman who saves the world', *Nanfang Zhoumo*, 13 January. http://eng.greensos.cn/showArticle.aspx?articleId=341 Accessed 26 August 2010.

He Tiantian (2009) 'Dandelion – Endless efforts on the journey', *China Global Fund Watch* Newsletter, 8 (July): 3–4.

—— (2008) 'Nuxing ganranzhe, zhanqilai, zouchulai!' [Infected women: Stand up and come out!], *Women de shengyin* [Our Voice] 6 (November), 7.

He Xiaopei (2006) *I am AIDS: Living with the Epidemic in China*. PhD thesis, University of Westminster.

He Xirong (1997) 'Collective identity and civil society', in Wang M, Yu X and Dy M, eds. *Civil Society in a Chinese Context*. Washington: Council for Research in Values and Philosophy.

HealthBridge (2008) 'Initial Steps towards a Healthy Urban Living Environment: Final report'.

Hedman E (2006) *In the Name of Civil Society: From Free Election Movements to People Power in the Philippines*. Honolulu: University of Hawai'i Press.

—— (2001) 'Contesting state and civil society: Southeast Asian trajectories', *Modern Asian Studies*, 35(4): 921–51.

Heinrich Böll Foundation (2006) *Active Citizens Under Political Wraps: Experiences from Myanmar/Burma and Vietnam*. Chiang Mai.

Hellberg L and Johansson A (2008) *Another Future for Thong Nhat Park: Public Spaces in Transition in the New Urban Reality of Hanoi*. Master's Thesis in Landscape Architecture, Swedish University of Agricultural Sciences.

Heng R (2004) 'Civil society effectiveness and the Vietnamese state – Despite or because of the lack of autonomy', in Lee HG, ed. *Civil Society in Southeast Asia*. Singapore: Institute of Southeast Asia Studies, 144–66.

—— (2003) 'Status of media in Vietnam', *Encyclopedia of International Media and Communications*, Elsevier Science (USA), Vol. 4, 561–71.

Hensengerth O (2010) *Sustainable Dam Development in China Between Global Norms and Local Practices*. Discussion Paper. Bonn: Deutsches Institut für Entwicklungspolitik, April.

Heyzer N, Riker J and Quizon A, eds. (1995) *Government-NGO Relations in Asia: Prospects and Challenges for People-Centered Development*. Basingstoke: Macmillan.

Hildebrant T (2009) 'Beyond nomenclature: Authoritarian governance in a democratic world', Edward Friedman Festschrift presented at the University of Toronto, October 24.

Hildebrant T and Turner J (2009) 'Green activism? Reassessing the role of environmental NGOs in China', in Schwartz J and Shieh S, eds. *Serving the People: State and Society Responses to Social Welfare Needs in China*. London: Routledge, 89–110.

Hinton P (2000) 'Where nothing is as it seems: Between Southeast China and Mainland Southeast Asia in the "post-Socialist" era', in Evans G, ed., *Where China Meets Southeast Asia: Social and Cultural Change in the Border Regions*. Singapore: Institute for Southeast Asian Studies, chapter 1.

Hirsch P (2010) 'The changing political dynamics of dam building on the Mekong', *Water Alternatives*, 3(2): 312–23.

Hirsch P and Warren C, eds. (1998) *The Politics of Environment in Southeast Asia*. London: Routledge.

Ho P (2008a) 'Introduction: Embedded activism and political change in a semi-authoritarian context', in Ho P and Edmonds RL, eds. *China's Embedded Activism: Opportunities and Constraints of a Social Movement*. London: Routledge, 1–19.

—— (2008b) 'Self-imposed censorship and de-politicized politics in China: Green activism or a color revolution?' in Ho P and Edmonds RL, eds. *China's Embedded Activism: Opportunities and Constraints of a Social Movement*. London: Routledge, 20–43.

—— (2001) 'Greening without conflict? Environmentalism, green NGOs and civil society in China', *Development and Change*, 32(5): 893–921.

Ho P and Edmonds RL, eds. (2008) *China's Embedded Activism: Opportunities and Constraints of a Social Movement*. London: Routledge.

Hoang Huy (2008) 'Ha Noi: Khoi cong khach san lon sat cong vien Thong Nhat' [Hanoi: Ground breaking of a large hotel adjacent to Reunification Park], *VietNamNet*, http://vietnamnet.vn/kinhte/2008/06/787111/ Accessed 6 August 2010.

—— (2007a) 'Tra gia dat neu Cong vien Thong Nhat thanh "dai nha hang"!' [High price to pay if Reunification Park becomes a 'big restaurant'!], *VietNamNet*, 7 August, http://vietnamnet.vn/xahoi/2007/08/726867/ Accessed 3 August 2008.

—— (2007b) 'Cong vien Thong Nhat se chi la noi nghi ngoi, thu gian' [Reunification Park will just be a place for rest and relaxation], *VietNamNet*, 19 August, http://tintuconline.vietnamnet.vn/vn/xahoi/158071/ Accessed 3 August 2008.

Hoang Lan Anh and Bui Phuong Anh (2008) *Review and Development of the Project on Building Civil Society Inclusion in Food Security and Poverty Elimination Network (CIFPEN)*. Hanoi: ActionAid Vietnam.

Hom S and Mosher S, eds. (2007) *Challenging China: Struggle and Hope in an Era of Change*. New York: Human Rights in China/Basic Books.

Howell J (2006) 'Gender and civil society', in Anheier et al, *Global Civil Society 2005–06*. London: Sage, ch. 1.

—— (2004b) 'Introduction', in Howell J and Mulligan D, eds. *Gender and Civil Society*. London: Routledge, 3–22.

—— (1996) 'Drops in the ocean: NGOs in China', in Clayton A, ed. *NGOs, Civil Society, and the State: Building Democracy in Transitional Societies*. Oxford: INTRAC.

Howell J, ed. (2004a) *Governance in China*. Lanham MD: Rowman and Littlefield.

Howell J and Mulligan D, eds. (2004) *Gender and Civil Society*. London: Routledge.

Howell J and Pearce J (2001) *Civil Society and Development: A Critical Exploration*. Boulder, CO: Lynne Rienner.

Hu Jia (2007) 'A tale of two crises: SARS versus AIDS', in Hom S and Mosher S, eds. *Challenging China: Struggle and Hope in an Era of Change*. New York: Human Rights in China/Basic Books, 13–31.

Hu Ping (2007) 'The Falun Gong phenomenon', in Hom S and Mosher S, eds. *Challenging China: Struggle and Hope in an Era of Change*. New York: Human Rights in China/Basic Books, 226–51.

Hughes C (2003) *The Political Economy of Cambodia's Transition*. London: Routledge-Curzon.

Human Rights Watch (2010a) Annual Report: China.

—— (2010b) Annual Report: Vietnam.

Inclusive Development Action (IDEA) (2009) Monthly Update, January.

—— (2008) Monthly Update, January–February.

—— (undated) Inclusive Development Action program brochure.

International Disability Rights Monitor (2005) *Vietnam IDRM Country Report*. http://www.ideanet.org/idrm_reports.cfm Accessed 1 June 2007.

International HIV/AIDS Alliance (2010) 'Case studies: How it works in practice', http://www.alliancechina.org/Alliance_China_Office/Case_Studies.html Accessed 26 August 2010.

James R and Malunga C (2006) 'The rise and pitfalls of civil society networks in Malawi', CADECO.

Jenkins JC (1987) 'Nonprofit organisations and policy advocacy', in Powell W, ed. *The Nonprofit Sector: A Research Handbook*. New Haven: Yale University Press.

Jeong Y (1997) 'The rise of state corporatism in Vietnam', *Contemporary Southeast Asia*, 19(2): 152–71.

Jia Ping (2009) 'Democracy in bud', China Global Fund Watch Research Report #1.

Jiang Gaoming (2009) 'The high price of developing dams', *China Dialogue*, http://www.chinadialogue.net/article/show/single/en/2707-The-high-price-of-developing-dams Accessed 4 November 2009.

Jiang Ru (2005) Testimony to the U.S. Congressional-Executive Commission on China, roundtable on 'Environmental NGOs in China: Encouraging Action and Addressing Public Grievances', 7 February.

Johnson I (2004) *Wild Grass: Three Stories of Change in Modern China*. New York: Pantheon.

Jorgensen L (1996) 'What are NGOs doing in civil society?' in Clayton A, ed. *NGOs, Civil Society, and the State: Building Democracy in Transitional Societies*. Oxford: INTRAC.

Jun Jing (2003) 'Environmental protests in rural China', in Perry E and Selden M, eds. *Chinese Society: Change, Conflict and Resistance*, 2nd edition. London: Routledge, 204–22.

Kadir S (2004) 'Singapore: Engagement and autonomy within the political status quo', in Alagappa M, ed. *Civil Society and Political Change in Asia: Expanding and Contracting Democratic Space*. Stanford: Stanford University Press, 324–56.

Kaldor M (2003) *Global Civil Society: An Answer to War*. Cambridge: Polity Press.

Kaldor M, Anheier H, Glasius M and Albrow M (2007) *Global Civil Society 2006–07*. London: Sage.

Kalland A and Persoon G, eds. (1998) *Environmental Movements in Asia*. Surrey: Curzon.

Katz H and Anheier H, 'Global connectedness: The structure of transnational NGO networks', in Anheier et al, *Global Civil Society 2006*. London: Sage.

Kaufman J (2010) 'Turning points in China's AIDS response', *China: An International Journal*, 8(1): 63–84.

Kaufman J, Kleinman A and Saich T, eds. (2006) *AIDS and Social Policy in China*. Cambridge MA: Harvard University Asia Center.

Keck M and Sikkink K (1998) *Activists Beyond Borders*. Ithaca, NY: Cornell University Press.

Keech-Marx S (2008) 'Airing dirty laundry in public: Anti-domestic violence activism in Beijing', in Unger J, ed. *Associations and the Chinese State*. Armonk NY: ME Sharpe, 14–47.

Kerkvliet B (2003) 'Introduction: Grappling with organizations and the state in contemporary Vietnam', in Kerkvliet, Heng and Koh, eds. *Getting Organized in Vietnam: Moving In and Around the Socialist State*. Singapore: Institute of Southeast Asian Studies, 1–24.

—— (2001a) 'Introduction: Analyzing the society in Vietnam', *Sojourn*, 16(2) (October), 179–86.

—— (2001b) 'An approach for analysing state-society relations in Vietnam', *Sojourn* 16(2) (October), 238–78.

Kerkvliet B, Chan A and Unger J (1998) 'Comparing the Chinese and Vietnamese reforms: An introduction', *China Journal*, 40: 1–7.

Kerkvliet B, Nguyen Quang A and Bach Tan Sinh (2008) *Forms of Engagement Between State Agencies and Civil Society Organizations in Vietnam*. Hanoi: NGO Resource Centre.

Kerkvliet B and Porter D, eds. (1995) *Vietnam's Rural Transformation*. Boulder: Westview.

Khagram S, Riker J and Sikkink K, eds. (2002) *Restructuring World Politics: Transnational Social Movements, Networks, and Norms*. Minneapolis: University of Minnesota Press.

Khiet Hung (2006) 'Dung so xa hoi dan su!' [Don't be afraid of civil society], *Tuoi Tre*, 21 May. http://tuoitre.vn/Chinh-tri-Xa-hoi/138839/Dung-so-xa-hoi-dan-su.html Accessed 16 August 2010.

Kim Tan (2009) 'Kien nghi dung du an khach san tai cong vien Thong Nhat' [Recommendation to stop hotel project in Reunification Park], *Dantri*,

26 February. http://dantri.com.vn/c20/s20-315615/kien-nghi-dung-du-an-khach-san-tai-cong-vien-thong-nhat.htm Accessed 31 March 2009.

King G, Keohane R and Verba S (1994) *Designing Social Inquiry: Scientific Inference in Qualitative Research*. Princeton: Princeton University Press.

King W (2010) 'Civic society as the nexus between formal democratic and informal engagement: the case of Taiwan', paper presented at conference on 'Civil Society in East and Southeast Asia: Understanding the Local Impact of the Global Promotion of Civil Society', University of Bristol, 14 January 2010.

Kingdon J (2003) *Agendas, Alternatives, and Public Policies*, 2nd edition. New York: Longman.

Klandermans B and Staggenborg S, eds. (2002) *Methods of Social Movement Research*. Minneapolis: University of Minnesota Press.

Knoke D (1990) *Political Networks: The Structural Perspective*. Cambridge: Cambridge University Press.

Knoke D and Kuklinski J (1982) *Network Analysis*. Newbury Park CA: Sage.

Koopmans R (2004) 'Protest in time and space: The evolution of waves of contention', in Snow D, Soule S and Kriesi H, eds. *The Blackwell Companion to Social Movements*. Oxford: Blackwell, 19–46.

Korten D (1990a) *Getting to the 21st Century: Voluntary Action and the Global Agenda*. West Hartford CT: Kumarian Press.

—— (1990b) 'NGO strategic networks: From community projects to global transformation', paper presented at the Asian Regional Workshop on Strategic Networking for Sustainable Development and Environmental Action, Bangkok, 26–30 November.

Krebs V (2004) 'Power in networks', www.orgnet.com Accessed 20 October 2010.

Kuhn A (2009) 'Beijing neighbors unite against incinerator plans', *National Public Radio*, 9 April. Transcript at http://www.npr.org/templates/story/story.php?storyId=102003993 Accessed 27 August 2010.

Kürten S (2008) 'The transformation of public space in Hanoi', *Asien*, 108 (July): 67–79.

Kyaw Yin Hlaing (2004) 'Burma: Civil society skirting regime rules', in Alagappa M, ed. *Civil Society and Political Change in Asia: Expanding and Contracting Democratic Space*. Stanford: Stanford University Press, 389–418.

Lam W (2007a) 'Chinks in the armour of the Hu Jintao administration: Can a harmonious society emerge in the absence of political reform?' *China Perspectives*, 3.

—— (2007b) 'China's debate over Vietnam's reforms', *China Brief*, 6(16), 9 May. http://www.jamestown.org/programs/chinabrief/single/?tx_ttnews%5Btt_news%5D=3966&tx_ttnews%5BbackPid%5D=196&no_cache=1 Accessed 4 October 2010.

Le Nhung, Thao Lam and Phuong Loan (2009) 'Ha Noi cho tiep tuc du an khach san gay tranh cai' [Hanoi's allowing hotel project to continue creates debate], *VietNamNet*, 14 February. http://vietnamnet.vn/chinhtri/2009/02/828851/ Accessed 6 August 2010.

Lederach JP (1997) *Building Peace: Sustainable Reconciliation in Divided Societies*. Washington: U.S. Institute of Peace.

Lee Ching Kwan (2007a) *Against the Law: Labor Protests in China's Rustbelt and Sunbelt*. Berkeley: University of California Press.

—— (2007b) 'Is Labor a political force in China?' in Perry E and Goldman M, eds. *Grassroots Political Reform in Contemporary China*. Harvard Contemporary China Series 14. Cambridge MA: Harvard University Press, 228–52.

Lee HG, ed. (2004) *Civil Society in Southeast Asia*. Singapore: Institute of Southeast Asian Studies.

Lee Seungjoo and Rhyu Sang-Young (2008) 'The political dynamics of informal networks in South Korea: The case of parachute appointment', *Pacific Review*, 21(1): 45–66.

Lee Yok-shiu and So AL, eds. (1999) *Asia's Environmental Movements: Comparative Perspectives*. Armonk NY: ME Sharpe.

Lehmann C (2011) 'An accelerated grimace', *The Nation* (21 March), 30–5.

Lewis D (2001) *The Management of Non-Governmental Development Organizations*. London: Routledge.

Li, Cheng (2009) 'Introduction', in Yu Keping, *Democracy is a Good Thing: Essays on Politics, Society, and Culture in Contemporary China*. Washington: Brookings Institution Press, xvii–xxxi.

Li Fangchao (2007) 'Public opposes Xiamen chemical plant', *China Daily*, 30 May, 4.

Li Jingrong (2009) 'Hydropower projects on Jinsha River ordered to halt', 22 June. http://www.china.org.cn/environment/features_analyses/2009-06/22/content_17992826_3.htm Accessed 30 August 2010.

Liang Congjie and Yang Dongping, eds. (2007) *The China Environmental Yearbook 2005: Crisis and Breakthrough of China's Environment*. Leiden: Brill.

Lin Nan (2001) *Social Capital: A Theory of Social Structure and Action*. New York: Cambridge.

Lin Teh-Chang (2007) 'Environmental NGOs and the anti-dam movements in China: A social movement with Chinese characteristics', *Issues & Studies*, 43(4), December, 149–84.

Lindau J and Cheek T, eds. (1998) *Market Economics and Political Change: Comparing China and Mexico*. Lanham MD: Rowman and Littlefield.

Linh Thuy (2009) 'Bao chi quanh vu xay khach san tai CV Thong Nhat' [Media reports on the case of hotel construction in Reunification Park], *Tuan Vietnam*, 19 February.

Link P (2002) 'The anaconda in the chandelier; censorship in China today', Woodrow Wilson International Center for Scholars Asia Special Report 102 (April): 3–7.

Linz J and Stepan A (1997) 'Toward consolidated democracies', in Diamond L et al, eds. *Consolidating the Third Wave Democracies: Themes and Perspectives*. Baltimore: Johns Hopkins University Press, 14–33.

Litzinger R (2007) 'In search of the grassroots: Hydroelectric politics in Northwest Yunnan', in Perry E and Goldman M, eds. *Grassroots Political Reform in Contemporary China*. Harvard Contemporary China Series 14. Cambridge MA: Harvard University Press, 282–99.

Liu Hong (2001) 'Sino-Southeast Asian studies: Towards an alternative paradigm', *Asian Studies Review*, 25(3): 259–83.

Liu Jianqiang (2007a) 'Fog on the Nu River', http://www.chinadialogue.net/article/show/single/en/811-Fog-on-the-Nu-River Accessed 4 November 2009

—— (2007b) 'Small, yet brave', *China Dialogue*, 22 June. http://www.chinadialogue.net/article/show/single/en/1117-Small-yet-brave Accessed 27 August 2010.

Liu Xiaobo (2007) 'China's robber barons', in Hom S and Mosher S, eds. *Challenging China: Struggle and Hope in an Era of Change*. New York: Human Rights in China/ Basic Books, 69–77.

—— (2006) 'Reform in China: The role of civil society', *Social Research*, 73(1): 121–38.

Liu Zhenting (2006) 'Yuenan zhengzhi gaige quanmian chaoyue zhongguo' [Vietnam completely surpasses China in political reform], *Yazhou Zhoukan*, 9 July. http://news.creaders.net/photo/newsViewer.php?id=668161 Accessed 4 October 2010.

Lo Sze-ping (2007) 'Environmental problems and Greenpeace in China', presentation at the Woodrow Wilson Center China Environment Forum, Washington DC, 19 September.

Logan W (2000) *Hanoi: Biography of a City*. Sydney: University of New South Wales Press.

London J (2009) 'Viet Nam and the making of market-Leninism', *Pacific Review*, 22(3): 375–99.

Lu Yiyi (2008) *Non-governmental Organizations in China: The Rise of Dependent Autonomy*. London: Routledge.

—— (2005) 'Environmental civil society and governance in China', Chatham House Briefing Paper ASP BP 05/04, August.

Luong Van Hy (2005) 'State, local associations and alternate civilities in rural Northern Vietnam', in Weller R, ed. *Civil Life, Globalization and Political Change in Asia: Organizing Between the Family and the State*. London: Routledge, 124–49.

Luong Van Hy, ed. (2003) *Postwar Vietnam: Dynamics of a Transforming Society*. Lanham, MD: Rowman and Littlefield.

Lux S and Straussman J (2004) 'Searching for balance: Vietnamese NGOs operating in a state-led civil society', *Public Administration & Development*, 24(2): 173–81.

Ma, Josephine (2005) 'Green groups fall under microscope', *South China Morning Post*, 18 August, 12.

Ma Jun (2004) *China's Water Crisis*. Norwalk CT: Eastbridge.

Ma Qiusha (2006) *Non-governmental Organizations in Contemporary China: Paving the Way to Civil Society?* London: Routledge.

Magee D (2006) 'Powershed politics: Yunnan hydropower development under great western development', *China Quarterly*, 185: 23–41.

Manahan MA (2010) 'A decade after the Cochabamba water wars: Inspiration for water justice and democratization struggles in Asia', *Focus on Trade*, 151 (30 May).

Marr D (2003) 'A passion for modernity: Intellectuals and the media', in Luong Van Hy, ed. *Postwar Vietnam: Dynamics of a Transforming Society*. Lanham, MD: Rowman and Littlefield, 257–95.

—— (1994) 'The Vietnam Communist Party and civil society', paper presented at the Vietnam Update 1994 Conference: Doi Moi, the state and civil society, 10–11 November, Australian National University, Canberra.

Marsh D and Rhodes R (1992) *Policy Networks in British Government*. Oxford: Clarendon Press.

Mattausch J (2000) 'The peace movement: Retrospects and prospect', in Cohen R and Rai S, eds. *Global Social Movements*. London: Athlone Press, 184–95.

McAdam D, McCarthy J and Zald M, eds. (1996) *Comparative Perspectives on Social Movements: Political Opportunities, Mobilizing Structures, and Cultural Framings*. Cambridge: Cambridge University Press.

McAdam D, Tarrow S, and Tilly C (2001) *Dynamics of Contention*. Cambridge: Cambridge University Press.

McCarthy H, Miller P and Skidmore P, eds. (2004) *Network Logic: Who Governs in an Inter-Connected World?* London: Demos.

McDonald, Kevin (2006) *Global Movements: Action and Culture*. Malden, MA: Blackwell.

McDonald, Kristen (2007) *Damming China's Grand Canyon: Pluralization Without Democratization in the Nu River Valley*. PhD diss., Environmental Science, Policy, and Management, University of California, Berkeley.

McGray H and McDonald K (2007) *China's Yunnan Province: Challenges and Opportunities in Environmental Governance*. World Resources Institute.

Melucci A (1996) *Challenging Codes: Collective Action in the Information Age*. Cambridge: Cambridge University Press.

Meng Dengke (2010) 'Media turns into NGOs', *Nanfang Zhoumo*, 13 January. http://eng.greensos.cn/ShowArticle.aspx?articleId=340 Accessed 27 August 2010.

—— (2009) 'A diminishing home for rare and endangered fish', *Nanfang Zhoumo*, 28 October. http://eng.greensos.cn/ShowArticle.aspx?articleId=279 Accessed 26 August 2010.

Meng Lin (2009) 'Ganranzhe caogen zuzhi zai Zhongguo minzhu yu fazhi jincheng zhong de zuoyong he fansi' [Reflections on the role played by PLWHA grassroots organisations in China's democratic and legal development], *Women de shengyin*, 2009/2, 1–2.

Meng Si (2011) 'Last ditch plea on Yangtze dam', *China Dialogue*, 9 March. http://www.chinadialogue.net/article/show/single/en/4152 Accessed 15 March 2011.

Mertha A (2008) *China's Water Warriors: Citizen Action and Policy Change*. Ithaca, NY: Cornell University Press.

Meyer M (2008) *The Last Days of Old Beijing*. New York: Walker & Company.

Milwertz C (2002) *Beijing Women Organizing for Change: A New Wave of the Chinese Women's Movement*. Singapore: NIAS Press.

Ministry of Environmental Protection (2009) 'MEP suspended approvals of EIA for hydropower development projects of China Huaneng Group and China Huadian Corporation to control illegal construction projects and energy-intensive and high-polluting overlapping construction projects', 11 June. http://english.mep.gov.cn/News_service/news_release/200907/t20090723_156677.htm Accessed 30 August 2010.

Ministry of Health (2010) *China 2010 UNGASS Country Progress Report (2008–2009)*.

Ministry of Labour, Invalids and Social Affairs (MOLISA) (2005) *Survey on Persons with Disabilities in Vietnam*. Hanoi.

Minkoff D (2002) 'Macro-organizational analysis', in Klandermans and Staggenborg, eds. *Methods of Social Movement Research*. Minneapolis: University of Minnesota Press, 260–85.

Minzner C (2006) 'Xinfang: An alternative to formal Chinese legal institutions', *Stanford Journal of International Law*, 42(2): 103–79.

Miraftab F (2004) 'Can you belly dance? Methodological questions in the era of transnational feminist research', *Gender, Place and Culture*, 11(4): 595–604.

Mohanty M, Mukherji PN with Törnquist O, eds. (1998) *People's Rights, Social Movements and the State in the Third World*. London: Sage Publications.

MqVU (2010) 'NGOs in China and Chinese investments overseas', blog posting, 14 July. http://mqvu.wordpress.com/2010/07/14/ngos-in-china-and-chinese-investments-overseas/ Accessed 23 August 2010.

Mulder N (2003) *Southeast Asian Images: Towards Civil Society?* Chiang Mai: Silkworm Books.

Mullings B (1999) 'Insider or outsider, both or neither: Some dilemmas of interviewing in a cross-cultural setting', *Geoforum*, 30: 337–50.

National Assembly of Vietnam (2010) *Luat Nguoi Khuyet tat* (Law on Persons with Disabilities) #51/2010/QH12, 17 June.

Ngoc Van (2005) 'Bao chi dien tu se tro thanh kenh thong tin doi noi, doi ngoai hang dau' [Online press will become leading domestic and international information channel], *Tien Phong*, 7 October. http://www.tienphong.vn/Tianyon/Index.aspx?ArticleID=24551&ChannelID=2 Accessed 16 August 2010.

Nguyen Bac (2009) 'Tu goc cong vien tro thanh khach san' [From the corner of a park into a hotel], *Tuan Vietnam*, 13 February.

Nguyen Huu Vinh (2007) 'Mo mam lang bao chi' [Searching around for the press], *Talawas*, 9 June. http://www.talawas.org/talaDB/showFile.php?res=10143&rb=0507 Accessed 16 August 2010.

Nguyen Manh Cuong (2009) *Co so ly luan va cac nguyen tac co ban de hinh thanh va quan tri cac to chuc xa hoi dan su tai Viet Nam* [Theoretical basis and basic principles to establish and govern civil society organisations in Vietnam]. Hanoi: Asia Foundation.

Nikitin V (2010) 'The new civic activism in Russia', *The Nation*, 8 November, 23–4.

Nooteboom S (2006) *Adaptive Networks: The Governance for Sustainable Development*. PhD thesis, Erasmus Universiteit Rotterdam, Netherlands. Delft: Eburon Academic Publishers.

Nørlund I (2008) 'International analyses and views on civil society in Vietnam', paper presented to the Central Institute for Economic Management, Hanoi, April 4.

Nørlund I, ed. (2006) *The Emerging Civil Society: An Initial Assessment of Civil Society in Vietnam*. Hanoi: CIVICUS.

O'Brien K, ed. (2008) *Popular Protest in China*. Harvard Contemporary China Series 15. Cambridge MA: Harvard University Press.

O'Brien K (2004) 'Neither transgressive nor contained: Boundary-spanning contention in China', in Gries PH and Rosen S, eds. *State and Society in 21st-Century China: Crisis, Contention, and Legitimation*. New York: RoutledgeCurzon, 105–22.

—— (1996) 'Rightful resistance', *World Politics*, 49(1): 31–55.

O'Brien K and Li Lianjiang (2006) *Rightful Resistance in Rural China*. Cambridge Studies in Contentious Politics.

O'Brien K and Stern R (2008) 'Studying contention in contemporary China', in O'Brien K, ed. *Popular Protest in China*. Cambridge MA: Harvard University Press, 11–25.

O'Donnell G and Schmitter P (1986) *Transitions from Authoritarian Rule: Tentative Conclusions about Uncertain Democracies*. Baltimore: Johns Hopkins University.

O'Rourke D (2002) 'Community-driven regulation: Toward an improved model of environmental regulation in Vietnam', in Evans P. ed. *Livable Cities? Urban*

Strategies for Livelihood and Sustainability. Berkeley: University of California Press, 55–131.

OpenNet Intiative (2007) 'Vietnam', accessed 13 September 2008.

Osa M (2003) 'Networks in opposition: Linking organizations through activists in the Polish People's Republic', in Diani and McAdam, eds. *Social Movements and Networks: Relational Approaches to Collective Action.* Oxford: Oxford University Press, 77–104.

Osborne M (2007) 'The water politics of China and Southeast Asia: Rivers, dams, cargo boats and the environment', http://japanfocus.org/-Milton-Osborne/2448 Accessed 14 February 2010.

Ougaard M and Higgott R, eds. (2002) *Towards a Global Polity.* London: Routledge.

Oxford Analytica (2010) 'Vietnam/China: Latent stresses threaten relationship', *Global Strategy Brief,* 15 July.

Painter M (2005) 'The politics of state sector reforms in Vietnam: Contested agendas and uncertain trajectories', *Journal of Development Studies,* 41(2): 261–83.

Patton MQ (1990) *Qualitative Evaluation and Research Methods.* Newbury Park CA: Sage.

People's Participation Working Group (2007) 'Overview on Collaborative Groups – CGs/CBOs', workshop report.

Peřinová M (2005) *Civil Society in Authoritarian Regime: The Analysis of China, Burma and Vietnam.* Thesis, Lund University, Sweden. www.scribd.com/doc/34773452/Civil-Society-in-Authoritarian-Regime Accessed 21 October 2010.

Perry E (1995) 'Introduction: Urban associations', in Davis D, Kraus R, Naughton B and Perry E, eds. *Urban Spaces in Contemporary China: The Potential for Autonomy and Community in Post-Mao China.* Cambridge: Cambridge University Press, 297–301.

Perry E and Selden M, eds. (2003) *Chinese Society: Change, Conflict and Resistance,* 2nd edition. London: Routledge.

Phung Suong (2007) 'Se co mot Walt Disney giua long Ha Noi?' [Will there be a Walt Disney in the Heart of Hanoi?], *Tien Phong,* 2 February. http://www.tienphong.vn/Tianyon/Index.aspx?ArticleID=74736&ChannelID=2 Accessed 7 July 2008.

Phung Trung Hau, Nguyen Le Minh and Nguyen Quan (2008) 'Hay giu nhung khoang khong quy gia con lai cua HN' [Preserve remaining open space in Hanoi], *VietNamNet,* 15 December. http://www.tuanvietnam.net/vn/sukien-nonghomnay/5587/index.aspx Accessed 16 December 2008.

Piven F and Cloward R (1977) *Poor People's Movements: Why They Succeed, How They Fail.* New York: Vintage Books.

Potter D (1996) 'Democratization and the environment', in Potter D and Taylor A, ed. *NGOs and Environmental Policies in Asia and Africa.* London: Frank Cass, 9–37.

—— (1993) 'Democratization in Asia', in Held D, ed. *Prospects for Democracy: North, South, East and West.* Cambridge: Polity Press, 355–79.

Potter D and Taylor A, eds. (1996) *NGOs and Environmental Policies in Asia and Africa.* London: Frank Cass.

Probe International (2009) 'A response to the Ministry of Environmental Protection's decision to suspend approval of hydro dam construction along the middle [Jinsha River]: Chinese NGO statement', 16 June. http://www.probe-international.org/three-gorges-probe/response-ministry-environmental-protection%E2%80%99s-decision-suspend-approval-hydro-dam- Accessed 5 September 2010.

—— (2008) 'Chinese environmentalists and scholars appeal for dam safety assessments in geologically unstable south-west China', 8 July, http://old.probe-international.org/catalog/content_fullstory.php?contentId=6871&cat_id=24 Accessed 5 September 2010.

Putnam R (1993) *Making Democracy Work: Civil Traditions in Modern Italy*. Princeton.

Pye L (1996) 'The state and the individual: An overview interpretation', in Hook B, ed. *The Individual and State in China*. Oxford: Clarendon, 16–42.

Qian Jing (2010) 'Yuenan Guohui keyi foujue "meng gongcheng"' [Vietnam's National Assembly is able to vote down 'dream project'], *Nanfang Zhoumo*, 4 August. http://www.infzm.com/content/48547 Accessed 25 August 2010.

Ragin C (1987) *The Comparative Method*. Berkeley: University of California Press.

Ragin C, Berg-Schlosser D and de Meur G (1996) 'Political methodology: qualitative methods', in Goodin RE and Klingemann HD, eds. *A New Handbook of Political Science*, 2nd edition. Oxford: Oxford University Press: 749–68.

Rawnsley G (2008) 'Media, Internet and governance', in Zheng Yongnian and Fewsmith J, eds. *China's Opening Society; The Non-State Sector and Governance*. London: Routledge, 118–35.

Read B (2009) 'The multiple uses of local networks: State cultivation of neighbourhood social capital in China and Taiwan', in Read B and Pekkanen R, eds. *Local Organizations and Urban Governance in East and Southeast Asia: Straddling State and Society* (Routledge Studies on Civil Society in Asia), 121–57.

Read B and Pekkanen R, eds. (2009) *Local Organizations and Urban Governance in East and Southeast Asia: Straddling State and Society*. London: Routledge Studies on Civil Society in Asia.

Reuters (2009) 'New Yangtze dam may be death sentence for rare fish', 19 June. http://www.reuters.com/article/idUSTRE55I1IG20090619 Accessed 26 August 2010.

Richburg K (2010) 'China's crackdown on nonprofit groups prompts new fears among activists', *Washington Post*, 11 May.

Robertson P (2007) 'Partnerships for impact: lessons from the Red Ribbon Center experience', case study written for the International Labour Organisation.

Rosemont H (2002) 'Commentary and addenda on Nosco's "Confucian perspectives on civil society and government"', in Rosenblum N and Post R, eds. *Civil Society and Government*. Princeton: Princeton University Press, 360–70.

Rucker P (2008) 'In US, A multitude of forces drains the spirit of giving', *Washington Post*, 23 May, A1.

Sabatier P and Jenkins-Smith H. eds. (1993) *Policy Change and Learning: An Advocacy Coalition Approach*. Boulder: Westview.

Saich T, ed. (1990) *The Chinese People's Movement: Perspectives on Spring 1989*. Armonk, NY: ME Sharpe.

Salemink O (2006) 'Translating, interpreting and practicing civil society in Vietnam: A tale of calculated misunderstandings', in Lewis D and Mosse D, eds. *Development Brokers and Translators*. Bloomfield CT, Kumarian Press, 101–26.

Sassen S (2002) 'Global cities and diasporic networks: Microsites in global civil society', in Anheier H, Glasius M and Kaldor M, eds. *Global Civil Society 2002*. Oxford: Oxford University Press, 217–38.

Schak D and Hudson M, eds. (2003) *Civil Society in Asia*. Aldershot: Ashgate.

Schiffer E and Waale D (2008) 'Tracing power and influence in networks: Net-map as a tool for research and strategic network planning', *International Food Policy Research Institute Discussion Paper #772*.

Schmitter P (1997) 'Civil society: East and West', in Diamond L et al, eds. *Consolidating the Third Wave Democracies: Themes and Perspectives*. Baltimore: Johns Hopkins University Press, 239–62.

—— (1974) 'Still the century of corporatism?' in Pike F and Stritch T, eds. *The New Corporatism: Social-Political Structures in the Iberian World*. South Bend IN: University of Notre Dame Press, 85–131.

Schwartz J (2004) 'Environmental NGOs in China: Roles and limits', *Pacific Affairs*, 77: 28–50.

Schwartz J and Shieh S, eds. (2009) *Serving the People: State and Society Responses to Social Welfare Needs in China*. London: Routledge.

Scott J (2009) *The Art of Not Being Governed: An Anarchist History of Upland Southeast Asia*. New Haven: Yale University Press.

Scott J and Kerkvliet B, eds. (1986) *Everyday Forms of Peasant Resistance in South-East Asia*. London: Frank Cass.

Shanks E, Luttrell C, Conway T, Vu ML and Ladinsky J (2004) *Understanding Pro-Poor Political Change: The Policy Process – Vietnam*. London: Overseas Development Institute.

She Le (2009) 'Sex main route to spread HIV/AIDS in China', *ReutersLink*, 21 November. http://www.reuterslink.org/news/chinahivaids.htm Accessed 29 September 2010.

Shi Fayong and Cai Yongshun (2006) 'Disaggregating the state: Networks and collective resistance in Shanghai', *China Quarterly*, 186: 314–32.

Shi Jiangtao (2009) 'Wen calls halt to Yunnan dam plan: Premier orders further environmental checks', *South China Morning Post* (Hong Kong), 21 May.

Shi Lihong (2010) 'Hejiang – women de jia' [Rivers – Our Home], documentary film produced by Wild China Films.

—— (2004) 'Nujiang zhi sheng' [Voices of an Angry River], documentary film produced by Wild China Films.

Shi Tianjian (1997) *Political Participation in Beijing*. Cambridge, MA: Harvard University Press.

Shieh S (2010) 'Why the chill in the air for NGOs?', blog posting, 12 May. http://ngochina.blogspot.com/2010/05/why-chill-in-air-for-ngos.html Accessed 7 November 2010.

Shieh S and Deng Guosheng (2011) 'An emerging civil society: The impact of the 2008 Sichuan earthquake on grass-roots associations in China', *China Journal*, 65 (January): 161–84.

Shigetomi S (2002) *The State and NGOs: Perspective from Asia*. Singapore: Institute of Southeast Asian Studies.

Shue V (2004) 'Legitimacy crisis in China?' in Gries PH and Rosen S, eds. *State and Society in 21st-Century China: Crisis, Contention, and Legitimation*. New York: RoutledgeCurzon, 24–49.

Sidel M (2010) 'Maintaining firm control: Recent developments in nonprofit law and regulation in Vietnam', *International Journal of Not-for-Profit Law*, 12(3), May, 52–67.

—— (1996) 'The emergence of a nonprofit sector and philanthropy in the socialist republic of Vietnam', in Yamamoto T, ed. *Emerging Civil Society in the*

Asia Pacific Community. Tokyo: Japan Center for International Exchange and Institute for Southeast Asian Studies, 293–304.

Silliman GS and Noble LG, eds. (1998) *Organizing for Democracy: NGOs, Civil Society, and the Philippine State*. Honolulu: University of Hawai'i Press.

Smart A and Smart J (1998) 'Transnational social networks and negotiated identities in interactions between Hong Kong and China', in Smith MP and Guarnizo L, eds. *Transnationalism from Below*. New Brunswick NJ: Transaction Publishers, 103–64.

Smil V (1993) *China's Environmental Crisis: An Inquiry into the Limits of National Development*. Armonk NY: ME Sharpe.

Socialist Republic of Vietnam (2007a) *Ordinance on Implementation of Democracy at the Commune Level* #34/2007/PL-UBTVQH11, issued by the Standing Committee of the National Assembly, 20 April.

—— (2007b) Resolution No. 32/2007/NQ-CP, 'On some urgent solutions to control transport accidents and traffic jams', issued 29 June.

—— (2003) Decree No. 88/2003/ND-CP, 'Providing for the organization, operation and management of associations', issued 30 July.

Stalley P and Yang Dongning (2006) 'An emerging environmental movement in China?' *China Quarterly*, 186 (June): 333–56.

Steinglass M (2009) 'More powerful than a tall building: Saving a bit of history in Hanoi', *Global Post*, 20 April (article and video).

Sun Yanfei and Zhao Dingxin (2008) 'Environmental campaigns', in O'Brien K, ed. *Popular Protest in China*. Cambridge MA: Harvard University Press, 144–62.

—— (2007) 'Multifaceted state and fragmented society: Dynamics of environmental movement in China', in Yang D, ed. *Discontented Miracle: Growth, Conflict and Institutional Adaptations in China*. World Scientific, 111–60.

Swarts H (2003) 'Setting the state's agenda: Church-based community organizations in American politics', in Goldstone J, ed. *States, Parties and Social Movements*. Cambridge: Cambridge University Press, 78–106.

Sztompka P (1993) *The Sociology of Social Change*. Oxford: Blackwell.

Tarrow S (2005) *The New Transnational Activism*. Cambridge: Cambridge University Press.

—— (1998) *Power in Movement: Social Movements and Contentious Politics*. Cambridge: Cambridge University Press.

—— (1996) 'States and opportunities: The political structuring of social movements', in McAdam D, McCarthy J and Zald M, eds. *Comparative Perspectives on Social Movements: Political Opportunities, Mobilizing Structures, and Cultural Framings*. Cambridge: Cambridge University Press, 41–61.

Teets J (2009) 'Post-earthquake relief and reconstruction efforts: The emergence of civil society in China?' *China Quarterly*, 198 (June): 330–47.

Thanh Nien (2009) 'Cho phep xay khach san trong cong vien Thong Nhat' [Granting permission to build hotel in Reunification Park], 11 February. www.thanhnien.com.vn Accessed 9 April 2009.

Thanh Thuy (2010) 'Strengthening the status of people with disabilities in the disability movement', www.dphanoi.org.vn Accessed 15 June 2010.

Tharp D (2009) 'Hanoi Disabled Independent Living Center', http://www.nippon-foundation.or.jp/eng/current/20090403.html Accessed 13 July 2010.

Thayer C (2010) 'The apparatus of authoritarian rule in Viet Nam', Presentation to the Conference on Authoritarianism in East Asia, Southeast Asia Research Centre, City University of Hong Kong, 28–30 June.

—— (2009) 'Vietnam and the challenge of political civil society', *Contemporary Southeast Asia*, 31(1): 1–27.

—— (2008) 'Vietnam: One-party rule and the challenge of civil society'. Paper presented to Surveying the Paradigm Shifts in Asia, Regional Outlook Forum, sponsored by the Institute of Southeast Asian Studies, Singapore, 8 January 2008.

—— (1995) 'Mono-organizational socialism and the state', in Kerkvliet B and Porter D, eds. *Vietnam's Rural Transformation*. Boulder: Westview, 39–64.

—— (1992) 'Political reform in Vietnam: Doi moi and the emergence of civil society', in Miller R, ed. *The Developments of Civil Society in Communist Systems*. Sydney: Allen and Unwin, 110–29.

The Dung (2007a) 'Phan ung gay gat viec "xe thit" Cong vien Thong Nhat' [Heated reaction to 'dismembering' Reunification Park], *Nguoi Lao Dong* [Labourers newspaper], 6 August. http://www.nld.com.vn/tintuc/chinh-tri-xa-hoi/199326. asp Accessed 3 August 2008.

—— (2007b) 'Vincom nhan loi ve mo hinh Disneyland' [Vincom admits fault with Disneyland model], *Nguoi Lao Dong*, 24 August. http://www.nld.com.vn/ tintuc/chinh-tri-xa-hoi/200243.asp Accessed 3 August 2008.

Thomas M (2002) 'Out of control: Emergent cultural landscapes and political change in urban Vietnam', *Urban Studies*, 39(9): 1611–24.

—— (2001) 'Public spaces/public disgraces: Crowds and the state in contemporary Vietnam', *Sojourn*, 16(2): 306–30.

Thomas N (1999) *Democracy Denied: Identity, Civil Society and Illiberal Democracy in Hong Kong*. Aldershot: Ashgate.

Thompson D and Jia Ping (2010) 'Dollar diplomacy can be healthy for China', *Foreign Policy*, 19 August.

Thu Ha and Linh Thuy (2009) 'Khach san gay tranh cai: khong the do loi cho qua khu' [Hotel debate: Can't blame it on the past], *Vietnam Week*, 16 February. http://www.tuanvietnam.net/vn/thongtindachieu/6121/index.aspx Accessed 9 April 2009.

Thu Huong (2007) 'Urbanisation must include green spaces', *Viet Nam News*, 27 May. http://vietnamnews.vnagency.com.vn/showarticle.php?num=01TAL-270507 Accessed 20 July 2008.

Thurber K (2009) 'Chinese doctor taking refuge in Midland to discuss AIDS with Washington officials', Midland Reporter-Telegram (Texas, USA), 29 November.

Thuy Du and Anh Dung (2007) 'Xe thuong binh tu tap phan Bo GT-VT' [Veterans' vehicles gather at the Ministry of Transport], 6 March. http://vietbao.vn/Xa-hoi/ Xe-thuong-binh-tu-tap-phan-Bo-GT-VT/20670072/157/ Accessed 26 July 2010.

Tien Phong (2007) 'Se khoi kien neu cac cong vien Ha Noi con bi loi dung vi loi nhuan' [Will sue if Hanoi's parks are misused for profit], 4 August. http:// www.tienphong.vn/Tianyon/Index.aspx?ArticleID=91835&ChannelID=2 Accessed 3 August 2008.

Tilly C (2004) *Social Movements 1768–2004*. Boulder, CO: Paradigm.

—— (1984) *Big Structures, Large Processes, Huge Comparisons*. New York: Russell Sage Foundation.

Tong Zhifeng (2009) 'Dongyuan jiegou yu ziran baoyu yundong de fazhan yi Nujiang fanba yundong weili' [Mobilization structures and environmental movement development in the Nu River anti-dam movement], *Kaifang shidai*, 9: 116–32. http://www.csscipaper.com/sociology/socitrend/51046.html Accessed 7 December 2010.

Tran Huy Anh (2009) 'Ha Noi can quy hoach vung cam xay dung' [Hanoi needs to plan for areas that ban construction], *Tuan Vietnam*, 1 March.

Tran Huy Anh and Linh Thuy (2010) 'Dat ngap nuoc Ha Noi' [Wetlands in Hanoi], draft of unpublished report for Hanoi University Centre on the Environment.

Tran Thanh Van (2009) 'Phan doi "xen" dat cong vien Thong Nhat de xay khach san' [Oppose 'tearing up' the land of Reunification Park to build a hotel], *Tuan Vietnam*, 9 February. http://www.tuanvietnam.net/phan-doi-xen-dat-cong-vien-thong-nhat-de-xay-khach-san Accessed 6 August 2010.

—— (2007a) 'Chi can 15 ty dong cho cong vien Thong Nhat la du!' [15 billion dong for Reunification Park is enough to improve it!], *VietNamNet*, 16 August. http://vietnamnet.vn/tuanvietnam/2007/08/730545/ Accessed 21 August 2007.

—— (2007b) 'KTS Tran Thanh Van cam on doc gia TVN' [Architect Tran Thanh Van thanks readers], *Tuan Vietnam*, 4 September. http://www.tuanvietnam.net/kts-tran-thanh-van-cam-on-doc-gia-tvn Accessed 7 August 2010.

Trang An Nguyen (2007) 'Cai tao Cong vien Thong nhat – long dong mai chua xong' [Upgrading Reunification Park – unfortunately still not complete], *VietNamNet*, 27 January. http://vietnamnet.vn/xahoi/dothi/2007/01/658284/ Accessed 8 August 2008.

Transparency International (2010) *Preventing Corruption in Humanitarian Practices: A Handbook of Good Practices*.

Trong Phu (2007) 'Cai tao cong vien Thong Nhat (Ha Noi): Se lay y kien dan truoc' [Upgrading Reunification Park: Will gather public opinion first], *Tuoi Tre*, 11 August. http://www.tuoitre.com.vn/Tianyon/Index.aspx?ArticleID=214824&ChannelID=3 Accessed 3 August 2008.

Trung Thuan (2010) 'Thay gi qua cuoc Hoi thao "Xay dung dinh huong phat trien giai doan 2010–2014 cua Hoi Nguoi Khuyet tat Ha Noi"?' [What are the results of the workshop 'Setting a development direction for DPO Hanoi in the period 2010–14'?], *Nang Xuan*, April, 34–6.

—— (2009) 'Vao Hoi Nguoi Khuyet tat de lam gi?' [Why join the Association of People with Disabilities?], *Nang Xuan*, October.

Tsai L (2007) *Accountability Without Democracy: Solidary Groups and Public Goods Provision in Rural China*. Cambridge: Cambridge University Press.

Tuan Vietnam (2009a) 'Dong gop cua ban doc cho chuyen muc' [Readers' comments on the special issue], 12 February. http://www.tuanvietnam.net/vn/thongtindachieu/6091/index.aspx Accessed 12 August 2010.

—— (2009b) 'Hoi Quy hoach VN de nghi Ha Noi xem xet DA khach san' [Vietnam Planning Association recommends Hanoi reconsider hotel project], 23 February. http://www.tuanvietnam.net/vn/thongtindachieu/6201/index.aspx Accessed 9 April 2009.

Turley W and Womack B (1998) 'Asian socialism's open doors: Guangzhou and Ho Chi Minh City', *China Journal*, 40 (July): 95–119.

UNAIDS (2010) 'Launch of China Red Ribbon Beijing Forum on HIV and Human Rights', 5 July. http://www.unaids.org.cn/en/index/topic.asp?id=677&classname=News&class=2 Accessed 31 August 2010.

—— (2009) 'Chinese civil society to be a strong partner in the response to AIDS', 7 May. http://www.aegis.org/news/unaids/2009/UN090505.html Accessed 16 August 2010.

—— (2006) *Report on the Global AIDS Epidemic*.

UNAIDS, UNDP and Marie Stopes International (2010) 'The Positive Talks Project – Talking positive about HIV', Experiences series No. 6, March.

Unger J (2008) 'Introduction: Chinese associations, civil society and state corporatism: Disputed terrain', in Unger J, ed. *Associations and the Chinese State*. Armonk NY: ME Sharpe, 3–13.

Unger J and Chan A (2008) 'Associations in a bind: The emergence of political corporatism', in Unger J, ed. *Associations and the Chinese State*. Armonk NY: ME Sharpe, 48–68.

—— (1995) 'China, corporatism and the East Asian Model', *Australian Journal of Chinese Affairs*, 33: 29–53.

United Nations (2006) *Disability at a Glance: A Profile of 28 Countries and Areas in Asia and the Pacific*. Bangkok: UN Economic and Social Commission for Asia and the Pacific.

United States Department of State (2009) Country Reports on Human Rights Practices: Vietnam, 2008, released 25 February 2009.

Uphoff N and Krishna A (2004) 'Civil society and public sector institutions: More than a zero-sum relationship', *Public Administration and Development*, 24(4): 357–72.

Vala C and O'Brien K (2008) 'Recruitment to Protestant house churches', in O'Brien K, ed. *Popular Protest in China*. Cambridge MA: Harvard University Press, 108–25.

Van Rooij B (2010) 'The people vs. pollution: Understanding citizen action against pollution in China', *Journal of Contemporary China*, 19(63): 55–77.

Van Tien (2006) 'Xa hoi dan su khong doi lap voi nha nuoc' [Civil society does not overlap with the state], *VietNamNet*, 12 June. http://vietnamnet.vn/chinhtri/doinoi/2006/06/580015 Accessed 16 August 2010.

Vasavakul T (2003) 'From fence-breaking to networking: Interests, popular organisations, and policy influences in post-Socialist Vietnam', in Kerkvliet, Heng and Koh, eds. *Getting Organized in Vietnam: Moving In and Around the Socialist State*. Singapore: Institute of Southeast Asian Studies, 25–61.

Vasavakul T, Le Viet Thai and Le Thi Phi Van (2009) *Public Administration and Economic Development in Vietnam: Remaking the Public Administration for the 21st Century*. Hanoi: United Nations Development Programme.

Vasiljev I (2003) 'The disabled and their organizations: The emergence of new paradigms', in Kerkvliet, Heng and Koh, eds. *Getting Organized in Vietnam: Moving In and Around the Socialist State*. Singapore: Institute of Southeast Asian Studies, 25–61.

Vietnam Studies Group (2009) 'Fwd: Thong nhat park', message posted by Michele Thompson on behalf of Burke Fishburn, 28 February.

—— (2007) Message posted by Chuck Searcy, 18 April.

Vietnam Union of Science and Technology Organizations (VUSTA) (2010) *Ban tin phat trien* [Development News] #1, October.

VietNamNet (2008) 'Hanoi deals with Catholic church's complaint', 21 September. http://english.vietnamnet.vn/social/2008/09/804772/ Accessed 1 October 2008.

—— (2007a) 'Bien cong vien Thong nhat thanh Disneyland: Nha khoa hoc len tieng' [Changing Reunification Park into Disneyland: Scientists Raise their

Voices], 7 August. http://vietnamnet.vn/bandocviet/2007/08/727135/ Accessed 3 August 2008.

—— (2007b) 'Dung vi loi ich kinh te ma lam mat cong vien' [Don't Let Economic Interests Destroy the Park], 8 August. http://vietnamnet.vn/bandocviet/2007/08/727383/ Accessed 2 August 2008.

Vu Duy Phu, ed. (2008) *Xa Hoi Dan Su: Mot so Van de Chon loc* [Civil Society: Some Selected Issues]. Hanoi: Nha xuat ban Tri Thuc.

Vu K (2009) 'Economic reform and performance: A comparative study of China and Vietnam', *China: An International Journal*, 7(2): 189–226.

Vu Thi Nga (2008) 'Bao cao ket qua hoi thao: Su tham gia cua cac to chuc phi chinh phu va cac to chuc cong dong trong van dong chinh sach: kinh nghiem thuc tien va khuon kho phap luat' [Workshop report on Participation of NGOs and community organisations on policy advocacy], 16 September, Hanoi.

Wainwright H (2005) 'Civil society, democracy and power: Global connections', in Anheier et al, *Global Civil Society 2004–05*. London: Sage, 94–118.

Wakeman F (1993) 'The civil society and public sphere debate', *Modern China*, 19(2): 108–38.

Walzer M, ed. (1995) *Toward a Global Civil Society*. Oxford/New York: Berghahn.

Wang Chen (2009) 'China embraces the information age', speech at Second Israeli Presidential Conference 'Facing Tomorrow 2009', 20–22 October, in *China Daily*, 1 November, 4.

Wang Yongchen (2008) 'Along the banks of the Nu: River, mountains, farms, and homes', online photo essay, http://eng.greensos.cn/showArticle.aspx?articleId=480 Accessed 11 August 2010.

Wang Yongchen and Zhou Chen (2010) 'From Lugu Lake to A Hai Power Plant', 5 January. http://eng.greensos.cn/ShowArticle.aspx?articleId=414 Accessed 26 August 2010.

Wasserstrom J (2009) 'China after Tiananmen: Middle-class mobilization', *Journal of Democracy*, 20(3): 29–32.

Watson A (2008) 'Civil society in a transitional state: The rise of associations in China', in Unger J, ed. *Associations and the Chinese State*. Armonk NY: ME Sharpe, 14–47.

Watts J (2011) 'Last refuge of rare fish threatened by Yangtze dam plans', *The Guardian*, 18 January.

—— (2007) 'China blames growing social unrest on anger over pollution', *The Guardian*, 6 July.

Weller R (2008) 'Responsive authoritarianism', in Gilley B and Diamond L, eds. *Political Change in China: Comparisons with Taiwan*. Boulder CO: Lynne Rienner, 117–33.

—— (1999) *Alternate Civilities: Democracy and Culture in China and Taiwan*. Boulder: Westview Press.

Weller R, ed. (2005) *Civil Life, Globalization and Political Change in Asia: Organizing between the Family and the State*. London: Routledge.

Wellman B and Berkowitz SD, eds. (1988) *Social Structures: A Network Approach*. Cambridge: Cambridge University Press.

Wells-Dang A (2011a) 'Environmental networks in Vietnam: A new form of civil society?', policy report, World Conservation Union (IUCN). Hanoi, October.

—— (2011b) 'The China women's network against AIDS, between donors and the grassroots', *China Development Brief*, www.chinadevelopmentbrief.cn.

—— (2010) 'Political space in Vietnam: a view from the "rice-roots"', *Pacific Review*, 23(1): 93–112.

—— (2007) 'Strangers on the road: Foreign religious organizations and development in Vietnam', in Taylor P, ed. *Modernity and Re-enchantment: Religion in Post-Revolutionary Vietnam.* Singapore: Institute of Southeast Asian Studies, 399–444.

Wexler R, Xu Ying and Young N (2006) *NGO Advocacy in China.* Beijing: China Development Brief.

White G (1996) 'The dynamics of civil society in post-Mao China', in Hook B, ed. *The Individual and the State in China.* Oxford: Clarendon Press, 196–222.

White G, Howell J and Shang X, eds. (1996) *In Search of Civil Society: Market Reform and Social Change in Contemporary China.* Oxford: Clarendon Press.

Wilson-Grau R and Nuñcz M (2006) *Evaluating International Social Change Networks: A Conceptual Framework for a Participatory Approach*, unpublished paper.

Wischermann J (2010) 'Civil society action and governance in Vietnam: Selected findings from an empirical survey', *Journal of Current Southeast Asian Affairs*, 2: 3–40.

—— (2006) 'Societal and political change in Vietnam. An instructive example for Myanmar/Burma? Introductory and conceptual reflections', *Active Citizens under Political Wraps: Experiences from Myanmar/Burma and Vietnam.* Chiang Mai: Heinrich Böll Foundation, 9–25.

Womack B (2006) *China and Vietnam: The Politics of Asymmetry.* Cambridge: Cambridge University Press.

—— (1987) 'The party and the people, revolutionary and postrevolutionary politics in China and Vietnam', *World Politics*, 39(4): 479–507.

Women's Network Against AIDS – China (2010) 'Gongzuo jianbao' [Work report], 2nd quarter.

Wong G (2010) 'China AIDS activist moves to US after harassment', *Associated Press*, 9 May.

Woodside A (2006) *Lost Modernities: China, Vietnam, Korea and the Hazards of World History.* Cambridge, MA: Harvard University Press.

—— (1998) 'Exalting the latecomer state: Intellectuals and the state during the Chinese and Vietnamese reforms', *China Journal*, 40 (July): 9–36.

—— (1988) *Vietnam and the Chinese Model.* Cambridge MA: Harvard University Press.

—— (1976) *Community and Revolution in Modern Vietnam.* Boston: Houghton Mifflin.

Wright T (2004) 'Contesting state legitimacy in the 1990s: The China Democracy Party and the China Labor Bulletin', in Gries PH and Rosen S, eds. *State and Society in 21st-Century China: Crisis, Contention, and Legitimation.* New York: RoutledgeCurzon, 123–40.

Wu Fengshi (2007) 'Institutionalizing public participation in AIDS governance in China: Notes from a unique meeting for activists and grassroots NGOs', Woodrow Wilson Center *China Environment Series*, 9: 69–74.

Xie Lei (2009) 'China's environmental activism in the age of globalization', City University of London Department of Transnational Politics Working Paper CUTP/006.

—— (2007) *Environmental Activism in Urban China: The Role of Personal Networks.* PhD diss., Wageningen Universiteit, Netherlands.

Xinhuanet (2006) 'Comprehensive regulations on HIV/AIDS prevention and treatment', Ministry of Public Health, 12 February.

Xu Donghuan (2010) 'Between a dam and a hard place', *Global Times*, 5 August. http://special.globaltimes.cn/2010-08/560293.html Accessed 21 August 2010.

Xu Nan (2009) 'The history of the development of NGOs for environmental protection in China', *Nanfang Zhoumo*, 9 October. http://eng.greensos.cn/ShowArticle.aspx?articleId=185 Accessed 27 August 2010.

Xu Xing (2006) 'Zhenggai, yuegong neng, zhonggong buneng' [Political reform: VCP can, CCP cannot], *Open Magazine* (Hong Kong). http://www.open.com.hk/2006_9p43.htm.

Xue Ye and Wang Yongchen (2007) 'Highly contentious hydropower development in Western China', in Liang Congjie and Yang Dongping, eds. *The China Environmental Yearbook 2005: Crisis and Breakthrough of China's Environment*. Leiden: Brill, 63–88.

Yamamoto T (1996) *Emerging Civil Society in the Asia Pacific Community*. Singapore: ISEAS.

Yan Yan (2009) 'China's media power evidenced in "anti-dam" movement', *Kexue Xinwen* [Science News], 22 October. http://eng.greensos.cn/ShowArticle.aspx?articleId=213 Accessed 11 August 2010.

Yang, Dali (1996) *Calamity and Reform in China: State, Rural Society, and Institutional Change Since the Great Leap Famine*. Stanford.

Yang Dongping, ed. (2009) *Annual Report on Environment and Development in China (Zhongguo Huanjing Lupishu)*. Beijing: Social Sciences Academic Press.

Yang Dongping (2007) 'China's environmental protection at a crossroads', in Liang Congjie and Yang Dongping, eds. *The China Environmental Yearbook 2005: Crisis and Breakthrough of China's Environment*. Leiden: Brill, xxi–lix.

Yang Guobin (2010) 'Brokering environment and health in China: Issue entrepreneurs of the public sphere', *Journal of Contemporary China*, 19(63): 101–18.

—— (2008) 'Contention in cyberspace', in O'Brien K, ed. *Popular Protest in China*. Cambridge MA: Harvard University Press, 126–43.

—— (2005) 'Environmental NGOs and institutional dynamics in China', *China Quarterly*, 181: 46–66.

Yang Guobin and Calhoun C (2008) 'Media, civil society, and the rise of a green public sphere in China', in Ho P and Edmonds RL, eds. *China's Embedded Activism: Opportunities and Constraints of a Social Movement*. London: Routledge, 69–88.

Yang M (1994) *Gifts, Favors and Banquets: The Art of Social Relationships in China*. Ithaca: Cornell University Press.

Yardley J (2004) 'Dam building threatens China's "Grand Canyon"', *New York Times*, 10 March.

Yauch B (2010) 'China's dam spree continues', 24 August. http://probeinternational.org/three-gorges-probe/china%E2%80%99s-dam-spree-continues Accessed 5 September 2010.

Yin R (1994) *Case Study Research: Design and Methods*. Thousand Oaks CA: Sage Publications.

Young N (2008) 'Chinese need better conversations among themselves', http://www.nickyoungwrites.com/?q=node/32 Accessed 30 December 2008.

Young N and Mian Liping (2008) 'AIDS: Anger and recrimination block progress in Henan', http://www.chinadevelopmentbrief.com/node/1276, 14 January.

—— (2007) 'HIV/AIDS: NGOs proliferate as the Global Fund steps in', http://www.chinadevelopmentbrief.com/node/1109, 23 May.

Yu Jiang and Zhu Tan (2007) 'Beijing Liulitun waste factory investigation: Residents struggling to live in rancid stench', 16 April. http://www.sinofile.net/saiweng/sip_blog.nsf/d6plinks/YZHI-72F5KX Accessed 27 August 2010.

Yu Keping (2009) *Democracy is a Good Thing: Essays on Politics, Society, and Culture in Contemporary China*. Washington: Brookings Institution Press.

Yuan Wenli (2010) 'Henan nuxing kang'ai shequ zuzhi wangluo choubeihui zai Zhengzhou shunli zhaokai' [Henan Network of Women's Community Organisations against AIDS successfully convenes preparatory meeting in Zhengzhou], 10 January. http://blog.sina.com.cn/s/blog_4e48f8040100g3b3.html Accessed 16 August 2010.

—— (2009) 'Promotion of women's participation – Hard work and good wishes', *China Global Fund Watch* Newsletter, 8 (July): 5–7.

Yuanfen New Media Art Space (2010) 'The secret language of women', http://www.yuanfenart.com/index.php?option=com_content&view=article&id=157&Itemid=123&lang=en Accessed 16 August 2010.

Zhao Tao (2010) 'A matter of love and sorrow for rivers', *China Youth Daily*, 3 June. http://eng.greensos.cn/showArticle.aspx?articleId=517 Accessed 26 August 2010.

Zhao Yuezhi and Sun Wusan (2007) 'Public opinion supervision: Possibilities and limits of the media in constraining local officials', in Perry E and Goldman M, eds. *Grassroots Political Reform in Contemporary China*. Harvard Contemporary China Series 14. Cambridge MA: Harvard University Press, 300–26.

Zhou Yongming (2002) 'Expanded space, refined control: The intellectual electronic press in China', Woodrow Wilson International Center for Scholars Asia Special Report 102 (April): 13–16.

Zhu Jiangang and Ho P (2008) 'Not against the state, just protecting residents' interests: An urban movement in a Shanghai neighborhood', in Ho P and Edmonds RL, eds. *China's Embedded Activism: Opportunities and Constraints of a Social Movement*. London: Routledge, 151–70.

Zweig D (2003) 'To the courts or to the barricades', in Perry E and Selden M, eds. *Chinese Society: Change, Conflict and Resistance*, 2nd edition. London: Routledge, 113–35.

Index

Accor Hotels, 115–16, 120, 124
ActionAid, 15, 39, 91, 95
Action for the City (Vietnam), xi, 121
advocacy, 2–3, 21–3, 25–9, 32–5,
    41–56
  Chinese civil society, 41–3
  community strategies, 16, 44, 45,
    53–8, 62, 72–3, 78, 82, 84, 90,
    94–6, 148–9, 154–7, 164–7,
    171, 172, 187
  embedded strategies, 44–50, 51, 53,
    55–8, 62, 69, 72–3, 75, 78, 82,
    84, 107, 109, 122–3, 125–6,
    129, 132, 135, 148–53, 154,
    164, 171, 172, 184, 187
  'inside-outside' model, 58, 107,
    123, 125, 133, 148, 171, 172
  'jujitsu' strategy, 59, 124, 151
  media strategies, 44, 45, 50–3, 55,
    57–8, 63, 68, 72, 77–8, 90,
    93–6, 101, 107, 109, 112–13,
    121–35, 136–7, 140–2, 145,
    148–9, 151, 153–6, 164, 166–7,
    171–2, 180, 183, 187
  Vietnamese civil society, 6, 13, 15,
    41–3
agency of network actors, 3, 8, 23, 27,
    29
Ahai dam, 138, 160
AIDS networks, see HIV
AIDS Care (China), 93, 103, 195
All China Women's Federation, 37,
    87, 99, 194
Amity Foundation (China), 20
architects, civil society role of, 106,
    108–13, 115–16, 120–1
art, as advocacy tactic, 94–6, 97,
    155
artists, civil society role of, 56, 83,
    136
ASEAN, 17, 79
  see also Southeast Asia
Asia Pacific Disability Forum, 61

Association of Support for
    Handicapped and Orphans
    (Vietnam), 64, 69–70, 83, 193
associations, 5, 7–8, 10–12, 25, 36,
    43, 64, 69, 71–3, 76–81, 83–4,
    102, 109–10, 120–2, 124, 126,
    131, 182
authoritarianism, 3–5, 7, 29, 31–2,
    174, 182
autonomy of civil society, 2, 4–8, 10,
    24, 50, 60, 149, 170, 179

Ba Dinh Square, 107, 133, 193
bauxite mining, 36, 37, 40, 133
Beijing, x, 10, 12, 20, 50, 55, 85–7,
    90–3, 95–6, 99, 104, 136,
    139–44, 153, 156–7, 159–60,
    162, 176
Bloc 8406, 36, 37, 40, 185
blogging, 41, 44, 45, 47, 50, 52–3, 88,
    111, 113–14, 121, 126–9, 133,
    154
'boomerang' advocacy strategy, 180
Bread for the World, 63, 74
Bright Future Group of people with
    disabilities (BFG, Vietnam), 21–2,
    37, 40, 61–84, 169–71, 175, 179,
    182–3, 185
Buddhism, 13, 54
business networks, 5, 25–6, 41, 190

CAP+ Network (China), 98, 101,
    194–5
Catholicism, 50, 57, 133, 185
Catholic Relief Services, xi, 74, 192
China
  laws and regulations, 5, 11, 60, 86,
    100, 160, 166–7, 182
  media, see media, China
  network history, 4–14
  politics, 16–21, 23, 29, 42–4, 48–50,
    162, 166
China Development Brief, xi, 41

China Environment and Culture
    Promotion Foundation, 136
China Foundation for Prevention of
    STD and AIDS, 100
China National Network of AIDS
    CBOs (CNNAC), 38, 101, 194–5
China Red Ribbon Forum, 100, 195
China Rivers Network (CRN), 22–3,
    37, 51, 136–68, 171–5, 177–80,
    182–3, 198
China-Vietnam comparison, 16–21,
    170, 196
China Youth Daily, 136, 140, 155, 198
China Youth Development
    Foundation, 12
CIVICUS, 25
civil society, 2–10, 24–9
    global/transnational, theories of,
        3, 32–3, 158, 186
    legal framework, 3, 5–8, 11, 16,
        18–19
civil society networks, 24–9
    Chinese, 10–16, 29, 37–40
    effectiveness, 15, 46–9, 52, 56–9,
        170–3, 175–6, 181–4
    formal/informal character of, 2, 8,
        10–14, 25, 29–30, 32–6, 84,
        104, 122, 130, 137, 144–7,
        161–2, 164, 172, 174–8, 180,
        184, 186–7
    formation, 11, 53, 63–5, 87–90,
        108–13, 123, 139–44, 155,
        169–70, 173–4, 183, 185
    leadership, 3, 8, 25, 30, 38–40, 42,
        60, 80, 84, 89, 94, 96, 102–5,
        121, 130, 140, 142, 144–8, 155,
        158, 163, 169, 172–5, 177, 179,
        183, 186
    strategies, *see* advocacy
    transnational influences, 32–3,
        73–5, 96–9, 124, 128, 139,
        157–8, 179, 186
    typology, 33–40
    Vietnamese, 10–16, 36–40, 179
    virtual, 34, 36, 40, 85, 88–9, 92,
        104, 107, 122, 128, 130, 169,
        176
Communist parties, 3–4, 7, 9, 31, 54,
    152, 195

comparative analysis, 3–4, 16–22,
    169–73
Confucianism, 17, 30
Conservation International, 157, 197
contentious politics, 27, 42–4, 185–6
corporatism, 5, 7, 44
corruption, 52, 54, 56, 106, 109, 133,
    184, 190
CSR Pioneers (China), 99
Cultural Revolution, 14, 174

dams, 39, 136–42, 158–60, 167
Dandelion Network (China), 88–92,
    94–5
Danish Society of Polio & Accident
    Victims (PTU), 79–80, 193
December 19th Market (Hanoi), 109
democratisation, role of networks
    in, 3, 29, 53, 100–1, 167, 185
DFID, 98
diasporas, 18, 20, 110–12, 124, 128,
    131
diffusion of network models, 73, 75,
    81, 171, 186
disability, 44, 61–84, 170, 182, 184,
    186
Disability Forum (Vietnam), 37, 62,
    77, 83, 192
Disability Resource & Development
    (Vietnam), 80–1
dissidents, 3, 9–10, 36, 82, 133, 180,
    184–5
doi moi (Renewal), 20, 63, 108
donors, 14–16, 19, 60, 67, 74–5, 86,
    87, 89, 91, 93–4, 96, 98–9, 102–5,
    128, 157, 161, 170, 173, 175–6,
    178–80
drug users' networks, 86, 89, 91, 98
Dujiangyan, 140–1, 197

environmental impact assessments
    (EIA), 151–2, 159–60, 167, 182
environmental networks, 10, 13–14,
    32, 42, 48, 52, 54–5, 137, 139,
    142, 144, 147, 149–50, 172, 184,
    186

Falun Gong, 10, 186
Family Health International, 91

Fatherland Front (Vietnam), 6
film, as advocacy tactic, 45, 61, 95,
    97, 142, 154–6
    see also art
framing, 23, 32, 41, 43, 39, 115, 119,
    124–5, 139, 141, 155, 158,
    162–6
Friends of Nature (FON, China), 55,
    140–1, 144–5, 147, 149, 159, 164
foundations, 14, 19, 60, 100, 157,
    161, 180
fundraising, 19, 51, 83–4, 85, 99, 143,
    161, 173, 176–7, 180
    see also donors

Gates Foundation, 98
gay/lesbian networks, 38, 89, 91, 98,
    194–5
gender, *see* women's networks
Global Fund, 91, 98–100, 102, 183,
    185
Global Greengrants, 142, 157
Global Village Beijing, 143–4, 197
Golden Hanoi Hotel, 108
GONGOs (Government-organised
    non-governmental
    organisations), 5, 8, 11, 13, 19,
    25, 46, 64, 69, 80, 81, 86, 91, 99,
    100, 106, 126, 136, 193, 195
    see also mass organisations
governance, 18, 28, 96, 139
Grassroots Democracy Ordinance
    (Vietnam), 113
Green Earth Volunteers (GEV,
    China), 140–2, 144, 148, 153,
    155, 157, 167, 197, 198
Green Watershed (China), 141,
    143–4, 149, 154, 156–8, 165,
    167, 197, 198
Guangdong province, 12, 92
Guangxi province, 12, 91–3, 96
Guangzhou, 20
guanxi, 1–2, 7, 11, 32, 44, 71, 132,
    176
Guizhou province, 12, 92

Habermas, Jürgen, 8, 134–5
Hai Duong province, 61
Hannah, Joseph, 42, 51

Hanoi, xi, 15, 20, 54, 57, 61–8, 76–7,
    80, 106–20, 129–30, 132–5, 179,
    183
Hanoi Association of People with
    Disabilities (DPO Hanoi), 62, 66,
    70, 76–7, 79–81, 83–4, 183
Hanyuan incident, 166
hats, as multiple roles of network
    members, 34, 58, 149, 166, 170
HealthBridge, 106–7, 110–12, 115–16,
    120–3, 125, 128, 130–1
Heinrich Böll Foundation, 143
Henan province, 86, 92–3, 101, 103
HIV networks, 10, 12, 37–9, 44,
    85–105, 170–3, 179–84, 186
Ho, Peter, 7, 48–9
Ho Chi Minh City Club of Disabled
    Youth, 81
Ho Chi Minh City, 20, 54, 80
Ho Chi Minh Mausoleum (Hanoi),
    76, 112
Hoan Kiem Lake (Hanoi), 107–9, 112
Hoi An, 62
Hong Kong, 12, 21, 61, 70, 74, 85, 91,
    108
Howell, Jude, 8–9, 43
Hu Jintao, 150
hydropower, *see* dams
hypotheses, research, 56–8, 164,
    170–3

Inclusive Development Action (IDEA,
    Vietnam), 77–8, 192
information technology, *see* Internet
Institute for Environment and
    Development (China), 144, 197
International Campaign to Ban
    Landmines, 32
International Labour Organisation, 80
International Republican Institute,
    19, 103
International Rivers (IRN), 141,
    157–8, 197
Internet, 2, 13, 20, 26, 34, 45, 50–3,
    57, 87–90, 94–5, 102, 104, 106,
    123–4, 127, 142, 151, 154, 160,
    176, 183
    see also civil society networks
    – virtual

Japan, 70, 74, 79, 115
Jinsha River (China), 137–8, 141, 150,
    155–7, 159–60, 166–7
    see also Yangtze River
journalists, *see* media
journalists' salons (China), 141, 154
Jubilee 2000, 32

Keck, Margaret, 32, 169, 180, 189,
    199, 200
Keech-Marx, Samantha, 12
Kerkvliet, Benjamin J. Tria, 7, 188,
    190
Korea, South, 17, 79
Kunming, 136, 139, 143, 156

labour networks, 10, 16, 18, 43
Lancang River, 137–8, 150, 158, 196
    see also Mekong River
land disputes, 54, 56–7, 107–9,
    118–19, 132, 134–5, 184
    see also protests
legal aid, 38, 54
Lenin Park, *see* Reunification Park
Li Peng, 150
Liang Congjie, 149, 198
Liu Xiaobo, 9
Liulitun landfill, 55
lobbying, *see* advocacy
Longkaikou dam, 138, 159
Ludila dam, 138, 159
Lu Yiyi, 7, 49

Ma Qiusha, 7
Mangrove HIV support group
    (Beijing), 95
Manwan dam, 138, 149, 156, 196
Marie Stopes International, 95
mass organisations, 6, 8, 20, 36, 37,
    77, 79, 80, 83, 192
    see also GONGOs, umbrella
    organisations
media, China, 18–19, 50–3, 90, 94–6,
    136–7, 140–2, 145, 149, 151,
    153–6, 164, 166–7, 183
media, Vietnam, 6, 18, 50–3, 61, 63,
    68, 72, 77–8, 107, 109–13,
    121–35, 183
    see also advocacy – media strategies

Mekong River, 138, 158, 197
    see also Lancang River
Meitlia, Andrew, 143, 165–6
Ministry of Agriculture (China), 150
Ministry of Civil Affairs (China), 8
Ministry of Construction (Vietnam),
    64, 70–1, 109, 112, 113, 119–20
Ministry of Environment and Natural
    Resources (Vietnam), 116
Ministry of Environmental Protection
    (MEP, China), 55, 136, 150–1,
    159–60, 167, 197
Ministry of Health (China), 86, 98,
    100
Ministry of Health (Vietnam), 73–4
Ministry of Information and
    Communication (Vietnam), 51,
    127
Ministry of Labour, War Invalids and
    Social Affairs (MOLISA, Vietnam),
    61–2
Ministry of Public Security (Vietnam),
    76–7
Ministry of Transport (Vietnam), 76–8
Ministry of Water Resources (China),
    150

National Assembly (Vietnam), 9, 51,
    64, 76, 133
National Coordinating Council on
    Disability (NCCD, Vietnam), 61,
    69, 70, 76–7, 78, 83, 191–2, 193
National Development and Reform
    Commission (NDRC, China), 150
National People's Congress (China),
    159
Nature Conservancy, 159, 197
networks, *see* civil society networks
network theory, 24–33, 57, 173–84
NGOs (Non-governmental
    organisations), 34–40, 54, 57,
    172, 176, 189
    as part of civil society networks, 25,
    32–4, 178, 180
    Chinese, xi, 4, 7–10, 12–13, 16, 20,
    41, 44, 46, 48–9, 52, 54–5,
    86–7, 91–2, 100–1, 103–4,
    136–55, 158, 163, 165–6, 169,
    174

international (INGOs), 15–16, 19,
61, 65, 70, 73–4, 80, 91, 106,
110–11, 121, 123, 128, 152,
163, 165, 169
registration of, 19
Vietnamese, xi, 3–6, 15, 19–20,
41–2, 61, 67, 121
Nguyen Tan Dung, 76
Nguyen The Thao, 116
Nu (Salween) River, 136–9, 141,
147–9, 151, 153, 155–6, 164, 167

Oxfam, 157, 197

parks, 107–9, 120, 123, 133
Peace Corps, 19
personal ties as basis of networks, 2,
10–12, 26, 28–9, 34–6, 41, 44–7,
57, 64, 66, 75, 139–40, 149, 163,
169, 171, 174, 176, 185–6
petitions, 41, 44–7, 55–6, 70, 72, 77,
107–8, 120, 122, 126, 136, 149,
151–2, 154, 159, 161
philanthropy, *see* donors, fundraising
Philippines, 34, 37, 62, 188
Poland, 119, 135, 185
political space, 18–21, 23, 60, 73,
82–3, 102–4, 114, 127, 131–4,
162, 164–7, 170, 174, 181–3,
186–7
Probe International, 158
protests, 10, 16, 42–5, 52, 54–7, 72,
76–8, 83, 104, 108, 114, 135, 137,
156, 166, 168, 186
see also land disputes
public space, 106–10, 113–15, 118,
121–5, 130–1, 133, 170, 176,
182–4
see also parks
public sphere, 4, 8–9, 134–5, 139,
141, 186
Pubugou dam, 166
Putnam, Robert, 25

QQ groups, 88–9, 104, 194

Red Cross, 85, 91
religion, 5, 7, 10, 19, 26, 135, 174
see also Buddhism, Catholicism

Reunification Park (Hanoi), 37, 40,
51, 106–35, 171–2, 183
rightful resistance, 45, 55, 57–8

Salvation Army, 19
Salween River, *see* Nu River
SARS epidemic, 53, 86
SAS Hotel project (Hanoi), 115, 119
scientists, civil society role of, 45, 47,
108, 112, 119, 136–7, 141–3,
145–6, 148–9, 155, 159, 178
SEPA, *see* Ministry of Environmental
Protection (China)
Shanghai, 13, 55, 85, 92, 95, 99, 153,
196
Sichuan earthquake (2008), 10, 12,
37–8, 137, 197
Sichuan province, 12–13, 92, 137,
140–1, 164–6
Sikkink, Kathryn, 32, 169, 180, 189,
199, 200
Singapore, 25, 115
social capital, 2, 5, 9, 25–6, 31, 44, 56,
65, 130–1, 146, 149, 154, 157,
172, 178
social movements, 8, 10, 16, 24, 27–8,
32, 42, 48, 137, 163, 172–3,
184–7
social work, 16, 96
socialism, 4, 14, 18, 62, 108, 119, 131,
134
Southeast Asia, 17, 158, 188
Southern Weekend (Nanfang Zhoumo),
155, 163, 198
state-society relations, 3–7, 44, 48, 59,
63, 102, 188
student networks, 13–14, 68, 81, 89,
112, 136–7
Sweden, 115–16, 118–20, 131

Taiwan, 13, 17, 21, 199
Tan Hoang Minh corporation,
113–14, 124, 195
Tarrow, Sidney, 185
Thailand, 48, 74, 158, 188
Thang Long Water Park case (Hanoi),
109, 112, 126
Thayer, Carlyle, 9–10
Thich Nhat Hanh, 54

Three Gorges dam, 136, 138, 150, 159, 169
Thu Le Park (Hanoi), 108, 109, 112, 122
Tibet, 136
Tiger Leaping Gorge, 138, 141, 157, 159, 196
Tilly, Charles, 187
Tsinghua University, 12
Tuan Vietnam (Vietnam Week), 127

umbrella organisations, 5–6, 36–7
UNAIDS, 86, 91, 95–9, 102–3, 105
United Nations, 70, 95, 105, 156
United Nations World Conference on Women (1995), 11, 14, 87
universities, civil society role of, 7, 12, 19, 63, 81, 121
urban planning, 106–9, 112, 131
USAID, 98

veterans, 73, 75–6, 78–9, 192
Vietnam
  laws and regulations, 5, 19, 43, 56, 64, 69, 70–1, 75–7, 79–80, 113, 119, 182, 192
  media, *see* media, Vietnam
  network history, 4–15
  politics, 16–21, 23, 29, 42–4, 48–50
  war legacies, 14, 174, 192
Vietnam Architects' Association, 108, 116, 121
Vietnam Association of People with Disabilities, 78–82, 182
Vietnam Blind Association, 81, 193
Vietnam Environment Association, 121

Vietnam History Association, 108
Vietnam Rivers Network, 37, 190
Vietnam Union of Science and Technology Associations (VUSTA), 36, 37
Vietnam Urban Planning Association, 106, 112, 116, 119–21, 125
Vietnam Women's Union, 36
VietNamNet (VNN), 112, 118, 122, 127
VinaCapital corporation, 116, 134
Vincom corporation, 112, 114, 116, 195
Vo Van Kiet, 119

Weller, Robert, 21
Wen Jiabao, 136, 149, 167
Wild China Films, 144–5
wildlife protection, 13, 140
Women's Network against AIDS – China (WNAC), 22, 37, 85–105, 169–70, 172–3, 175, 178–9, 182
women's networks, 10, 12–14, 37, 39, 87, 182
World Bank, 77, 132

Xiamen, 53, 55
Xiangjiaba dam, 138, 166, 197
Xiaonanhai dam, 138, 159

Yang, Mayfair, 11, 13, 32
Yangtze River, 136–8, 140, 196–7
  see also Jinsha River
Yen, James, 54
Yunnan province, 12, 20, 37, 91–3, 98, 136–7, 140, 143, 149–50, 152, 158, 164, 197